BLOOD AND PROGRESS

In memory of Stephanie Hewlett (Teff), 1950–2016

BLOOD AND PROGRESS
Violence in Pursuit of Emancipation

Nick Hewlett

EDINBURGH
University Press

Edinburgh University Press is one of the leading university presses in the UK. We publish academic books and journals in our selected subject areas across the humanities and social sciences, combining cutting-edge scholarship with high editorial and production values to produce academic works of lasting importance. For more information visit our website: edinburghuniversitypress.com

Edinburgh University Press Ltd
The Tun – Holyrood Road
12(2f) Jackson's Entry
Edinburgh EH8 8PJ

Typeset in 11/13 Sabon by
Servis Filmsetting Ltd, Stockport, Cheshire,
and printed and bound in Great Britain by
CPI Group (UK) Ltd, Croydon CR0 4YY

A CIP record for this book is available from the British Library

ISBN 978 1 4744 1059 5 (hardback)
ISBN 978 1 4744 1060 1 (paperback)
ISBN 978 1 4744 1061 8 (webready PDF)
ISBN 978 1 4744 1062 5 (epub)

CONTENTS

ACKNOWLEDGEMENTS

Many people have contributed in different ways to the creation of this book. I would like to thank the following, for reading either parts of the draft manuscript or the book proposal: Gary Browning, Elizabeth Frazer, Gus Hewlett, Emily Hewlett, David Jelley, Finbar Lillis and two anonymous readers. In particular, I would like to thank Gregory Elliott and Philippe Le Goff for reading the entire manuscript and making extremely insightful and useful comments on many aspects of it. The final version is, of course, my responsibility alone. (Translations into English, unless otherwise indicated, are also my own.) Special thanks also to Bridget Taylor. I am also grateful to all those at Edinburgh University Press who either encouraged me in this project at an early stage or helped with the later stages, including design, editing and production. An earlier version of Chapter 4 was published in August 2012 in *The European Legacy*.

Nick Hewlett
March 2016

INTRODUCTION

The practice of physical violence is one of the very worst aspects of human behaviour and it has been a defining feature of the way in which members of the Homo sapiens species have related to one another since their appearance on Earth some 200,000 years ago. Over time, humans have developed the means to pursue violence against one another in increasingly deadly and ingenious ways, and these have frequently been used either to pursue or prevent social or political change. Hegel ([1837] 2009: 21) described this as the 'slaughter-bench of history'. Today, a gruesome range of techniques and devices is available to those seeking or preventing change, from age-old stabbing, poisoning and strangulation to aerial bombardment, killing by remote-controlled drones and cyber-attack, not to mention chemical and nuclear warfare. Indeed, we live in times that often seem defined by violence. The conflicts in the Middle East, for which the West bears so much responsibility, the almost-daily suicide attacks in either advanced capitalist or poorer countries, revolutions and their suppression in North Africa, civil wars in other parts of the African continent and drug-related killings in South America – together these have contributed to stamping the era in which we live with the mark of violence.

These are gloomy thoughts. But in this book my other starting point is an optimistic one, namely a belief in the potential of human beings to move beyond violence and to live in a world that is characterised by equality, justice and – most importantly given the subject matter of this book – ongoing and profound *peace*. Despite the setbacks and failures such a project has suffered in the past, despite the appalling violence committed in the name of equality and freedom in the Soviet Union, China, Cambodia and elsewhere, I argue that the only way to move beyond the injustices, hardships and seemingly perpetual violence of

1

the world as we know it is to continue to explore pathways to a very different, far more equal and humane world. There are clear indications in the world in which we live that such a future is possible as well as desirable.

When thinking about radical social and political change, we very quickly encounter the question of how change will be brought about. Will it be via party politics and election campaigns (for those countries that have parliamentary democratic systems), perhaps followed by slow and patient reform, or will it involve the building of mass movements that undertake struggle for transformation in peaceful or semi-peaceful ways? Will it involve armed uprising? Will it involve acts of individual terrorism where a few or many non-combatant individuals are killed? Will there be Terror on the part of the new regime, as was the case in the 1789 French Revolution, the Russian Revolution of 1917 and arguably many other dramatic changes of regime in the twentieth and twenty-first centuries? The media is full of reports from around the world of wars between nations and parts of nations, of suicide bombings, of massacres and mass imprisonment, of aerial bombing and of assassinations. These reports remind us that many groups, individuals and governments have already thought about questions relating to violence for change and have come to particular conclusions.

In this book we are dealing with the paradox of committing violent acts in the name of a future non-violent society and questions raised in this context include: 'Under which circumstances (if any) is violence justified?'; 'Who is justified in pursuing violence in revolt?'; 'If and when violence is legitimate, what are the limits to permissible violence?'; 'Do some radically different ends justify more intense violence?'; 'Does the nature of violent revolt affect the nature of the goal?'; 'Is pacifism or semi-pacifism an appropriate means of struggle in some (or all) circumstances?'; and 'How does a profound commitment to a peaceful and non-violent goal relate to the means by which this is achieved?'. All of these questions are ones regarding the legitimacy or otherwise of the use of violence in pursuit of change. Any thoughtful response needs to take into account the violence and extreme hardship caused by the current world economic system, the relationship between inequalities and violence and also the possible futures that capitalism as a socio-economic system may or may not have. Of course, none of these questions has an easy answer and each case of violence in revolt needs to be debated according to the circumstances in which it is taking place. But we can offer a framework for thinking about violence for progressive ends and engage in a number of debates, and now is a particularly appropriate time to be doing so.

We are living in an age where violence either to enable or to prevent change is widespread. But we are also living in an age that is characterised by the end of historical communism, that is the end of communism in the Eastern bloc in particular, but also the end of communism in a more traditional sense in China, which now has a thriving capitalist economy. This casts a different light on the question of the relationship between violence and struggles for emancipation. First, the demise (or nearly so) of historical communism means the end of what was the most significant social, economic, political and cultural experiment that the world has seen in the name of freedom from oppression and in favour of equality and emancipation, with very mixed results. It brought many material benefits in terms of work, housing, healthcare and education, for example, but among the costs were severe repression against any dissent expressed by groups or individuals, and the virtual absence of any type of democracy. Second, the end of communism means the passing of societies that practised a great deal of violence themselves, perhaps not quite rivalling violence by capitalist regimes over the same period, but nevertheless significant as counter-examples of what this book is arguing we should be aiming for, namely peace. This means that despite the failure of what once seemed to offer great hope, there is an opportunity in terms of thinking about violence in pursuit of emancipation that has not presented itself for several generations, namely a sort of tabula rasa upon which we can sketch some new ideas; out of the ashes of the failed communist experiments of the twentieth century, beyond the immediate Western triumphalism of 'end-of-history' arguments and in light of the catastrophic Western interventions in the Middle East in the early twentieth century, there can emerge thinking that can perhaps help us move on.

It is necessary to explain briefly what I mean by violence, which I define primarily as deliberately causing physical pain, injury or death to others, and political violence will therefore be deliberately causing physical pain, injury or death to others with political goals in mind. This is sometimes described as personal, or agent-related violence, where the perpetrator or perpetrators are often easily identifiable. However, it is also necessary to take into account what is sometimes described (after Galtung 1969) as 'structural', or society-related violence, meaning harm inflicted, for example, as a result of particular conditions of work, or harm as a result of uneven distribution of resources in society, perhaps resulting in ongoing pain, illness or premature death. Inequality and structural violence are often closely related – the one frequently leading to the other – and it becomes highly relevant when discussing, among other things, the ethics of violence in revolt compared with the ethics of established states and governments that may be deemed responsible for structural violence. I should add that I do not include damage to property in my definition of violence, so smashing the windows of a government ministry building or cutting down a fence surrounding a military airbase are not forms of violence, although burning crops or destroying a person's house may cause so much hardship and suffering that it becomes a form of violence. Certainly, the boundary between violent and non-violent forms of action is not always clear-cut, nor is the difference between agent-related and structural violence, but the discussion must be had nonetheless.

It should also be said that, although violence causes some of the worst forms of suffering, there are some experiences that can be even more brutal. The following examples may be deemed even worse than some physical violence: homelessness and displacement from one's community and culture over an extended period as a refugee; severe isolation due to mental health problems and inadequate welfare support; emotional bullying over a number of years at the hands of a partner, parent or colleague. Again there is no doubt an overlap between these sorts of suffering and violence, but for the sake of the clarity of argument in this book we will not generally consider such phenomena as being examples of violence.

Let us now turn to the question of emancipation. Human emancipation involves going beyond the state of affairs where there is oppression and exploitation. In order to achieve emancipation it is necessary to abolish forms of relations between individuals and groups that prevent the flourishing of human beings. Associated with the philosophical lineage of Rousseau, Hegel and Marx, it is far more ambitious than the liberal idea that freedom equates to absence of constraints on individual actions. Rather, emancipation implies that the way in which individuals and groups relate to one another and to the world in which they live must change in order to enable realisation of people's full potential, and a change in personal circumstances on its own is not sufficient. So emancipation necessitates changes in the social, economic and political circumstances in which people live in addition to changes in people's attitudes and consciousness. In other words, employing the notion of emancipation not only reflects a view that human beings are perfectible, but that the material conditions in which they exist have a profound effect on their ability to reach their full potential. It reflects a view that in many – and perhaps all – cases people are being held back by their social circumstances from flourishing as individuals and as part of wider groups and communities. The term 'emancipation' was originally used in relation to slavery, one of the most extreme versions of exploitation of humans by other humans, and in the twentieth and twenty-first centuries the word has often been used in relation to the oppression of women and moving beyond it. In each of these examples, a profound change in social circumstances and attitudes, not to mention rules of behaviour (including legal change), is necessary in order for emancipation or partial emancipation to take place. A change of individual circumstances or individual consciousness is necessary, but is not sufficient.

In this book I am using the term 'emancipation' in a broad sense, in other words suggesting that wherever there are relations involving exploitation and oppression, the process of moving beyond them will be a process of emancipation. Exploitation and oppression always involve inequalities of various kinds and emancipation involves overcoming inequalities; full emancipation in all areas would therefore involve radical equality of many types, certainly including material equality in terms of people's material needs being met, but also equality in terms of life opportunities, including work, arrangements for bringing up children, healthcare, access to fulfilling leisure activities and as comfortable an old age as possible. It would also involve equality in terms of decision-making, both in the family unit (or perhaps communal living arrangements), at work and in local, national and international politics. Thus, broad human emancipation would involve profound democracy as part of radical equality. Erik Olin Wright (2010: 10) discusses the way in which progressive thought can enable the process of emancipation and suggests that 'any emancipatory social science faces three basic tasks: elaborating a systematic diagnosis and critique of the world as it exists; envisioning viable alternatives; and understanding the obstacles, possibilities, and dilemmas of transformation'. He argues that diagnosis and critique of social processes that generate harm is important, and feminism, theories of racial oppression and radical environmentalism have all done this effectively, but that this has probably been done almost to the exclusion of thinking of worked-out alternatives. The idea of emancipation *from* various forms of oppression and exploitation should be put together with the alternative conditions under which one could live after emancipation has taken place; what we are seeking emancipation *from* should be combined with what we are aspiring *to* in order to have a more complete set of ideas about both transformation and the longer-term goals. My primary concern here is not the subject of emancipation itself, of course, but of violence in pursuit of emancipation. Nevertheless, emancipation is a theme to which we will return, especially in Chapter 1 when we look at the possibility of non-violent futures.

We may describe this as a dialectical approach to the question of emancipation, where the end goal is linked to and interrelates with the means by which emancipation takes place. The way in which we struggle for change affects the goal we are pursuing, and the more we know about the type of society we are struggling for the more this will affect the way we pursue it. I suggest we should also develop a dialectical approach to the question of violence in pursuit of emancipation. On the one hand, this means that we must both imagine a plausible version of, and assert the need for, a society characterised by non-violence and peace, suggesting that there are indications in the current state of things that this is a viable objective. On the other hand, we need to examine the violence of modern capitalism; although capitalism has allowed the emergence of certain phenomena that offer hope in the pursuit of peace and non-violence, there is at the same time the potential for contemporary global capitalism to become far more violent as it enters further periods of deep crisis. These two assertions – that late capitalism has both a peaceful dynamic and a violent dynamic – may seem to be at least partially in contradiction with each other. But this is a real and significant paradox and I argue that engaging with this paradox is important if we are to develop a humane and constructive approach towards the question of violence in the pursuit of emancipation. It will be clear that I am not opposed to liberating violence in all circumstances, but consideration of the means of emancipation needs to be mediated by a discussion of the ends being sought. In other words there is some violence that is in contradiction with the goals being pursued.

The latter part of this argument may appear to have similarities with Just War Theory, especially as expressed by Michael Walzer in his landmark book *Just and Unjust* Wars ([1977] 2006a) that is about when states should and should not go to war. I have more to say about this debate in subsequent chapters, but for the moment I simply suggest that Walzer's book is too weak a condemnation of capitalist wars of the twentieth century and not critical enough of violence encouraged or tolerated by the conditions of the status quo. Indeed, Just War Theory was used by some (but not Walzer) to justify the 2003 invasion of Iraq, an invasion that was followed by a calamitous war and occupation. It is also too modest in its ambitions for a different world, condemning violence 'motivated by ideology' (surely also an apt description of so many wars that are supposedly 'just'?) and defending violence in favour of the type of world that itself generates a great deal of violence.

I do not believe it is possible to draw up a general list of 'dos and don'ts' of violence in pursuit of emancipation that covers every eventuality, which Just War Theory appears to set out to do, and that the growing literature on Just War regarding insurgency also appears to attempt. Rather, I consider various different approaches to violence in relation to historical struggles and their broader contexts and draw conclusions from these, set against my more general philosophy of peace and emancipation. In particular, I look at Fidel Castro's use of violence in revolt in Cuba in the 1950s and in related struggles in the 1960s and beyond, and argue that there are important lessons to be learned from his and other Cuban rebels' more ethical approach to the question of struggles for emancipation. Castro's approach is in some ways an improvement on the theory and practice of Leninism and Bolshevik insurgency during the Russian Revolution and its aftermath, where the fight against the status quo seemed to mirror the methods of the old order and its allies to a far greater degree than in Cuba. There are many differences between the two revolutions, of course, not least that the stakes were far higher in Russia than in Cuba, including from the point of view of the place of Russia and the place of Cuba in relation to rest of the world. But Castro's greater concern for humanism, combined with a more highly developed view of the type of society he and his comrades were fighting for, made a significant difference.

I also look at an underlying source of much modern left-wing thought on violence for social and political change, namely the writings of Marx and Engels, and argue that their analysis of violence is rather different from the one that they are usually associated with. They are often presented as approaching violence in revolt as a mere tool for enabling transition to another form of society, as the 'midwife' of a new order and a way of clearing away the 'muck of ages' in preparation for what will follow. I argue for a more subtle reading of their thought, which detects a view that any violence is deeply regrettable and indeed examines what we now call structural violence, especially in Engels's *The Condition of the Working Class in England* ([1844] 1999), but also in Marx's *Capital* ([1867] 1954).

Many studies or interventions regarding political violence written from a left-wing perspective are exclusively concerned with questions of strategy, such as how to get rid of a dictator, how to achieve national liberation or revolution, how to move beyond discrimination based on race or ethnicity or how to overthrow capitalism. Many are successful in these respects, but hardly any deal with how violent the struggle for a better world can be without compromising the goal. Written in or close to the heat of battle, they concentrate on violence purely as a means to an end and dwell very little on the effect that insurrectionary violence will have on the later order of things.

Moreover, rather oddly, very few studies written from such a perspective deal with the question of what the better world will look like if it is achieved. My contention is that these two questions – the ethics of violence in revolt and the nature of the better world – are intimately related; we need to know in some detail why we are in revolt and what our goals are before we can ask the question as to whether it is legitimate to resort to violence, and if so to what type of violence. Not to think about the nature of the better world makes generalised thinking about violence in pursuit of emancipation almost impossible. Often, those who advocate violence in the name of emancipation develop a romantic attachment to it and fail to take adequately into account the dehumanising effects of 'liberating' violence on the people who carry out such violence and also on the nature of the post-liberation order. They fail to reflect on whether the violence of liberation is not in the longer term in a very practical sense in contradiction with the aims being pursued.

In the first two decades of the twenty-first century, the question of terrorism has been very much to the fore. Since 9/11, successive US governments, with support from some allies, have made sure that terrorism is constantly on the agenda. They have done this by pursuing 'Wars against Terror' and also discussing at great length the 9/11 and subsequent attacks in the West, although there have been countless times more victims of terrorist attacks in poorer countries than in the richer ones and many, many more civilians killed in the Wars against Terror than in terrorist attacks in the West. But of course the catch-all word 'terrorism' is far more complex than many governments are inclined to make out, in part because many governments themselves perpetrate terror. Use of the word does, however, raise some crucial questions, which include: 'Who are – and who are not – terrorists?'; 'Is it ever justifiable to kill non-combatants, even in a legitimate cause?'; and 'How does killing non-combatant individuals, in terrorism or moments of Terror, affect the nature of the society being fought and killed for?'. The relatively new and highly disturbing phenomenon of ISIS, or Islamic State, is also relevant, of course, with its appeal for some young adults the world over, who see themselves as going to fight for a cause with a just end.

It will already be clear that this book is written from a broadly Marxist perspective. But it takes what is – as far as I know – a novel approach towards the question of the ethics of struggles in pursuit of emancipation, precisely because it puts at centre stage the goal of a profoundly equal, democratic and peaceful society and makes this an integral part of the argument about violent strategy and tactics. Arguing that the goal of a wholly peaceful society should be an explicit part of the way in which we think about violence in pursuit of emancipation changes the way in which we approach and understand the topic. But it is also important to integrate into the argument an understanding of both violent and peaceful dynamics found in late capitalist society. My argument is not pacifist, but it does relate means and ends dialectically to each other to such an extent that the terms of the debate are altered substantially.

Chapter 1

NON-VIOLENCE AS AN IMPERATIVE GOAL

> The elimination of violence, and the reduction of suppression to
> the extent required for protecting man and animals from cruelty
> and aggression are preconditions for the creation of a humane
> society.
>
> Herbert Marcuse ([1965] 1969: 96)

Over the last 150 years, vast numbers of people have been killed by
regimes of different hues, and even greater numbers have suffered and
died due to 'natural' disasters such as famine and preventable diseases;
this is not to mention the widespread and extreme suffering of many of
the living. In light of this extreme violence and ongoing suffering, with
no obvious end in sight, it is imperative that progressive thought should
ally itself explicitly and emphatically with the pursuit of peace and
non-violence. This may seem an obvious point. But socialist thought
in particular has often shied away from this position, believing that to
talk of peace and non-violence even as a distant goal was a distraction
from the task of fighting (often in a literal sense) opponents who were
set on maintaining the status quo, or making it worse for many people.
While such objectives as equality, democracy and freedom from exploitation and oppression are often correctly held up as crucial, the pursuit
of peace and non-violence are seen as desirable but as areas that will
emerge almost automatically as other goals are achieved. Any overt talk
of peace, even in the longer term, is often taken as an indication of lack
of resolve to overcome capitalist exploitation and capitalism's own violence, or as a misunderstanding of the entrenched nature of capitalist
exploitation and violence. Non-violence, even as a distant goal, seems
to be viewed as a sign of weakness or naivety.

My argument is that progressive thought must *begin with* an assertion of the profound importance of peace and non-violence, alongside other, more conventionally discussed areas. In the twenty-first century there is an unprecedented opportunity to advance the project of peace among human beings, given the scientific knowledge we have acquired in many areas combined with various progressive impulses present in the twentieth and twenty-first centuries. But we also have a duty to advance the project in a way that is reminiscent of Kant's peace imperative, which promotes the nurturing of human life above all else; and this may become increasingly urgent because it will perhaps be the only way for the human race to survive in the longer term, given the threat of global annihilation in war, perhaps in conjunction with ecological catastrophe. I argue this in part because of the extreme violence of both the capitalist and historical communist worlds (discussed in Chapter 2), but also because of the simultaneous peace dynamics that have become apparent and that are signs that a non-violent future is now plausible.

My suggestion, then, is that there needs to be a bold and comprehensive statement of the type of society being sought, namely a society characterised by peaceful and profoundly democratic egalitarianism, where a process of emancipation is combined with a struggle for peace. Such a statement regarding peace, democracy and equality may be called utopian, an approach that the left shunned for much of the twentieth century and largely does today. Socialists traditionally do not stress the goal of peace in this utopian fashion, in part because they concentrate on a critique of capitalism and on resistance against aspects of the status quo. A great deal of energy has also been devoted to the task of thinking about a moment of radical transition (revolution, overthrow of the existing order, liberation and so on). All this is necessary, but any talk or thought that has a utopian element is often treated with disdain. Thus, the – perhaps violent – means are not related dialectically with the peaceful, egalitarian and just ends, which makes for a weaker critique of the present, a weaker view of the future and, in particular, a weaker approach to our immediate concern, namely the rights and wrongs of violence for emancipation.

In addition, the near absence of a clearly stated aspiration for peace is explained by violence being seen as integral to the toolbox of the struggle for a better world. There is fear that too much talk of peace and non-violence, even in the longer term, may suggest that one signs up lock, stock and barrel to Gandhi's views and practices, to a fully fledged *satyagraha*.

UTOPIAS

Imagining how a radically egalitarian and profoundly just society may look has not enjoyed a great deal of success over the past 150 years. Marx's and Engels's dismissal of the 'utopian socialists' Robert Owen, Saint-Simon and Charles Fourier as producing unhelpful and 'fantastic pictures of future society' and as indicating merely 'the first instinctive yearnings for a general reconstruction of society' (Marx and Engels [1848] 1968: 60), rather than a proper contribution towards getting rid of capitalist society and creating a better one, is influential on many socialist approaches to thinking about a better future. This, and in particular Engels's blistering attack on utopian thought in the section of *Anti-Dühring* entitled 'Socialism: Utopian and scientific', have passed into Marxist orthodoxy and have influenced socialist thought more generally. However, all radically progressive thought without exception has an imaginary and optimistic vision of the future and by definition takes the view that it is quite possible to make the world a far fairer and more humane place than it currently is. This always involves a view of the future that may be called 'utopian'. When someone sketches out some detail of what this world may look like, as Saint-Simon, Fourier and Owen did in some detail, and as William Morris did in the late nineteenth century in *News from Nowhere* (1890), this may be seen as a logical project to undertake for anyone who believes that emancipation is possible. If, on the contrary, progressive thought has nothing to say on what the future may consist of, this would seem to offer little hope that things could be different. When Marx and Engels wrote the *Communist Manifesto* they were in the process of establishing their theory of 'scientific' socialism and in attacking utopian socialism arguably they over-stated their anti-utopian position. As I suggest in Chapter 4, they were not always as anti-utopian as much received wisdom makes out and even Engels (the more anti-utopian of the duo) conceded in 1870:

> German theoretical Socialism will never forget that it stands on the shoulders of Saint-Simon, Fourier and Owen, three men who despite their fantasies and utopianism are to be reckoned among the most significant minds of all times, for they anticipated with genius countless matters whose accuracy we demonstrate scientifically. (Engels ([1875] 1970: 246)

More importantly, however, we do not need to throw out the scientific socialist approach if we wish to include a utopian element in our approach to socialism. An important writer in terms of the reconciliation of classical Marxist thought with the notion of utopia is the German philosopher Ernst Bloch, who, in his *The Principle of Hope* ([1938–47] 1986) and *The Spirit of Utopia* ([1918] 2000), suggests that a 'warm stream' (utopian) Marxism is crucial if the 'cold stream' realism of scientific socialism is to be fully useful. But Bloch goes beyond a re-reading of Marx and Engels and offers a philosophy of his own. Glimpses of an emancipated utopia, he argues, which are profoundly motivating in terms of the will to change the circumstances in which human beings live, are already present in many forms of art, including painting, literature, architecture and music, but also in religion and ethics: 'every work of art, every central philosophy had and has a utopian window in which there lies a landscape which is still developing' (Bloch cited in Panitch and Gindin 1999: 2).

Various authors have sought more recently to reassert elements of utopian socialist thinking, including Erik Olin Wright in his outstanding work *Envisioning Real Utopias* (2010). In this, he explores examples of existing institutions or practices that may inform emancipation and the creation of a better world. The notion of 'real utopias', he argues, addresses the tension between dreaming on the one hand and practical activity on the other, and suggests that our imagination has an important part to play in the practice of creating a better future. Olin Wright examines practical alternatives to typical current practices, including worker cooperatives, a sophisticated 'unconditional basic income' that would replace conventional welfare payments and participatory city budgeting as practised in Porto Alegre, Brazil (Wright 2010: 6). 'Nurturing clear-sighted understandings of what it would take to create social institutions free of oppression is part of creating a political will for radical social changes to reduce oppression' (ibid.). Thus, there is emphasis on notions of well-being, happiness and in particular 'flourishing', where individuals are able to realise their potentials, whether these be intellectual, artistic, physical, social, moral or spiritual, with no suggestion that one domain is more worthy than another. All of this requires equal access to resources and this sort of approach condemns all inequalities, such as those currently based on class, gender, race and physical disabilities, and indeed all others that get in the way of such access to resources (15–16). Like Bloch, Olin Wright engages in a critique of contemporary capitalism, but insists that thinking in some detail about alternatives is necessary if we are to begin to construct a realistic, but far fairer, way forward.

Leo Panitch and Sam Gindin, in their introduction to a volume on *Necessary and Unnecessary Utopias*, argue slightly differently that

> [w]hat the socialist project needs today . . . is not so much the details of how socialism would work or what we would do if we took state power, not more measures of why capitalism is not good enough. Rather it needs something transitional between these, beginning with a commitment to developing capacities to 'keep the goal clearly visible', as Bloch puts it. (Panitch and Gindin 1999: 23–4)

The 'motivating vision', then, influenced by a utopian approach, would include such elements as 'overcoming alienation', 'attenuating the division of labour', 'transforming consumption', 'alternative ways of living', 'socialising markets', 'planning ecologically', 'internationalising equality' and greater democracy.

These are important contributions to a view of a far more humane future that addresses practical ways in which we can move in such a direction and others too have made important contributions (for example, Jameson 2004; Levitas 2013). But none are explicit about a commitment to peace and non-violence, although each author's commitment to this in the longer term is not in doubt. David Harvey gets far nearer to such a spelled-out position when he recounts a *News from Nowhere*-style utopian dream about a world in which people live in small, semi-self-sufficient communities where the division of labour is far less rigid than it is in the advanced capitalist countries as we know them, where relations between individuals are entirely constructive, where sexual relations are more fluid and less fraught with problems and where conflict is resolved before it gets out of hand. Most importantly, for us, there is no sign of any violence – no domestic violence, no sexual violence of any kind, no armed robbery or murder, no political violence, no police force, no army. Peace, it seems, has broken out. Harvey suggests that this state of affairs may have been achieved after a breakdown of capitalism following a massive financial crisis combined with rapid global warming and that after a brief global militarised-repressive interlude, a 'peaceful, non-violent mass movement, led almost entirely by women, swept across the globe' (2000: 262). For the moment, the way in which Harvey's dream world came about is less relevant, although the fact that the movement was led by women is relevant to my argument as it develops. His statement of what a more peaceful and egalitarian society may look like is germane, and reminds us that to dream remains important, as long as the dream is based upon a collective ability to realise it; we see how we could get from A (our lives and societies today) to B, a future, emancipated world.

Perhaps the clearest exception to the general rule of shunning utopian thought and/or the inclusion of an explicit peace element within it comes from Herbert Marcuse, who believed it possible that in a future, far more humane society, physical violence between human beings would be so anathema and so repellant that violence may make them physically sick. In an essay entitled 'Ethics and Revolution' the assumption throughout is that the revolution he is discussing only has validity if it enables the birth of a society that allows the non-violent blossoming of individuals and groups; his stated aim is

> to recapture a basic concept of classical philosophy which has been all too often repressed, namely, that the end of government is not only the greatest possible freedom, but also the greatest possible happiness of man, that is to say, a life without fear and misery, and a life in peace. (Marcuse 1968: 134)

In a slightly later work, Marcuse argues that one could in fact speak of the 'end of utopia' because it was no longer merely part of an idealised dream to believe in a world where freedom reigned and there were entirely new types of relations between human beings, because '[a]ll the material and intellectual forces which could be put to work for the realization of a free society are at hand' (Marcuse 1970: 64). 'Today', he suggests, 'we must try to discuss and define – without any inhibitions, even when it may seem ridiculous – the qualitative difference between socialist society as a free society and the existing society' (68). He describes certain 'vital needs' that would emerge in such a society, in which destructive and repressive urges would be displaced by a 'vital biological need for peace' that would, for example, 'be expressed in the impossibility of mobilizing people for military service'. Certainly, non-violent conflicts would continue to exist, but to think that these conflicts could be resolved 'without oppression and cruelty' was entirely feasible (79–81).

A – for the moment imaginary – world where peace and non-violence prevailed would be a world where there was no direct (agent-related) violence of any kind, not on the part of agents of the state (what we now call police officers or soldiers or prison officers), or people in the street or parents or guardians towards their children or other family members towards children or between sexual partners or former sexual partners. There would be no attacks by one country on another, no civil war. There would be no armed insurgency either, because political differences would be resolved via widespread discussion and implementation of democratically arrived-at decisions in a way that engaged many people. It is likely that vegetarianism would be more widespread and the killing of animals managed in a far more humane way than is the case in most countries at present. If all this seems far-fetched, we should ask ourselves what our ideal sort of society would in fact be, and if it does after all incorporate these sorts of ideas then what are the reasons why we (many of us at least) are prepared to set our sights so low and accept the high levels of violence of so many kinds that currently exist.

More immediately, my suggestion is thus that non-violence and peace should be fully part of all progressive aspirations, manifestos and programmes as a matter of urgency, but a life lived free of violence and intense suffering should also be framed as a human right. We might even formulate this human right along the lines of a clause in a charter, and one that would have very far-reaching consequences if it were implemented. It might read something like this:

All human beings without exception have the right to a life which is, to the extent which modern medicine and other areas of science allow, free from physical pain and from severe discomfort. They also have a right to a life that lasts as long as modern medicine and more generally modern science will allow. Such pain, severe discomfort and curtailment of life might be caused by physical (including armed) attack by: agents of one's own country's national government, or by another national government (foreign incursion), or by an international organisation; by other individuals or groups, including by relatives and/or individuals in positions of authority over others, at work, in the home, or in the local community. Such pain, physical suffering and curtailment of life might also be caused by avoidable illness or malnutrition or other deprivation which could be stopped or alleviated by recourse to medical and/or other treatment or change of circumstances such as improved diet, enhanced leisure, or reduction in working hours.

Freedom from physical pain and from severe discomfort and enjoyment of full longevity whenever and wherever this is scientifically possible would thus become an absolute right. Lack of resources – which both within individual nations and internationally is often a question of distribution, in other words of inequality – would no longer be a legitimate reason for people to have different experiences of pain, suffering and life expectancy. It may be argued that such a state of affairs would be impossible because so many other aspects of societies as we know them would have to change before this would be possible. Many things would of course need to change greatly, but that particular fact does not make the goal any less just or less worth struggling for, and if we make a right to a long, peaceful and pain-free life the starting point and make any other state of affairs ultimately indefensible, other changes would indeed flow from this. Certainly, making this a goal has echoes of a 'transitional demand', namely one that could only be fully realised in a radically egalitarian society, but this should not mean that it is presented as an insurmountable obstacle. On the contrary, it is a demand that could serve both as a means both for pushing for reform for the time being and as a way of mobilising around building a different, more equal, more just and peaceful society.

One question that arises in relation to the realisation of a state of affairs where human lives were free from violence and suffering in a far more just and equal society would be the matter of responses to the breaking of laws, a question that every society would, realistically, need to address, at least in the medium term. In particular, there is the question of whether imprisonment of serious or serial law-breakers would still be practised, a punishment that in its current form in most societies is a form of violence according to many definitions, including my own. My answer is that prison would almost certainly need to exist, but that in a profoundly equal and peaceful society the prison system would have far more emphasis on reform of the individual and on their reintegration into society, wherever possible, than it has at present. This would be in stark contrast with the highly punitive, under-resourced prison regimes in most countries today, which are largely places to park law-breakers out of sight of the wider society and that are often institutions where criminal behaviour is consolidated, not to mention places where there is a large amount of unjustified misery, as the large number of suicides in many prison systems demonstrates. The prison system in some Nordic countries, however, may offer some indication of how there could be emphasis on reform, education and rehabilitation, rather than on punishment and vengeance. The Norwegian penal reform system, for example, is exemplary in this respect. In Halden Prison, a maximum-security jail in Norway, which opened in 2010, the 245 prisoners live communally in groups of eight, in which they are able to cook for themselves if they wish and engage in many work and educational activities (Gentleman 2012). There is great emphasis on rehabilitation and the authorities try to ensure that all prisoners who go back into the community have both adequate accommodation and a job. Carefully designed not only from the point of view of security but also in order to create pleasing aesthetics and ease of living, there is hardly ever a fight. Warders who work in the Norwegian prison service have two years of training in a university, which places emphasis on human rights, ethics and law. Of course this sort of prison service is expensive, but it also leads to a far lower rate of reoffending than in many countries (20 per cent in Norway compared with 50 per cent in Britain, for example) and in this sense it also saves money. More importantly, however, it constitutes a far more humane approach to the treatment of serious offenders than do most other prison systems in the world and is an indication that such an approach does work.

MODERNITY, LIBERALISM AND NON-VIOLENCE

The coming of modernity offered tremendous opportunities for the emergence of the peaceful aspirations we are discussing here. As Marx and Engels suggest in the *Communist Manifesto*, modernity is certainly brutally destructive of traditional ways of life that had offered safety and nurture to many people, albeit alongside much hardship as well. But modernity also cleared the way for an unleashing of human potential that only the 'creative destruction' of capitalism could bring. For the first time, it was clear that the future was not merely an endless repetition of the past, with the predictability of changing seasons and the secular and religious rites and celebrations that went with them, and the seemingly immutable patterns of social organisation and exploitation. The future would certainly not be the socio-economic and political replica of the past and the potential was for it to be far more just, far more equal, far better. But it could alternatively be worse if people did not organise themselves properly and replace capitalism and all the injustices and exploitation that go with it, with something much better. This was the point: human beings needed to seize the opportunity offered to them by modernity, take control of their own fate and establish a very different sort of society, where 'the free development of each is the condition for the free development of all' (Marx and Engels [1848] 1968: 53). Human beings and human society – and this was also a broader, Enlightenment notion – were now seen as perfectible, indeed so much so that for Marx and Engels it was now possible to imagine a society based on mutual support and cooperation, on equally shared wealth, on progress in the interests of all, on flourishing of all individuals in supportive social circumstances, instead of a society based on conflict, division, inequality, exploitation and alienation. Peace could at last reign and all that gave rise to violence would be left behind.

By contrast with much thought and ideology in pre-modern eras, modern thought takes violence to be intrinsically wrong and from the Enlightenment onwards there is an anti-violence dynamic. Emphasis is put on the experience of the individual, on the rights of the individual and on individual happiness, all of which has a peaceful dynamic. Groups emerged that campaigned against slavery, torture, the death penalty and some particularly cruel practices in warfare. The question of domestic violence began to be raised as well, including violence against women and violence against children. Modern socialist thought had the potential to make a particularly constructive contribution to this process and to offer the framework in which to realise this anti-violence. But as socialist thought and practice developed, its immediate priorities lay elsewhere. Modern socialist thought was largely formed in nineteenth-century Europe, where the bourgeoisie was winning the battle against the feudal order and where the urban proletariat was growing fast. Marx and Engels's core prediction in the *Manifesto* seemed convincing: the demise of capitalism was imminent because it was creating rapidly a huge class of wage slaves that would rise up and destroy the system that was keeping it in chains, and many socialists in the nineteenth century came to believe that capitalism would be swept

away quickly. The emphasis was therefore put on getting rid of capitalism, on transition, on revolution. Marx, Engels and before long Lenin
became the outstanding, eloquent communicators of this approach and
the Russian Revolution seemed to confirm the correctness of the view
that the capitalist world's days were numbered, even if it seemed that
socialist revolutions were at least as likely to take place in developing
countries as in the heartlands of industrial capitalism.

As the twentieth century wore on, subsequent revolutions and
uprisings – in Germany, Spain, China, Vietnam, Cuba, Bolivia, Algeria,
Guinea-Bissau and countless others – seemed to confirm not only
that a better world beyond capitalism was achievable but that it would
come soon to many countries. All this had the effect of rooting socialist
thought in the 'science' of Marx's later writings, where the emphasis
was on understanding the nature of capitalism and on the struggle for
its overthrow and on transition to post-capitalism, where revolution
was the immediate goal, but where the nature of the ultimate goal
of socialism was hardly discussed. Debates also focused on whether
Russia and China and other post-capitalist countries were on the road
to proper communism, real emancipation, and whether it was possible
to achieve revolution in advanced capitalist countries and, if so, how.
In all of this debate and practical campaigning, not to mention uprising
and armed struggles in many parts of the world, virtually no time was
given to discussing the question of non-violence and peace as an ultimate goal, and such notions were often deemed to belong to the realm
of 'bourgeois' morality, or even just morality, by which many Marxists
and others in pursuit of emancipation were frightened of being tainted.
Peace campaigners were often seen as woolly liberals who lacked the
analytical insight and precise logic of scientific socialism, who failed
to understand that the source of much violence was class society, that
violence would always reign as long as capitalism existed and that it
would disappear once socialism was properly established. To discuss
the goal of non-violence and peace was seen as both a distraction from
the struggle against capitalism and also lacking foundation, because we
could not know what a society free from class struggle – or else from
Soviet or Chinese communism – would look like.

In some respects, of course, these arguments were not wrong.
Violence did often have its roots in class society, and it was necessary to
seek out the underlying causes of violence in order for peace eventually
to reign. As Isaac Deutscher puts it with characteristic insight,

[a]s Marxists, we have always preached . . . the need to overthrow capitalism by force [yet we retain] the aspiration to transform societies in such a way that violence should cease forever as the necessary and permanent element in the regulation of the relationship between society and individuals, between individuals and individuals. In embracing the vision of a nonviolent society, Marxism . . . has gone further and deeper than any pacifist preachers of nonviolence have ever done. Why? Because Maxism has laid bare the roots of violence in our society. (Deutscher 1984: 256)

But such a view of the relationship between the relevance of violence in the past, present and (non-violent) future was very rare, and in the more conventional process of being hard-nosed and 'scientific' about causes, transition and the inability to predict the nature of socialism, the peaceful heart of socialism was often overlooked, and the goals of a socialist society were ignored.

Liberalism, perhaps *the* quintessential ideology of capitalist modernity, is at best a double-edged sword and at worst profoundly hypocritical. It has been associated with and has been used to justify the most appalling practices, including full-scale war and colonial massacres. But there are aspects of liberal ideology that are essential to any thinking about peace and non-violence. As we have noted above, with its emphasis on the individual and freedom, on the preservation of life and protection of the individual, liberalism offers inspiration and encouragement as far as ending violence is concerned. There is, after all, a special relationship between the individual and violence, including the obvious but important point that both physical pain and death are in many respects experiences that are acutely individualistic: however much one may talk about 'collective pain', physical suffering is experienced by the individual and the physical pain experienced by one individual stops with them, with their body, due to the obvious fact that one individual's nervous system operates independently from any other individual's nervous system. This does not mean that we cannot feel empathy – sometimes very intensely – but we can move on from and leave behind emotions like empathy, pity and solidarity in relation to others' suffering as we do not share other people's pain in a physiological sense. Thus, modernity and the rise of the individual have enabled increased sensibility to, and aversion from, pain, violence and death.

Although capitalism combined with liberalism places emphasis on the importance of the individual, including an ideology of non-violence and protection of the human body, it is incapable of producing the circumstances for a fuller flourishing of the individual and, therefore, for the full realisation of the Enlightenment project in this respect. Only a far more egalitarian and just society could do this, one where the peace and well-being of certain sections of society was no longer at the expense of the oppression and (sometimes dire) suffering of other groups of human beings, including in developing countries. Even freedom from actual violence in many parts of the world, whether this be more conventional violence (including violence against women) or structural violence, is not possible under current circumstances; many people live in appalling circumstances that liberal regimes allow to continue, because the liberal state is reluctant to go beyond certain bounds when it comes to alleviating individuals' hardship and material want. This is just one part of the enormous hypocrisy of liberalism. Moreover, even the most minimal liberal norms regarding human rights are easily abandoned in times of war or in search of 'security', as the USA's War on Terror has shown in so many ways, including the systematic use of torture on detainees. Nevertheless, as Norman Geras argues, although it allows millions of people to go hungry and even more to live in extreme poverty:

> liberalism historically has been about trying to set limits to the accumulation and abuse of political power, about protecting the physical and mental space of individuals from unwarranted invasion, and about evolving institutions and practices, political and juridical, that contribute to such ends. (Geras 1999: 48)

Liberalism does offer some protection against cruel practices and should be drawn upon and built upon in a more egalitarian, just and peaceful society.

THE POST-WAR PERIOD IN THE WEST

The post-war period in the West was in various respects a time when there was a strong, peaceful dynamic, when various forms of violence seemed to become increasingly unacceptable. In numerous countries in the West, there was unprecedented economic growth lasting several decades when near full employment and sharply rising living standards for many people meant overall reductions in material inequalities and improved quality of life including, for example, better housing, reduced working time and longer paid holidays. Some of this was a reaction against the death, destruction and multiple hardships of the Second World War, and in the post-war period the people of many countries expected improvements after years of hardship and what was seen as reward or at least compensation for sacrifices of many kinds during the war. But this was also the heyday of Keynesian economic policy, when governments were keen to redistribute a sufficient share of profits to workers in order to ensure that the wheels of consumer capitalism were turning effectively. Often led by social democratic parties, governments sought to ensure cooperation between capital and labour and employers were prepared to offer a greater share of profits in the form of wage rises and corporate taxes in return for cooperation on the part of trade unions and employees. In Britain, this was summed up in the phrase 'beer and sandwiches at Number Ten', describing how in the 1960s and 1970s British trade union leaders were in the habit of meeting the Prime Minister in London to discuss industrial relations and other issues, before Margaret Thatcher became Prime Minister in 1979 and put an abrupt stop to the practice and all that went with it. This type of Fordist compromise was accompanied in many countries in the West by the establishment and consolidation of the welfare state, meaning far greater access to healthcare for the less well off, together with state benefits for unemployment, sickness, maternity and old age. To some extent greater prosperity and consensual politics brought greater interest in a peaceful way of life. A new generation grew up that, in many countries in Western Europe, had no direct experience of the violence of war. The tenor of politics in the post-war period suggested that violence and even material hardship was a thing of the past, or at least soon would be. This made the Vietnam War (1955–75) all the more shocking, and the anti-Vietnam War movement seem all the more worthy. Similarly, the threat of nuclear war between super powers made the anti-nuclear weapons movements in various countries urgent as well.

We must be careful not to paint too rosy a picture of this period in the West, which also continued to see significant hardship for the lower paid and saw, for example, governments preparing to resort quite readily to state violence when labour protested vigorously in strikes, pickets or street demonstrations. Ethnic minorities in predominantly white North America, but also Western Europe, often suffered severe discrimination. Feminist movements were beginning to change ideas and practices regarding women, but what would soon be regarded as deeply sexist attitudes and practices were still taken for granted or at least tolerated. Moreover, advanced capitalist countries' economies were still benefiting greatly in material terms from their intrinsically violent relations with colonies and former colonies, and governments did not hesitate to use significant and ongoing violence in relation to less developed countries (including colonies and former colonies) when it suited them. To take just one example, the (ultimately failed) attack against Egypt in 1956, when British, French and Israeli troops were sent to invade after President Nasser nationalised the Suez Canal, was a classic case of the West assuming that it could continue to use violence in other countries and indeed entire regions of the world in order to defend commercial and strategic interests.

Nevertheless, certain post-war developments in defence of human rights are of relevance to our argument. In 1948, in direct response to the mass killings of the Second World War, the United Nations drew up the Universal Declaration of Human Rights (UDHR), which was signed by forty-eight countries and included the right to live a life free from slavery, torture and 'cruel, inhuman or degrading treatment or punishment'. This was the first time an international agreement had been signed along these lines and although there was doubtless hypocrisy involved on the part of some – and perhaps many – signatories (South Africa being among them), the fact that the Declaration came into being at all is of real significance. (The Declaration also included a positive individual right to resistance against 'tyranny and oppression' as a last resort.) Public attitudes towards what became known as human rights have certainly changed, as the widespread support for the international human rights organisation Amnesty International demonstrates. Established in 1961, by 2015 it had a declared membership and activist base of approximately three million and more than 2,000 staff worldwide. The World Health Organization (WHO) was also established in 1948 and has played a crucial role in reducing the scale of, or eradicating, certain diseases, including tuberculosis, malaria, smallpox, human immunodeficiency virus (HIV)/acquired immune deficiency syndrome (AIDS) and Ebola. In 2002, WHO published the first *World Report on Violence and Health*, documenting and suggesting ways to prevent interpersonal violence, mainly by people against other members of their own family, whether they be children, adults (often but not always women) or older people.

During the same period there was also what is sometimes called the Rights Revolution, where, in reaction to strong and effective campaigns in many areas, legal and attitudinal changes took place in relation to the rights of women, ethnic minorities, children, homosexuals and people with disabilities. This 'revolution' has meant increased awareness and decreased tolerance of violence against each of these groups and, for example, a reduced level of corporal punishment in schools and less domestic abuse. There is, of course, still a long way to go before various forms of violence related to these groups disappears completely, but there has been movement in the right direction. We may say the same about health and safety both in the workplace and in the home, where – in many countries in the West, at least – far fewer accidents occur today than in the immediate post-1945 period.

ELIAS, PINKER AND THE 'CIVILISING PROCESS'

In *The Civilising Process* ([1939] 1994), Norberto Elias argues that over the past five centuries and in particular with the rise of the modern state and – after Max Weber – its monopoly of legitimate violence, society's general attitude towards both violence and fear of violence has changed considerably. At the same time, individuals have become more empathetic towards one another. Whereas in the Middle Ages violence was an accepted part of life at all levels, from the family, the school and local manifestations of power to the war-mongering nation state, the coming of modernity and in particular later modernity brought a decreasing level of violence in all spheres. Industrialised countries in particular had gone or were going through this 'civilising process'; violent impulses that had once been given free rein were now increasingly being controlled and constraints were also becoming enshrined in law. Various objections may be made to Elias's thesis, of course. First, simultaneously with the publication of the first edition of the book in 1939, unprecedented destruction of human life began in the Second World War. Elias (himself a German Jew) stuck to his argument in the post-war years, arguing that it was still valid if the general sweep of 'civilisation' was examined and that the process was bound to be an uneven one. Second, Elias's description of the alleged decline of violence as characteristic of 'civilisation' had, to say the least, a colonial or neo-colonial ring about it, although he maintained that his argument was universally valid and not just applicable to Western societies. Related to this, we may point out that at least some of the relative peace of advanced capitalist societies is dependent on both past and present violence being exported to poorer parts of the world; whether it be agent-oriented violence or structural violence, the West's relative peace, linked with prosperity, depends to some extent on, to take the more extreme examples, wars fought in other countries (for example, in pursuit of cheaper oil) and on the far harder living and working conditions for people in developing countries compared with those living in the West. Etienne Balibar (2004: 125) describes this as the division of the world into 'death zones' in developing countries and 'life zones' in the advanced capitalist nations, with the latter highly dependent on the former in order to enjoy a relatively peaceful environment. Finally, it may be objected that the peaceful logic of modernity may in the future be reversed, or at least suffer a drastic setback, as it did in the twentieth century during the Second World War.

Nevertheless, it will be clear from what I have argued in the previous few pages that I have some sympathy with Elias's argument and believe that there is indeed a certain peaceful logic to modernity, albeit one that can suffer serious reverses, and one that cannot be realised properly within capitalism. Steven Pinker argues in similar fashion to Elias in a lengthy and controversial book that there has been a generalised decline in violence over a long period of time and that 'today we may be living in the most peaceable era in our species' existence' (2011: xxi). Inspired in conceptual terms by Elias – his third chapter is entitled 'The Civilizing Process' – but, by contrast with Elias, relying on very substantial amounts of data, Pinker argues not only that wars between major powers have become a thing of the past (the Long Peace), but that violence in all its forms has diminished. Since 1989, then, 'organised conflicts of all kinds – civil wars, genocides, repression by autocratic governments, and terrorist attacks – have declined throughout the world' in what he calls the New Peace (xxiv; see also 295–377).

My argument in this opening chapter is perhaps superficially similar to Pinker's but in fact is rather different. Pinker maintains that there is a decline in violence in all spheres of life and that, while we cannot be sure that this will continue, it is a distinct trend. There is certainly something in the spirit of Pinker's argument to agree with. It is true (although he does not put it quite like this) that modernity has created some of the preconditions for peace and non-violence; it is also true that some 'modern' societies have in themselves – albeit highly unevenly – become more peaceful, or at least more publicly concerned with the promotion of peace and non-violence. However, he relies far too heavily on *proportions* of populations when arguing about the sharp decline in violence. Moreover, he appears at least partially to ignore large swathes of the world in the form of the developing world, commenting that the 'inaccessible or inhospitable territories of the world' are exceptions that prove the rule of the civilising process (81). Neither does Pinker seem to see the irony in suggesting that very high levels of violence in the USA during the 1960s, 1970s and 1980s have been addressed and reduced in part, at least, by mass imprisonment of criminals (120–1). According to many definitions of violence, this process has helped reduce one form of violence outside of prison while increasing another within their walls. By 2015, the number of prisoners in the US had risen to approximately 2.3 million, a seven-fold increase since the 1970s, five times the number in Britain per head of population, nine times that of Germany and fourteen times that of Japan. *The Economist* puts it starkly: '[a]t any one time, one American adult in 35 is in prison, on parole or on probation. A third of African-American men can expect to be locked up at some point, and one in nine black children has a parent behind bars' (2015b: 18). Thus, violence in the form of imprisonment reflects closely the inequalities in society more generally.

Most importantly, Pinker's highly optimistic approach seems at times to border on complacency, to be almost accepting of the current levels of violence of all different kinds in the world today, which are still extremely high by any standards. To devote an entire 800-page book to the argument that violence is on the decline relative to the (rapidly growing) world population seems at least by implication to be over-accepting of appallingly high current levels of violence of many kinds. To take one example, the World Health Organization found that globally in 2014 one in four children had been physically abused, one in five girls had been sexually abused and one in three women had been a victim of physical and/or sexual violence at some point in her lifetime (WHO 2014b). Many other examples spring to mind, of course, the point being that there is a great deal of violence in contemporary societies and this is tragic, to say the least. In his preoccupation with the developed world and over-reliance on a 'modernising' schema, Pinker appears almost to ignore counter-developments in poorer countries and, more importantly in terms of the conclusions we may draw, he seems to miss the point that on a highly globalised planet the developed world has a crucial effect on less developed parts, and in many ways one that helps maintain the poverty, inequality and violence (including structural violence) of less developed countries. It is crucial that we should take a stand against this violence and reflect on how to get rid of it, rather than simply attempt to prove that violence has declined in proportion to populations as a whole.

We need to take a nuanced approach to both Elias and especially to Pinker, then. The logic of their positions appears to be that peace will arrive without us trying very hard. Buried in the mass of data, we do find that Pinker is arguing that 'gentle commerce' helps the cause of peace a great deal, which is rather different from my own argument. Ultimately, they both appear to be attempting to support fully the liberal democratic and capitalist order, whereas my view is that, although there are peaceful aspects of capitalism and liberalism, especially in the West, this order is maintaining a great deal of violence and is in danger of perpetuating a great deal more of it in the future.

More convincingly, Richard Bessel (2015: 10) argues that, although Pinker may be wrong to assert that violence worldwide is actually diminishing:

> we have witnessed a transformation in *attitudes* towards violence, with profound consequences for our political, social and personal lives. It may be debated whether we really 'have been getting kinder and gentler' [as Pinker argues], but we do live in a world where being kinder and gentler increasingly is regarded as admirable and where violence is routinely condemned. (Bessel 2015: 10; emphasis in original)

He suggests that the causes of this transformation in attitudes include a reaction against the devastating violence of two world wars, the post-Second World War economic boom, more stable state structures that are 'more capable of maintaining civil peace' (274), improvements in public hygiene and medical provision making death more remote and therefore violent death more horrific, changes in the position of women in society and the existence of more women in positions of public prominence and a mass media more able than ever before to transfer reports and images very quickly from violent conflicts virtually anywhere on the globe.

FEMINISM, FEMINISATION AND MATERNALISM

The increasing influence of women in many societies, together with a greater inclination towards non-violence and peace on the part of many women means that the potential for peace in the longer term has increased and is likely to continue to increase as the influence of women becomes greater.

This area is, however, far more complex than this initial remark may suggest, and our approach must be more nuanced. According to many indicators, the tendency on the part of girls and women in most situations is to be less violent than their male counterparts, whether this be in the school playground, in the home or on the street; much of the relevant literature suggests that there are evolution-related reasons for this that at least in part explain more peaceful behaviour, whether or not we then draw the conclusion that men are more 'biologically inclined' towards violence due, perhaps, to higher levels of testosterone (Archer 2006). However, it is just as true that women tend, for example, to be wholly supportive of (often male) soldiers, particularly when the men are engaged in combat. As mothers, wives, partners, non-combat army personnel and more generally citizens in support of war, women often approve of the actions and assist the men who are often in the front line of fighting. Traditionally, they have nurtured, praised, organised, tended the wounded and mourned the dead, all in the cause of war. Indeed, there are notable examples of women shaming men who are not involved in combat and taking an explicitly pro-violence approach; in 1914, the Order of the White Feather was created in Britain, which arranged for women, including suffragettes Emmeline and Christabel Pankhurst, to present white feathers to men who were not in uniform. The white feather was a symbol of cowardice. In Germany in the 1930s, the Nationalsozialistische Frauenshaft, or National Socialist Women's League (NSWL), played an important role in offering women party leadership and more specifically supporting routine violence perpetrated mainly by men. By 1938 the NSWL had in the region of two million members, accounting for 40 per cent of total National Socialist Party membership (Payne 1995: 184). A more recent example of women perpetrating or encouraging extreme violence is female supporters of Islamic State, many of whom were brought up in countries of the Middle East, but some of whom have travelled to the region from elsewhere in order to support the military and political campaign of IS, which includes systematic and extreme violence, including, inter alia, killing or enslaving religious minorities.

Indeed in virtually all major conflicts in history for which we have records, women have supported men's violence; Aristophanes' play *Lysistrata*, where Greek women refuse to have sex with their men in order to persuade them to end the Peloponnesian War, is not only a rare exception to a more general rule of women supporting war, but is also a work of fiction, albeit an encouraging one. It would indeed be rather surprising if a major armed conflict neatly placed men in one, pro-fighting camp and women in another, peace-promoting camp, given that men and women are often bound so closely together emotionally, ideologically and materially. Indeed, in some armies, including in Europe and the USA, and in less formal fighting groups, women today are increasingly involved in actual combat, although the numbers involved are, for the time being, small. However, as war and other forms of fighting come to depend increasingly on sophisticated equipment such as unmanned aerial combat vehicles, or drones, electronic surveillance and cyber warfare and less on troops on the ground where men are often preferred, women will be increasingly at the heart of the battle machine.

Nevertheless, women have often had a particular affinity with peace movements of various kinds, offering profound commitment in day-to-day activities and also taking on leadership roles. Cynthia Cockburn (2012) discusses such movements and their gender dimension and describes peace and anti-violence movements in many countries, including Japan, the Palestinian territory of Gaza, Spain, France, Germany and Britain. In each case, women play a particularly important role. One may also mention the Women for Peace movement in the North of Ireland, which later became the Community for Peace People. It was led by Mairead Maguire – whose sister's three children were killed in 1976 by a car driven by a republican who had been fatally shot by a soldier – Betty Williams and Ciaran McKeown. Another outstanding example of women organising for peace in recent history was the Greenham Common Women's Peace Camp in Britain, which was in place uninterruptedly from 1981 to 2000. It was set up in order to protest against the deployment of Cruise missiles at the US air base at Greenham, but became a much broader movement against all military violence. It was run by a women-only core of activists who stayed at the camp around the clock, seven days per week, and organised successful mass (and sometimes mixed) days of action, one of which, in December 1982, involved encircling the base with a roughly 30,000-strong (women only) human chain. The base was closed in 1993 but the camp remained in place in order to ensure that the base was not re-opened. Throughout, a link was made by those organising the protest between women, mothers, life and non-violence as opposed to men, violence, war and death. (For debates among feminists regarding the effectiveness of Greenham see Frazer and Hutchings 2014a.)

This is, then, a particularly difficult area to find one's way through and one that is full of paradoxes. Is there something 'essentially peaceful' about women, and in particular mothers, a characteristic that can be identified as a source of hope as women gain greater equality and more influence in public affairs, or are women (including mothers) intrinsically as violent and pro-war as men? Even if they are not as violent as many men as individuals and ordinary citizens, once they gain more power, do women simply tend to 'act like men' in relation to war and violence more generally? For analytical guidance, let us turn to Sara Ruddick and her book *Maternal Thinking: Towards a Politics of Peace* (1995). Ruddick points out that, certainly, mothers and women more generally often play their part in wars, including (in her eyes) unjust wars. Although violence and war is usually thought of as particularly male, and support for military action is often thought of as an approach that is associated with masculinity, '[w]omen's peacefulness is at least as mythical as men's violence' and 'there is nothing in a woman's genetic makeup or history that prevents her from firing a missile or spraying nerve gas over a sleeping village if she desires this or believes it to be her duty'. Women have always been involved in war in one way or another, often finding it as exciting as do men, and taking the opportunity that war offers to escape from domestic duties and to enjoy different experiences from those of peacetime (Ruddick 1995: 154).

However, Ruddick also argues that there is indeed a special relationship between mothering and the politics of peace:

All of women's work – sheltering, nursing, feeding, kin work, teaching of the very young, tending the frail elderly – is threatened by violence. When maternal thinking takes upon itself the critical perspective of a feminist standpoint, it reveals a contradiction between mothering and war. Mothering begins in birth and promises life; military thinking justifies organized, deliberate death. (Ruddick 1995: 148)

Moreover,

[i]f they have made training a work of conscience and proper trust a virtue, if they have resisted the temptation to dominate their children and abrogate their authority, then mothers have been preparing themselves for patient and conscientious nonviolence ... if military endeavours seem a betrayal of maternal practice, nonviolent action can seem a natural extension. (Ruddick 1995: 150)

Ruddick argues that there is no such thing as a 'pure maternal peacefulness' but something much more complicated in the form of 'a deep unease with military endeavors' linked with 'maternal impulses to applaud, connect and heal' and although mothers are not necessarily peace-loving, the practice of mothering is a 'natural resource' for the politics of peace (156–7). She insists that

[t]he contradiction between violence and maternal work is evident. Wherever there are wars, children are hurt, hungry and frightened; homes are burned, crops destroyed, families scattered. The daily practice and long-term aims of women's caring labour are all threatened. Though mothers may be warlike, war is their enemy ... Although mothers may not be peaceful, 'peace' is their business ... Although a group of mothers, like any other group, includes ordinary militarists and peacemakers as well as fierce fighters and saintly pacifists, the practice of mothering taken as a whole gives rise to ways of thinking and acting that are useful to peace politics. (Ruddick 1995: 220)

While not all individual women, or even mothers, are intrinsically peace-loving, then, Ruddick is arguing that this is a contradiction – and we may add that to nurture and to fight simultaneously is a 'dialectically contradictary' phenomenon that is ripe for resolution.

The rise of the influence of women in many spheres since the Second World War has increased the likelihood of moving towards more enduringly peaceful societies. There are now far more women than there used to be in positions of influence in the workplace, in politics, in the media and in the arts. There is no automatic correlation between the presence of women and a greater orientation towards peace and non-violence, but relevant issues are more likely to be raised by women than men. Moreover, as men have become more involved in child rearing and domestic work, there is greater sensibility towards these issues on the part of men as well. In other words, gender stereotypes have broken down somewhat and this has brought with it a changing attitude towards fighting and violence more generally. Feminism has brought with it a change in attitudes on the part of many women and men to the question of 'everyday life' and this has included altered attitudes in this domain.

MODERN MEDICINE

In the West, the last two centuries – and in particular the period since the Second World War – have seen tremendous advances in medicine and healthcare (Jackson 2014; Porter 2002). Certainly, socio-economic, demographic and political changes brought with them threats to human health as well as benefits; in the nineteenth century, rapid urbanisation of work and housing saw increasing prevalence of infectious disease and poor mental health, which affected the working classes hugely disproportionately. Urban slums and intensive working conditions meant high levels of mortality from diseases such as tuberculosis, cholera, dysentery and smallpox. Places of work often became more dangerous as the industrial revolution got under way, particularly factories and coal mines, where the risk to workers of all ages was not only of industrial injury and accidental death but also of silicosis, asbestosis and sometimes cancer.

However, the expansion of towns and cities and the establishment of large hospitals also brought substantial improvements in the care and treatment of the sick, including what are today considered as minimum levels of cleanliness and hygiene. In the course of the nineteenth century, surgical techniques improved greatly and became more humane, with the introduction of effective and safer anaesthesia, notably ether, nitrous oxide and chloroform. The use of antiseptic in operating theatres, associated in particular with Joseph Lister in Britain, had a substantial effect on survival rates during and after surgery. The late nineteenth century also brought the development of vaccines against infectious disease, including the tropical diseases malaria, yellow fever and sleeping sickness, administered at first mainly to missionaries and soldiers working or fighting in hot countries. Such advances in medicine, together with increased state expenditure on healthcare and welfare more generally, and combined with rising living standards and better nutrition, meant far greater resistance to infectious disease. By 1950, the health of general populations living in advanced capitalist countries had improved almost beyond recognition compared with a century earlier and average life expectancy had increased by twenty to thirty years, largely (but not entirely) due to a massive decline in infant and adolescent mortality.

The period from the Second World War to the present has again brought substantial advances in medicine and healthcare in developed countries, and a very significant increase in public resources devoted to these areas. James Le Fanu (2011: 3) identifies the following as being among the most significant moments of medical research since the Second World War: the discovery of penicillin (1941); the commercial production of cortisone for various uses, including reduction of pain and swelling (1949); the identification of smoking as the cause of lung cancer (1950); the effective treatment of tuberculosis using streptomycin and 4-aminosaliclic (1950); the creation of intensive care after the Copenhagen polio epidemic (1952); the use of chlorpromazine in the treatment of schizophrenia (1952); open heart surgery (1955); the development of vaccination against polio (1955); hip replacement (1961); kidney transplantation (1963); breakthroughs in the prevention of strokes (1964); and the discovery of helicobacter as the cause of peptic ulcers (1984). We should also mention advances with regard to contraception, the treatment of HIV/AIDS and of heart conditions and their causes, such as high blood pressure.

In terms of prevention of disease, many countries have seen the introduction of state-funded public health and welfare systems, established or greatly expanded after the Second World War. These systems often allow almost everyone access to a full range of healthcare, including regular monitoring of children in schools, inoculation against infectious diseases, and free school meals. One glaring exception was the USA, where access to healthcare remained far from universal until 2010, when reforms partially rectified this situation. Meanwhile, sophisticated equipment such as lasers, ultrasound, computerised tomography (CT) and magnetic resonance imaging (MRI) meant that early detection and treatment of certain diseases changed out of all recognition. Enormous amounts of money, both public and private, were spent on research into new drugs, equipment and procedures, in what became an extremely lucrative business. In the early twenty-first century, many countries banned smoking in public places, which began to help reduce the number of people who smoked and lower the incidence of various diseases, especially lung cancer, heart attack and stroke. Nevertheless, various chronic diseases such as cancer, heart disease, arthritis and diabetes were still (and in some countries were increasingly) prevalent, in part but not solely because people were living longer. Moreover, people's state of health varied greatly between social classes and different levels of income, with significant differences between rich and poor according to various key criteria such as longevity, incidence of heart disease, cancer and diabetes, and frequency and length of hospital visits.

The above account applies far more to higher-income countries than to lower-income countries, of course. Nevertheless, substantial – if highly uneven – improvements were made in some less-developed countries. According to the World Health Organization (2014a), and looking at the question of longevity on a global basis, a girl who was born in 2012 will live on average to the age of 72.7 years, and a boy to 68.1 years. This is a six-year increase compared with the equivalent figures for children born in 1990, and a twenty-five-year increase compared with children born in 1948. The global under-five mortality rate dropped from ninety-one per thousand live births in 1990 to forty-three in 2014. The figures for low-income countries have improved the most, with an increase in life expectancy of 9 years from 1990 to 2012, from 54.0 to 63.1 years for women and from 51.2 to 60.2 years for men. In 2014, WHO published the *Global Status Report on Violence Prevention*, which found that homicide rates had dropped 12 per cent over ten years, with approximately 475,000 people murdered in 2012 (WHO 2014b). The existence of such an inquiry, and the fact that a majority of countries worldwide had cooperated with the research for the report, seems to be an indication that attitudes were changing in this domain as well.

The evolution of the state of human health during the period we call modernity, then, has been mixed; urbanisation and industrialisation caused – and in some parts of the world continue to cause – a large amount of illness and many untimely deaths. However, my main point is that there has been a strong impulse to make very substantial advances in many areas of medicine and healthcare and these have indeed been made. Certainly, after Foucault, we can agree that there are negative aspects of the development of modern medicine, including a degree of unwelcome control that healthcare systems can exercise over populations, and it is also true that capitalism needs a reasonably healthy proletariat in order for the system to function properly; a workforce that is often sick will not allow the wheels of capitalism to turn as effectively, both because it is not working properly and because it is not consuming commodities and services as it should. It may also be argued that scientific 'progress' in part led, for example, to eugenics and theories of race, which in turn contributed to some of the ideological support for the systematic extermination of Jews and others by the Nazis. But it was not scientific discoveries in themselves that led to the Holocaust, any more than, for example, the development of flight led, in itself, to the firebombing of Dresden in 1945 or the splitting of the atom led in itself to the dropping of the atom bomb on Hiroshima and Nagasaki; the same discoveries and inventions can be put to various different uses, some of them horrifically destructive of human life and some of them beneficial to many people. A recent example of this, so far on a smaller scale, is the invention and development of drones, which can be put to use in rescue operations, for example, as well as in the 'war against terrorism' where people who have nothing to do with violent actions are often killed alongside 'suspected terrorists'.

What does all of this tell us about peace and non-violence? It tells us that there is an underlying urge and an underlying desire for good health, absence of pain, preservation of the human body intact, and a widespread impulse to move in the opposite direction from suffering and violence. Modern medicine combined with the welfare state has been pushing in this direction for many years and there is now the possibility and the scientific understanding to eradicate or prevent many conditions and improve the health of many people worldwide; the possibility is now there, even if the will is only partially there.

*   *   *

In this chapter I have made a strong argument for the starting point of any analysis of violence in pursuit of emancipation to be the eventual eradication of violence and the establishment of lasting peace. Any progressive, egalitarian and socialist project must place far greater emphasis on the objective of non-violence and peace than has been the practice hitherto, and must link the goal of non-violence clearly and explicitly with the quest for equality and democracy. As we shall see in the next chapter, the long history of violence in human societies is often closely connected with inequality and a drastic reduction or eradication of inequality must go hand in hand with the promotion of non-violence and peace. Many who have struggled for socialism have shunned the idea that it is worth dreaming a little and imagining what a far more equal and just society may be like, alongside a hard-headed approach to the tactics and strategy of struggle. But implicit in any quest for a very different sort of society is always a set of ideas about the nature of that imagined society. My suggestion is that we need to incorporate peace and non-violence in a very central way in a more explicit exploration of what we may call a utopian vision. We need to do this via an assertion of the importance of a peaceful, non-violent society, alongside other values that are more commonly associated with emancipatory politics, such as equality and deep democracy, freedom from oppression and freedom from exploitation.

To argue that we have an obligation to strive for peace is a view that is commonly associated with a deontological position, or one based on the idea of duty. Immanuel Kant is often cited in relation to this way of arguing about human behaviour, as he maintains that it is our duty to treat the protection of human life as more important than any other objective. In Kant, the right to live a life free from pain and untimely death is raised above all others and a threat to the life of one human being is a threat to humanity as a whole. I make no apology for taking a position that has Kantian overtones and suggest that such an approach is necessary if we are to understand properly the relationship between a struggle for emancipation, including peace, on the one hand, and on the other perhaps necessary violence in the course of the revolt against the established order. However, it will already be clear that I believe there are also limits to the usefulness of a deontological approach, which can itself be employed in order to disguise the violence of the status quo. Marxist thought, by contrast, is sometimes dubbed 'consequentialist', that is, a form of thought that judges actions according to the consequences that these actions lead to rather than according to the rights and wrongs of the actions themselves; critics suggest that Marxist thought therefore leads to the acceptance of morally unacceptable behaviour in the short term for the sake of justice and ethically correct behaviour in the longer term, or to put it another way, accepts ultimately unjustifiable means for the sake of desirable ends. The tension between these two positions – deontological and consequentialist – will be present in the remainder of this book, as we examine the nature of violence of the recent past and ways in which insurgents approach the moral dilemmas regarding use of violence in favour of a just end.

I have suggested that contained within modernity and particularly within late modernity are elements that suggest that there is a general impulse for peace. This is highly uneven, of course, and there are many counter-indications. But there are enough encouraging signs, particularly in the richer countries – from the more progressive elements of liberalism to the Rights revolution, from the increasing influence of women in society to the enormous advances made in modern medicine – to suggest that there has already been an anti-violence dynamic afoot for a long time. It is true, of course, that, for example, the science behind modern medicine can be used for deeply reactionary purposes and some of the most appalling examples of this can be found in the history of Nazi Germany. But this does not in itself negate the progressive elements of modern medicine and, to put it in Habermasian terms, modernity is a project that needs completing; until this project has been completed it will remain very uneven in its benefits.

This profound commitment to a peaceful future may prompt the question of why my argument is not pacifist – why do I not argue that the method of struggle for emancipation should reflect a refusal under all circumstances to engage in violence. My response to this question begins with the comment that methods of struggle should always be as minimally violent as possible, that is, that they should use as little violence as possible in all circumstances. To go beyond this minimum violence is to contradict the goal that is being sought, which includes the elimination of violence of all types. Next, it is necessary to point out that the status quo itself is very often violent and that it generates a great deal of violence of various kinds. This still does not in itself justify violence in pursuit of emancipation, unless this violence is truly effective in beginning to move beyond oppression. Most importantly, however, the defenders of the status quo, or the ruling class, are very often prepared to use violence in order to defend the current order, an order that may be profoundly unjust. In this case, violence may indeed be necessary in order to combat this unjust status quo. Nelson Mandela (1995: 194) was clear about this; despite being an advocate of avoiding violence wherever possible, he argued that the terms of the struggle are set by the enemy, namely the defender of the unjust order, and if they insist on using violence in order to defend the current order, it may be necessary to use violence against them. It must still, however, be a measured use of violence that seeks to avoid a descent into a blood-bath (or a still worse bloodbath, in the case of South Africa under the Apartheid regime) and seeks to avoid the use of violence that is at risk of continuing or generating further violence after the transition.

In practice, pacifism often entails acceptance of the status quo, espe-cially when the powers that be are prepared – which is almost always the case – to resort to violence in order to maintain the status quo. This would certainly have been the case in Vietnam and Algeria during the struggles for emancipation from Western control, where France and the USA were almost entirely without boundaries in their use of violence; although in both cases there were undoubtedly practices on both sides that were unacceptable (and probably affected the nature of the order post-independence) the victory of the insurgents is hard to imagine without violence. This is not to say that one should be as violent as the oppressor and it is not to say that revolutionaries and freedom fighters in anti-colonial struggles have always limited themselves to legitimate violence and no more; from the Russian Revolution to the Chinese revolution, from Algeria to the North of Ireland, from the Spanish Civil War to South Africa, there are examples of excessive violence on the part of rebels fighting for just causes. But they would, in almost all cases, have achieved far less without at least some recourse to arms.

To put this slightly differently, history itself is profoundly unjust and violent. To be able to draw a line suddenly under the injustice and vio-lence without shedding a further drop of blood would be excellent, but this is unimaginable. Most arguments against any form of emancipa-tory violence are therefore likely to accept much of the status quo. The history of the major revolutions of the twentieth century is now domi-nated by writers who seek to show that ongoing bloodshed and cruelty were an inevitable result of the revolution itself, an interpretation that has the effect of suggesting that a profound belief in emancipation is necessarily accompanied by the intention to perpetrate excessive violence. One challenge, then, is to show that a commitment to a profoundly egalitarian future, far from promoting violence, offers a future that is far fairer and more peaceful than anything we have known to date and can be achieved via minimum use of violence.

Chapter 2

CAPITALISM, COMMUNISM AND VIOLENCE

The torture squad was so well trained that they were performing almost perfect crimes, avoiding leaving any obvious evidence. Nothing was left to chance.

Mohamedou Ould Slahi (2015: 73)

Human history is replete with political violence. Both maintenance of the status quo (preventing change) and effecting political and socio-economic change, whether it be from below or by the ruling class (from above), have involved large quantities of violence, whose quality has often been grimly inventive. Usually the powerful have been the perpetrators of violence and the weak the victims, including in what is now thought of as 'conventional' warfare; Paul Valéry commented that 'war is a massacre between people who don't know each other, on behalf of others who know each other very well but don't massacre each other'. A conservative estimate for the death toll from such warfare in the twentieth century is 100 million. If we add repressive, insurgent and structural violence to the equation, the number of violent deaths since 1900 has been truly vast, and it is still growing steadily; for example, in any one day in 2013 the number of children dying from preventable diseases worldwide was more than 17,000. Taking another example, estimates for the number of civilians – that is non-combatant men, women and children – killed in Iraq due to the war since 2003 vary from 121,000 (according to Iraq Body Count) to half a million. This continuous, embedded violence is of course known about widely, but today it is rare for anyone to stand back and ask how long this enduringly unjust state of affairs can be allowed to continue, still less how it may be overcome permanently, in other words to look at the politics of the situation. Such 'grand narratives' as communism, which did look to a very

41

different future and argued for egalitarian and peaceful alternatives, are now usually dismissed as unworkable, totalitarian and in themselves necessarily leading to ongoing violence. Based on the evidence of the behaviour of communist regimes in the twentieth century, such claims have some basis in historical fact, but the alternative offered is usually a variant of the politics, economics and ideology of the West, which is at least as violent as communism, and it is, moreover, ongoing, with no salvation offered from the violence of the past and the present. Political liberalism, especially when combined with market capitalism, continues to be intensely lethal. Religious fundamentalist regimes offer no hope of a peaceful alternative either.

We often deal in numbers of deaths and not with the detail of individual cases, so before we proceed further it is worth reminding ourselves that for each person killed or dying prematurely as a result of almost any violence there are family members whose lives are ruined through ongoing bereavement, loss of a carer, loss of income, loss of home, forced migration and much beyond. Moreover, we tend to overlook the effect of serious injuries, which often mean that people suffer terribly for the rest of their lives, and those injured may well outnumber deaths in any particular scenario.

If we accept, as I argue in Chapter 1, that we have a duty to attempt to achieve lasting peace and non-violence and that such a goal is achievable, before exploring more fully various ideas regarding violence and emancipation we must examine the nature of some of the violence in the recent past and the present, and in particular the relationship between capitalism and violence on the one hand and between historical communism and violence on the other. In what follows I look fairly briefly at the violence perpetrated by regimes claiming to be communist in the twentieth century, and in more detail at violence perpetrated by the 'free world'. The failure of historical communism is particularly tragic given that for the pioneers of communism and for many millions of rank-and-file communists, these regimes should have delivered profound equality of many different kinds, together with a wide range of freedoms, peace and non-violence. Whatever the reasons for communist regimes' failure – and the capitalist West certainly bears some responsibility – the period of classic communism is all but over and I wish therefore to concentrate on violence perpetrated by capitalist regimes. Despite weaknesses and recurring crises, capitalism as a mode of production is for the moment in a position of almost absolute dominance and has a tendency to invent new ways of overcoming crises each time they arise. Therefore ordinary people are subjected to extreme hardships and cruelties in the name of upholding capitalist 'freedoms' of various kinds – freedom of enterprise, freedom to exploit resources (including people) for profit, freedom to intervene militarily in poorer countries. Notwithstanding what I argue in the previous chapter, namely that there are now signs that a peaceful and non-violent future is a possibility, it is also possible that capitalism will become more, rather than less, violent in future; the brief period of relative consensus and compromise in the post-war period, which also combined the end of formal colonialism with dangerous but relatively stable Cold War relations, has given way to a potentially more perilous global system, where the USA and its allies are determined to defend their interests internationally, but where the 'enemy' is far less clearly identified, less united and less stable.

THE OTHER SIDE OF MODERNITY

In Chapter 1, I outlined the progressive, peace-oriented aspects of the legacy of the Enlightenment and of modernity more generally. The other side of the coin, namely the broad facts regarding violence during the development of capitalism and modernity, are fairly well known, but it is worth re-stating some of them briefly. If we begin with slavery, this is one of the most obviously violent and extreme forms of exploitation and has existed in almost all types of human society since the Neolithic period. We can think of slavery as the ownership and extreme commodification of one human being by another, to the extent not only that people are bought and sold but also that countless enslaved individuals have been either deliberately killed by their owners or have died from neglect and/or overwork. Slavery involves various forms of exploitation, always achieved and maintained by violence and the constant threat of further violence, often including torture and rape. It exists to this day in a variety of forms, from forced labour to sexual exploitation and the Global Slavery Index estimates that there are fourteen states worldwide with more than one per cent of the population that is enslaved (*The Economist* 2015: 52).

What we now think of as 'traditional' slavery, much of which was the Atlantic slave trade, played a key role in the development of capitalism. In his classic study of the relationship between slavery and early capitalism in Britain, Eric Williams ([1942] 1990: 33) suggests that somewhere in the region of two million slaves were transported to British colonies from 1680 to 1786 and he describes the major role that slavery played in establishing Britain as a successful capitalist nation:

> The Negroes were purchased with British manufactures; transported to the plantations, they produced sugar, cotton, indigo, molasses and other tropical products, the processing of which created new industries in England; while the maintenance of the Negroes and their owners on the plantations provided another market for British industry, New England agriculture and the Newfoundland Fisheries. By 1750 there was hardly a trading or a manufacturing town in England which was not in some way connected with the triangular or direct colonial trade. The profits obtained provided one of the main streams of that accumulation of capital in England which financed the Industrial Revolution. (Williams [1942] 1990: 52)

Next, it would be difficult to overstate the violence involved in the West's conquering and maintaining colonial territories, which also played an important role in the development and consolidation of capitalism. To take but three examples and leaving aside countless others, first, David Stannard, in *American Holocaust* (1992: 95), estimates that from sixty to eighty million native Americans died during the conquest of the New World. Moreover, the surviving members of the indigenous population were forced to live marginal existences and are still suffering the consequences to this day. Second, when Belgian King Leopold II ruled the Congo Free State at the end of the nineteenth century and the beginning of the twentieth, millions died and many thousands were mutilated – often by amputation of hands or feet of wives or children of plantation workers – as a form of punishment for failing to meet rubber production quotas; this was another crystal-clear example of extreme cruelty carried out in the pursuit of profit. Third, in 1952, the Mau Mau rebellion took place in Kenya, which was an uprising by the Kikuyu people demanding the return of their land. Britain reacted by placing almost one and a half million of the Kikuyu population in camps over the following eight years and such was the hardship and brutality meted out in these camps that an estimated one hundred thousand people died (Elkins 2005).

Colonial rule was invariably not only deeply repressive but it also involved constant and systematic brutality, and it was defended, when challenged, with the argument that indigenous people were far inferior to the colonisers. An important aspect of colonial rule, beyond the declared reasons that included bringing 'civilisation' or Christianity to barbarous people, was what Marx describes as 'primitive accumulation'; the colonies offered capitalists the opportunity to accumulate large amounts of capital quickly, and as time went by colonies also became profitable market places for goods, again offering established colonial capitalists an advantage over emerging capitalists. Colonial activity involved both direct exploitation of human labour, often under the harshest of conditions, but also manipulation of the economies and resources of colonised countries for the benefit of the colonising country. This compounded the suffering of the colonised people as they became locked into a system created for the benefit of the occupying country and that was often quite contrary to the needs of the indigenous population. To describe modern capitalism as coming into existence 'dripping from head to toe, from every pore, with blood and dirt' (Marx [1867] 1954: 77) is no exaggeration. Insubordination, let alone resistance, on the part of indigenous populations in colonies was always repressed harshly, but in two world wars, soldiers were recruited widely from various empires to fight in European wars and countless numbers of these colonial recruits died as a result. As A. J. P. Taylor commented regarding the First World War, 'some 50 million Africans and 250 million Indians were involved, without consultation, in a war of which they understood nothing' (cited in Losurdo 2015 [1996 and 1998]: 309) and Domenico Losurdo adds that for a 'master race' to use people as cannon fodder in this way in some important respects resembles genocide (ibid.).

Zygmunt Bauman, perhaps more effectively than any other writer, investigates the relationship between modernity and genocide. For him, the Holocaust was very much in keeping with the highly developed rationalism of modernity and 'it was the spirit of instrumental rationality, and its modern, bureaucratic form of institutionalization, which had made the Holocaust-style solutions not only possible, but eminently "reasonable" – and increased the probability of their choice' (1989: 18). In particular, the Nazis used modern bureaucracy, science and industrial techniques in order to transport millions of people hundreds of miles in order to either use them as slave labour, or kill them, or to do one followed by the other. According to Bauman this was not an aberration as far as the logic of modernity was concerned, but wholly in keeping with it. My own argument is that modernity embodies both significant positive and peaceful elements, but that there is nothing in its logic that guarantees a straight path towards greater progress and peace; the tragedy of the Nazi genocide contains echoes of earlier genocides, including the extermination of native Americans and the mass killing of Armenians by the Ottoman government in the early twentieth century. Bauman argues that

> [a]s the promotion of rationality to the exclusion of alternative criteria of action, and in particular the tendency to subordinate the use of violence to rational calculus, has been long ago acknowledged as a constitutive feature of modern civilization – the Holocaust-style phenomena must be recognized as legitimate outcomes of civilizing tendency, and its constant potential. (Bauman 1989: 28)

As we shall see in the rest of this chapter, although the scale of the killing in the Second World War has not been repeated in one country or area, there has been a great deal of capitalist and communist violence since 1945, even if we confine our enquiry to a few thematic areas. Nor is the future certain to be any more peaceful, by any means.

Liberalism is often seen as the paradigmatic ideology of Enlightenment and post-Enlightenment thinking, with its emphasis on the freedom of the individual, individual rights, tolerance and promotion of peace. I suggest in Chapter 1 that some aspects of the theory and practice of liberalism do indeed have an anti-violence and peaceful dynamic and are to be welcomed. However, alongside this dimension lies a far bleaker one as well. In terms of the history of liberal ideology, Losurdo describes in some detail the way in which prominent European and North American liberals supported slavery, how they not only tolerated but also supported the extermination of native Americans and how they took a similar attitude towards the racist brutality of colonial rule. John Stewart Mill himself claimed that there were 'savage tribes so averse from regular industry, that industrial life is scarcely able to introduce itself among them until they are . . . conquered and made slaves of' (cited in Losurdo [2006] 2011: 226). Britain and Holland, famous defenders of the moral superiority of liberalism, committed the most appalling crimes in their colonies; the USA, another champion of liberalism, facilitated and encouraged systematic violence against African-Americans that included lynching, especially in southern states, and the USA commits barbarous acts in the name of spreading democracy and liberalism (and of course liberal economics) around the world to this day, with a special place for the Central Intelligence Agency (CIA) in all of this. In short, there is plenty of evidence that the history of liberalism is not simply one of promoting peace.

The general notion of 'liberal peace' encompasses various subsidiary ideas that do, however, take liberalism to be inherently peaceful. For example, some historians and international relations specialists have claimed that liberal democratic states do not go to war with one another, in what is sometimes known as the 'democratic peace' thesis. This – originally Kantian – notion has become particularly prevalent since the end of the Cold War. Related to the democratic peace thesis is the doctrine of 'gentle commerce', which again suggests that nations that trade with one another do not go to war. Both claims are highly contestable, and have been challenged successfully using historical data (see, for example, Dillon and Reid 2009: 106–27). Mark Neocleous (2014: 7) goes further than simply refuting claims of liberal peace and argues that 'liberalism has from its inception been a political philosophy of war, has been fully conscious of this and, as a consequence, has sought to bury this fact under various banners', including 'peace and security' and 'law and order'. I suggest what may be an alternative way between these views, namely that liberalism combined with capitalism tends to promote peace in advanced capitalist societies as long as the interests of capital, in other words the pursuit of profit, are not jeopardised seriously. Liberalism is true to its word and is peaceful as long as it is able to promote 'freedom' in order to make money. This is not because political liberalism combined with capitalism is inherently altruistic, but because this system relies largely on mass consumption and mass salaried employment, combined with universal suffrage, to remain in place. In capitalist societies, at least in the heartlands of capitalism, the ruling class can often rule without excessive coercion and depends on economic domination in order to keep people in line, by contrast with pre-capitalist societies where the ruling class practised more coercion and violence. Unlike the situation in pre-capitalist societies and in numerous dictatorships around the world today, it does not rely on widespread and active state and private violence in order to maintain its rule, although both the state and private entities (such as 'security' firms) do of course practise some violence, particularly on demonstrators, strikers and certain minority groups. Gramsci's notion of ideological hegemony is also relevant here, where consent is at least as important as coercion for maintaining the status quo, at least outside of periods of crisis. However, once this relatively stable and relatively peaceful state of affairs is threatened, or more bluntly once capital's ability to continue to accumulate is threatened, liberal democratic regimes will not hesitate to use direct force on their own electorate, quite apart from violent intervention in other, poorer countries. This is all deeply hypocritical on the part of liberal ideology, of course. But for many people living in the countries where liberal ideology and liberal democratic rule prevails, this is a distinct improvement on pre-capitalist arrangements or on contemporary dictatorships, for that matter, where there are no claims made regarding equal rights or freedom of expression, and where maintaining the status quo is far more directly dependent on violence.

We will return to the question of structural violence and its relationship with inequality at greater length below, but let us now remind ourselves that liberalism makes the individual the centre of attention in virtually all domains. Thus, in the liberal view of things, violence only takes place where there is an agent, a perpetrator. But this means that those suffering from neglect, from poor living conditions, homelessness, untreated mental health problems or overwork, or who have truncated lives due to poor medical care or malnutrition, leave the liberal democratic scheme of things free of any responsibility. No-one is responsible for these areas of suffering and death according to the liberal outlook, but as Bikhu Parekh suggests, if we begin our enquiry by placing the victims at the centre of it, things look very different:

> Rather than ask if and how we, who are too refined to hurt even a fly, are causally and morally responsible for physical harm to others, we should ask why millions suffer distress, injury, pain, and premature deaths and what we could do to prevent and alleviate them. (Parekh 1990: 137)

Just War Theory (JWT), which seeks to offer guidance as to when states are and are not justified in going to war, has a long history rooted in pre-Christian thought, but in its modern form, it is often a liberal argument that permits certain types of military violence and rules others out. In a nutshell, JWT posits that ethical issues in relation to war fall into two main categories, *jus ad bellum* – justice of (going to) war – and *jus in bello* – justice of (being in a) war. According to this approach, any group or country planning to start a war must make sure that it abides by a series of stipulations, including *just cause*, which would include being under attack, or severe threat of attack, and intervention in a humanitarian capacity. Excluded from the list of legitimate reasons for going to war is pursuit of a particular ideology or enlarging the extent of one's territory. The war that is initiated must be *proportionate*; in other words the net result must be to save lives rather than cause a higher number of deaths. It must also be a last resort, be likely to achieve its goals and have *legitimate authority*; in other words those going to war must be authorised to do so. Once the war has started, *jus in bello* applies and again fighting needs to be proportionate to the behaviour of the enemy, so, for example, carpet bombing should not be used against an enemy that is killing a relatively small number of one's own people. Certain people should not be attacked if at all possible, including the elderly, children and pregnant women, and schools and hospitals should be untouched. Prisoners of war should be treated well.

Much of this seems to Western liberals like common sense and some of it has strongly influenced international law or guidance, including the United Nations Charter. Certainly, the general spirit of keeping bloodshed to a minimum is to be applauded, but there are various aspects of even the above thumbnail sketch of JWT that leap out as being potentially more violence-causing than peaceful in the long run. The stipulation that war should not be pursued for ideological reasons assumes that, first, the established order is not influenced by any ideology, that is, that it is ideology-free and is ruled by value-free reason and, second, that any ideology that is not liberalism is bound to bring a worse fate than the liberal status quo. We already know that liberalism and capitalism have caused, tolerated and turned a blind eye to countless numbers of deaths in the modern era. Part – but by no means all – of this is due to the fact that material inequality, of which liberalism is very tolerant, is itself the root cause of a great deal of suffering and premature death.

Moreover, the notion of legitimate authority is highly contentious. Does legitimate authority mean that liberal democratically elected governments (or international bodies representing them) are the only entities that have the authority to start or remain in a war? This raises all sorts of questions, of course, including one regarding the legitimacy of governments that, due to high numbers of abstentions in elections and/or because of the nature of the party system, represent a minority of the electorate as a whole. Does a President or government with formal support of less than 30 per cent of eligible voters or 36 per cent of the electorate – these are the proportions of the total electorate supporting George W. Bush and the British Labour Party respectively in the elections that preceded the decision to invade Iraq in 2003 – have authority to decide to wage war? Do insurgents ever have legitimate authority against a minority elected government? Quite apart from the general legitimacy or otherwise of JWT, one may also ask how often it has been invoked when in fact the war being pursued is clearly unjust; Michael Walzer, author of the classic modern text on JWT, believes that the invasion of Iraq was in contravention of JWT and that 'regime change is not part of the paradigm' (2006b: x).

One of the striking aspects of JWT is that it has a firm belief in the justice of the society and polity that is making decisions regarding just war. It rules out the idea that the forces opposing it may bring about an eventual state of affairs that is more just (and less violent in the medium and longer term) than the current state of affairs. It is, in fact, accepting of the status quo in a manner that is characteristic of liberal democracy. As a theory of the morality of, and limits to, violence in war, JWT may also be expected to inform the conduct of violence in revolt, but it is in fact too accepting of the status quo and assumes the status quo is not itself violent. At the same time it is too permissive in its recommendations for how to conduct war, and not radical enough with regard to the ends sought. Certainly, there are now attempts to apply JWT to insurgents (for example, Finlay 2015; Gross 2015), but general rules are as difficult – or more so – to make in the case of insurgency as in the case of conventional warfare, and ideology must in fact always be taken into account. In other words, JWT raises more questions than it answers. It would seem to reflect some of the positive, humanitarian aspects of liberalism, but also the limited ambitions of liberalism in terms of creating a more enduringly humane world.

Liberalism is certainly profoundly *un*-ambitious when it comes to reducing violence and ongoing suffering in societies that are thought of as liberal. Certainly, it seeks to minimise the most obvious forms of violence in the most obvious ways, so it outlaws murder, offers universal or semi-universal healthcare and introduces legislation to reduce accidents at work and on the road. But it does not tackle the root causes of many of these problems, many of which are caused or greatly exacerbated by poverty and deprivation, and ultimately by the ruthless pursuit of profit. In its eagerness to be anti-ideological it allows these injustices to persist and encourages the conclusion to be drawn that it is the fault of individuals if they are poor, poor and black, in sub-standard housing, can only afford an unsafe motor car and take on dangerous work. Questions of violence and suffering are often presented as being beyond the reach of politics. In fact liberalism is a philosophy of the status quo and seeks to de-politicise in order to defend the established order. This means accepting the agent-less suffering and deaths mentioned above for fear of upsetting the liberal-capitalist apple cart. The failure of communism in the twentieth century has very much served liberalism's purpose in its bid to show that there is no better alternative.

COMMUNISM AND VIOLENCE

Violence is by no means peculiar to regimes operating under the banner of capitalism. In the twentieth century in particular, governments claiming to be communist committed appalling acts of violence and cruelty against their own people. In one of the most extreme cases, Pol Pot and the Khmer Rouge killed in the region of 1.5 million Cambodians and left millions more in extreme poverty, out of a total population of approximately eight million. From 1975 to 1979, in a concerted campaign against intellectualism and urban living, borrowed in part from the Great Leap Forward in China, millions of Cambodians were made to leave towns and cities to go to work on collective farms. The resulting food shortages brought widespread disease and malnutrition, leading in themselves to many deaths. The Tuol Sleng Genoice Prison, often known simply as S-21, became the infamous centre of torture and execution, with roughly 14,000 prisoners dying within its walls; researchers in the decades after the regime had fallen found in the region of half a million pages of confessions extracted from the inmates of the prison (Kiernan 2008).

The Soviet Union, and then the rest of the Eastern bloc as well after 1945, also failed dramatically to bring peace and non-violence either to its own people or to those whose countries it went to war with. Forced collectivisation of agriculture and industrialisation, from 1929 onwards, caused the deaths of millions of peasants through starvation and disease, largely because of the speed with which it was implemented. The Gulags also caused incalculable suffering to millions of political dissidents and others interned within them, many of whom died. The Great Purge of the late 1930s, designed to weed out Communist Party members who were less than wholly in support of the Stalinist party line, involved the execution of hundreds of thousands of rank-and-file members as well as Communist leaders. In China, the worst excesses were twenty to thirty million deaths in the famine of 1959–61 that followed the Great Leap Forward and the prosecutions, humiliations, torture and killings during the Cultural Revolution of the late 1960s, which sought to purge remnants of capitalist thought. Thus there is some irony that in today's China, which is a bizarre blend of hyper-capitalism and state communism, poor working conditions and long working hours cause thousands of deaths per year, especially in coal mining.

Two remarks should be made regarding communism and violence at this point. First, particularly under Joseph Stalin, the relationship between the political, social and economic organisation and practices of the Soviet Union bore little relationship to what we may properly call communism, and the same may be said of China for much of the period since the revolution of 1948. This would apply even more to Cambodia under Pol Pot. Second, these countries, especially the Soviet Union, were often working against the odds in order to bring the standard of living of the mass of the population up from the very low starting point before the advent of communism. This does not in any manner excuse, and indeed only partially explains, the violence that was committed in the name of communism. But repression, mass executions and famine caused by forced collectivisation of agriculture and industrialisation, inexcusable though these factors were, were in part elements of a strategy designed to achieve a society more conducive to the conditions where communism could flourish, and also to compete sufficiently with the capitalist West that abject failure became less likely. Moreover, as Amartya Sen (1981) has shown, famines that take place in capitalist countries, while often triggered by natural phenomena, are often made far worse by the actions and inactions of governments. Yet these famines are rarely blamed on 'capitalism' in the way the Chinese famine is on 'communism'.

The historiography of communism since the fall of the Berlin Wall in

1989 and the break-up of the Soviet Union in 1991 has largely become one of asserting that ruthless violence of communist regimes was there from the very start; in these narratives, the very nature of Marxist ideology and especially Leninism meant that descent into barbarity and systematic cruelty was inevitable, rather than widespread violence constituting a deformation and indeed a betrayal of the original project. Writing about 'communist violence' has become very much part of a way of trumpeting the advantages of capitalism against *any* form of regime claiming to be communist, from Cambodia to Cuba. This is about as meaningful as arguing that when Nelson Mandela was President of (capitalist) South Africa he represented the same values as Margaret Thatcher, or General Pinochet for that matter.

A particularly notable example of reducing communism entirely to violence came with the publication of the *Black Book of Communism* (Courtois [1997] 1999), originally published in French and subsequently translated into several other languages. Estimating the total number of deaths attributable to communism at 100 million, the book prompted widespread debate regarding both its approach and its conclusions, ranging from the methodology used to arrive at the number of deaths to the extent to which it was communist ideology itself that was responsible for them. Domenico Losurdo's position is that the USSR and China committed truly terrible crimes, but that the *Black Book* ignores, especially, the way in which the Nazi regime followed the example of the West's deeply criminal activities in its colonies when devising its own murderous behaviour. Moreover, while the Great Leap Forward was catastrophic, Mao did not set out to kill so many people, so why, Losurdo asks, 'equate political responsibility and deliberate homicide?' (Losurdo [1996 and 1998] 2015: 311). The *Black Book*, he argues, compares the misdeeds of communists with an idea of liberalism, not with the reality of liberalism:

> The fact is that in the Black Book ... the deeds and misdeeds of Communism are compared not with the actual behaviour of the world it sought to challenge (about which the strictest silence reigns), but with liberalism's declarations of principle ... As we know, the latter did not hesitate to theorise slavery or despotism for barbarians (not to mention war) and, in states of emergency, made provision for dictatorship in the metropolis ... The tragic history of Communism, denounced as the very embodiment of

totalitarianism, is set against an idyllic portrait of Britain and the USA, or other countries governed by the liberal rules of the game. But what of such rules in the colonies and in relations with populations of colonial origin? And what of such rules in situations of acute crisis?' (Losurdo 2015: 313)

Losurdo does not challenge the idea that many crimes were committed in the name of communism, then, but he does highlight the historiographical hypocrisy practised in the process of defending capitalism. We may add that the question of arriving at precise numbers of deaths is certainly important. But the question of how we judge violence in history does not depend on strictly accurate quantification; do we judge the actions that caused the famine in China less harshly if ten million died rather than twenty million? Both figures imply mass, avoidable deaths, not a few unfortunate and anomalous casualties in an otherwise positive and humane exercise.

The question arises, then, as to whether we should decide that the experience of communism in the twentieth century was so bloody and generally such a failure that we should dispense with the notion of communism altogether. My own view is that we should not draw this conclusion. Faced with the ongoing bloodshed, suffering, injustices, waste, potential destruction due to ecological catastrophe and profound economic crises with all their ramifications under capitalism, and indeed the failure of capitalism in terms of providing the circumstances for meeting material needs and providing fulfilling lives for the vast majority in a sustained way, there is still an urgent need for a system of social and political organisation that is based on radical equality, fulfilment of everyone's needs and peace. This will not happen within a socio-economic system where profit is the driving force. The experience of communism in the twentieth century was in a number of ways appalling, although at risk of being seen to defend the indefensible, I would point out that it did provide the vast majority of the population with employment, housing, healthcare, greatly enhanced life expectancy and a much improved education system compared with precommunist regimes. Moreover, when capitalism was restored in the Soviet Union, the following decade saw in the region of an extra four million deaths compared with the decade that preceded the restoration of capitalism (Therborn 2013: 171).

As I have argued and continue to argue below, capitalism has certainly been no better than communism and has in some ways been worse, and as far as cruelty towards innocent individuals is concerned there is often little to choose between communist and capitalist violence. For example, was it better to be a peasant tilling the land and raising animals in North Vietnam in the 1960s and 1970s when America was bombing, burning, and dropping napalm, or to be a peasant in Ukraine in the 1930s when death from starvation was likely? As mentioned above, it is notable that historians who are deeply hostile to communism tend to attribute the horrors that were perpetuated in its name to a sort of 'essence of communism', which will reoccur whenever communism is introduced, whereas the extraordinary violence and injustices suffered by many as a result of capitalism's ruthless pursuit of profit and sustained inequality are somehow in every case anomalous; they are not properly part of capitalism itself, but form an extraordinary excess due to local factors such as fascism (not capitalist fascism, whereas Stalinism is simply equated with communism), psychopathic individual dictators or deadly weapons ending up in the 'wrong hands'.

Having made the above points, it is necessary to reiterate that there were appalling crimes committed in the name of communism, but also to emphasise the importance of drawing the lessons of these crimes when thinking about the construction of alternative futures. It is in part the simplicity of the idea of communism, based on radical equality and its axiomatic justness, which means that the notion and the desire to bring about communism are unlikely ever to disappear completely, and communism is likely to bounce back however great a fall it has taken. Allowing the idea of communism to evolve and making peace an integral and highly explicit part of such thinking is crucial. Indeed, the virtual disappearance of the twentieth-century's 'historical' communism offers greater opportunities now than for many decades for thinking about the creation of a very different type of society, as Badiou and others have argued so convincingly (Badiou ([2009] 2010); Douzinas and Žižek 2010).

US VIOLENCE OVERSEAS SINCE 1945

Even if we confine ourselves to the period since the Second World War, we are tragically spoiled for choice when it comes to identifying examples of violent intervention abroad on the part of advanced capitalist nations; many of the world's major powers (and numerous weaker ones) have engaged in or supported violent activities in other countries. In many instances, history has condemned these interventions and they have become, retrospectively, a source of collective shame within the countries that have intervened, not only on the left and among progressive liberals, but across a broad political spectrum. Examples abound, but we may include: the brutal British repression in Kenya in 1952, mentioned above, for which details of widespread torture and summary execution are beginning to come to light more fully, due in part to legal proceedings brought by now-elderly victims; France's war against the struggle for Algerian independence with widespread torture and roughly half a million deaths; the USA's 'war against communism' in Vietnam; and the USA's and Britain's invasion and occupation of Iraq from 2003 (the two latter conflicts being discussed below) – these are among the wars by advanced capitalist countries against developing countries that have cost many millions of lives and that are generally deemed to have made the situation pre-dating the wars much worse. In particular, during the post-war period of wars of national liberation, Britain, France, the Netherlands and Portugal clung on to their empires against the rising tide of independence movements. France's role in Algeria is of especial relevance, where French tactics of extreme violence including assassination, execution of prisoners and widespread torture failed to prevent the Front de Libération Nationale (itself guilty of excessive violence) from achieving independence in 1962. Benjamin Stora (1995: 91) estimates that half a million people were killed in the conflict, most of them Muslim Algerians.

The foreign interventions on the part of the USA since 1945 are highly significant, not only because the USA has caused and continues today to cause large numbers of deaths and large amounts of additional, non-lethal suffering abroad, often in alliance with other countries, but also because it is in many respects the archetypical example of a country that has long combined capitalism with liberal democratic government, with the associated leeway in terms of relatively few constraints on a bloody overseas policy. The US population is highly depoliticised, with only about half the electorate actually turning out to vote in national elections, mainly for two parties that are politically close in important respects, especially in the realm of foreign affairs. As in many advanced capitalist countries, but perhaps in particular in the USA due to its size and the fact that it has barely been attacked for centuries, foreign policy is indeed of little regard for many North Americans, who limit themselves to generalised patriotic expressions, such as outrage at the 9/11 attack on the Twin Towers, and broad support for US soldiers abroad. This relative indifference on the part of the general population – still more than in many other advanced capitalist countries – allows for a more ruthless foreign policy and proper consideration of this domain is left, as Perry Anderson (2014: 5) points out, to ministers, diplomats, bankers, industrialists and, of course, the military.

In the first half of the twentieth century, the USA had already pursued much violent intervention abroad, but from 1945 onwards the decline of European global hegemony encouraged the US to increase the scale of both direct and indirect intervention, alongside a great deal of effort in the economic, political and ideological spheres. During the Cold War, the 'fight against communism' was the reason offered in a host of hugely lethal interventions from the late 1940s to 1990, ranging from large-scale aerial bombing to economic sanctions, via military coup, naval blockade, burning down villages, destroying crops vital for the subsistence of the local population, use of chemical defoliants causing chronic health problems including cancer, assassination and torture, not to mention the occasional threat of dropping an atomic bomb. Crucial to all this was the CIA, created in 1947 with a brief to collect and analyse intelligence, but also to carry out covert operations. Its activities over the years included advice on coups d'état against numerous governments deemed hostile to US interests, assassination of political leaders, training for counter-insurgency and training on interrogation and torture techniques for countless, some of them transient, allies of the US.

We have space to mention only some of the USA's most destructive interventions overseas since 1945, so let us start with the Korean War of 1950–3. The war was the first large-scale, and in some ways the defining, armed conflict of the Cold War, involving massive destruction of human life, with North Korean, South Korean, Chinese, American and other United Nations soldiers dying in large numbers, including more than a million Chinese and about three million Korean civilians. The US diplomat Gregory Henderson suggests in relation to South Koreans dying at the hands of their own government that 'probably over 100,000 were killed without any trial whatsoever' (cited in Blum 2014: 52). In the last two years of the war, the US under President Truman and then Eisenhower became decidedly more aggressive in the pursuit of an end on American terms to the increasingly unpopular war. This involved carpet bombing North Korea for three years with virtually no concern for civilians and using napalm extensively, although firebombing was even more common (Cummings 2010: 149). By the end of the war there were in the region of five million refugees.

It is, however, the Vietnam War that has become the depressingly iconic example of Cold War US aggression, synonymous with huge and ultimately futile destruction in order to stop the spread of communism, involving, inter alia: saturation bombing, the widespread use of napalm, Agent Orange defoliant and crop-destroyer (with serious detrimental effects on people's health for many years), burning down of countless villages whose inhabitants had supposedly helped the Viet Minh, numerous massacres of civilians (not only at My Lai by any means) and torture of prisoners either directly by American soldiers or by South Vietnamese who were often trained by the CIA. The intensity of firepower was unprecedented in the history of warfare: from 1965 to 1968, twenty-six times more ammunition was fired per soldier in Vietnam than in the Second World War and over the same period on average thirty-two tons of bombs were dropped on North Vietnam every hour of the day and night. There were heavy casualties among both the US professional army and US conscripts, but far, far more casualties among the Vietnamese. From 1955 to 1975 there were more than 58,000 US military personnel killed in the war and more than 300,000 wounded, while South Vietnamese deaths amounted to about 254,000 with approximately 783,000 wounded; in the region of 1.7 million North Vietnamese soldiers were killed (Turse 2013: 11, 79). Roughly half a million North Vietnamese were killed in US air raids, often regardless of whether they were combatants or not. Wholly characteristic of such wars, there was a dramatically unequal number of deaths and seriously injured people if we compare the richer with the poorer nation. Ho Chi Minh's grim dictum was: 'You will kill ten of us, we will kill one of you, but in the end, you will tire of it first.' In the end, he was indeed broadly correct, but he greatly underestimated the ratio of North Vietnamese to American deaths.

Turning to Indonesia, we have an example where the US offered unequivocal support for one of the most extensive massacres of the twentieth century. In September 1965 there was an attempted coup against the anti-imperialist President Sukarno, which was almost certainly organised by elements close to the army and was used as a pretext for what followed. In the ensuing months there was a pogrom in which 500,000 to a million communists were killed by the army and its collaborators, who often murdered family members and communist sympathisers as well. Although there was little direct involvement by the US in the bloodbath, beyond supplying lists of communists and sympathisers, US policy enabled the massacre, and the US government and the CIA made sure that General Suharto was aware of America's support. In a formal, diplomatic sense, the US ignored the mass murder they knew was taking place (Robinson 1996: 125–7). After the largest Communist Party in the 'free' world was physically annihilated in a matter of months, Suharto was made head of state and became a close ally of the West and Indonesia was soon a major beneficiary of economic and military aid, especially from the US.

The recent history of US intervention in Central and South America is particularly telling from the point of view of the USA's determination to crush popular struggles and especially anything that smacked of communism or other forms of radical egalitarianism. By contrast with its attitude towards many other regions of the world, well before 1945 the US was in the habit of armed incursion in Central America and the Caribbean, and counted many authoritarian and repressive regimes as its close allies.

In 1954 the US backed a coup against Guatemala's President Jacobo Árbenz, using the CIA to train and arm mainly exiled Guatemalans who attacked on the ground while the US air force threatened an offensive from the sky; the reform by the Árbenz government that finally triggered US action had been redistribution to landless peasants of roughly 1.5 million acres of land, much of which belonged to the American-owned United Fruit Company. After the success of the Cuban revolution in 1959, popular movements emerged in many countries in Latin America and, while the US could not intervene directly in Cuba because of Soviet protection after the failed Bay of Pigs invasion of April 1961, it more than compensated for this by orchestrating CIA-abetted counter-insurgency and/or giving large amounts of military aid to reactionary movements in various other countries, including Venezuela, Peru and Bolivia. The 1964 coup by the Brazilian army against the elected government enjoyed direct US military support, and in the Dominican Republic, Uruguay and Argentina military dictatorships violently suppressed popular movements for change with the blessing of the US. Then Chile became the arena where the US showed itself to be particularly unscrupulous. Salvador Allende assumed the presidency of Chile after elections in 1970, despite the millions of US dollars spent on parties hostile to Allende. A left social democrat, Allende pursued policies of nationalisation of copper-producing companies, planned the nationalisation of the American-owned International Telephone and Telegraph Company (ITT) and established diplomatic relations with Cuba, China and North Korea. Three years later, after careful planning in conjunction with the CIA, the Chilean military overthrew the Allende government, prompting Allende's suicide, and General Augusto Pinochet became head of one of the most repressive and bloodthirsty regimes known to Central or Latin America.

When Jimmy Carter became President in January 1977, the only countries in Latin America to have governments formed after elections involving free competition between political parties were Venezuela, Costa Rica and Colombia (Coatsworth 2010: 205). Carter began raising questions regarding human rights in the region and apparently trying to push it in a liberal democratic direction, but in Nicaragua things went badly for the Carter administration when, in July 1979, the radical and widely supported Sandinistas overthrew the Somoza dictatorship, receiving a tumultuous welcome as they entered Managua. This inspired a popular uprising against the military-led government in El Salvador, prompting Carter to set aside his concern for human rights as he backed the military in the ensuing struggle, with snipers firing into crowds of demonstrators, killing scores of them and injuring many more. There were numerous assassinations, including the killing of the Archbishop of San Salvador, Óscar Romero, and then, at his funeral, a bomb was thrown into the crowd of mourners and gunfire followed, killing at least forty and injuring hundreds. After Ronald Reagan became President in January 1981, the Salvadorean Junta received large amounts of money, military hardware and training from the US and the consequential repression was truly terrible, with the by-now bleakly familiar fare of massacres, napalm and firebombing, widespread killing by death squads, together with sexual abuse and torture. In the meantime, Reagan declared that the Sandinista government was the arch enemy of the US in the region, despite the alleged threats to US interests having no basis in reality, and he instructed the CIA to train and fund Nicaraguan exiles as they grouped together under the name of the Contras. With help from the Honduran and Argentine regimes as well, the Contras began attacks on Nicaragua in 1982 and the White House approved the mining of Nicaraguan harbours by the CIA in the winter of 1984, in clear violation of international law. In 1986 the International Court of Justice in the Hague found the US to be in breach of international law and required it to compensate Nicaragua financially for the damage done in a war where in the region of 30,000 Nicaraguans had died. The US ignored the ruling.

In the meantime, the Reagan administration supported successive, murderous regimes in Guatemala, including the Ríos Mont government of 1982–3, which destroyed almost 9,000 indigenous villages, killing at least 50,000 people and creating a million refugees. Reagan also gave military aid to El Salvador for 'counter-insurgency' purposes, which involved the brutal slaughter of approximately 40,000 people from 1979 to 1984, most of whom were unarmed and were not involved in fighting. The war created approximately half a million refugees. In both countries, again, massacres, death squads and torture became commonplace.

John Coatsworth sums up the human cost of US activity in Central America during this period as follows:

> Between the onset of the global Cold War in 1948 and its conclusion in 1990, the US government secured the overthrow of at least twenty-four governments in Latin America, four by direct use of US military forces, three by means of CIA-managed revolts or assassination, and seventeen by encouraging local military and political forces to intervene without direct US participation, usually through military coups d'état . . .
>
> The human cost of this effort was immense. From 1960, by which time the Soviets had dismantled Stalin's gulags, until the Soviet collapse in 1990, the numbers of political prisoners, torture victims and executions of non-violent political dissenters in Latin America vastly exceeded those in the Soviet Union and its East European satellites. In other words, from 1960 to 1990, the Soviet bloc as a whole was less repressive, measured in terms of human victims, than many individual Latin American countries. The hot Cold War in Central America produced an unprecedented humanitarian catastrophe. From 1975 to 1991, the death toll alone stood at nearly 300,000 in a population of less than thirty million. More than one million refugees fled from the region – most to the United States. (Coatsworth 2010: 220–1)

'Humanitarian catastrophe' is indeed a fitting description for the USA's interventions in various parts of the world during the Cold War, not only in Central America. But this catastrophe did not cease once many of the Communist countries had become part of the capitalist world after 1991. On the contrary, the end of the Cold War meant that the US went on to act in a way that befits the world's only superpower – as global policeman. In what follows we will concentrate on the Middle East and in particular on Iraq since 2003, where violence at the service of the capitalist West is amply illustrated.

The West's intervention in the Middle East in the early twentieth century was in many ways summed up when, in December 2014, the US Senate intelligence committee released a report that appeared to come nearer than any previous official report to revealing the full extent of torture by the CIA in the long wake of September 11. The still heavily censored account described in detail the torture techniques, which included 'water boarding' (simulated drowning), mock executions, hanging by wrists, prolonged sleep deprivation and lowering the temperature of interrogation rooms to around freezing point for long periods, not to mention the use of loud and disturbing noise, routine verbal abuse and all manner of threats. Many of these techniques had been employed in Vietnam, Latin America and elsewhere. The report detailed how one man froze to death under interrogation, and how many others suffered permanent physical or psychological damage, but this and all other aspects of the report no doubt greatly underestimate the fuller picture that includes well-documented accounts of more than 100 detainees dying under CIA torture in the years after the invasion of Iraq (Greenwald 2009). The Senate report does confirm that nine countries hosted secret CIA prisons, including Morocco, Poland and Thailand, and forty-seven others facilitated CIA torture, in some cases by cooperating in the 'rendition' of prisoners from one country to another in order to be tortured; these countries included Australia, Belgium, Canada, Ireland, Italy, Sweden and the UK. Thus, the most powerful country on Earth, with the full cooperation of many of its allies, took part extensively in activities that gravely breached the Geneva Conventions on Human Rights.

Paradoxically, important though publication of the report was, it detracted from the suffering that the Iraqi people had been going through for decades, much of it as a result of the actions of the US government and its allies, combined with the brutal dictatorship of

Saddam Hussein, the erstwhile ally of the US and the West. In the Iran–Iraq War of the 1980s, which had a total death toll of about one million, half of them civilians, the US strongly supported Iraq politically and militarily. The West remained silent when Iraq used chemical weapons against the Iranians and, what is more, they remained silent when Saddam used chemical weapons against his own people in March 1988 in Halabja, Southern Kurdistan, killing approximately 7,000 people, mainly civilians. Indeed, it was not these war crimes that turned the US and its allies against Iraq, but Saddam Hussein's attack on Kuwait (a major supplier of oil to the US) in 1990, prompting the US, with support from numerous other nations including Russia and many countries in the Middle East, to launch a massive air attack in early 1991, followed by the briefer but intensely bloody Operation Desert Storm land campaign. However, the years from the invasion of Kuwait until 2003, taken as a whole, saw what was possibly the most lethal attack on the population of Iraq of the past thirty years, namely the imposition of UN sanctions. Healthcare was devastated and there has been much debate as to the number of children who died as a result, with various analysts suggesting as many as half a million and others two hundred thousand.

In Iraq since the US–British invasion of 2003, again the number of deaths, people seriously injured and the extent of war-related homelessness has been extensive. The US refuses to make public its own estimates of the number of Iraqi deaths, but Iraq Body Count has documented accounts of the deaths of 121,000 civilians between 2003 and 2015. The war and its aftermath also created a million refugees. *The Economist* (2013a) adds that in 2013 there was 25 per cent unemployment, and that 25 per cent of families were living below the poverty line. By 2007, according to the annual survey of Iraqis conducted by ABC News, USA Today, the BBC and ARD, already 78 per cent of Iraqis opposed the presence of US troops and 51 per cent believed that violence against the US military was legitimate (Cockburn 2007: xvii). With the rise of ISIS (see Chapter 5), things have gone from bad to worse, with the seizure of territory in both Iraq and neighbouring Syria. Robert Fisk, one of the most experienced Anglophone writers working on the Middle East, commented in June 2015:

[I]t's worth knowing just how General Pierre de Villiers, chief of the French defence staff, summed up his recent visits to Baghdad

Table 2.1 US military spending, 1997–2014

Year	Amount ($billions 2011)
1997	276
1998	274
1999	280
2000	301
2001	312
2002	356
2003	415
2004	464
2005	503
2006	527
2007	556
2008	621
2009	668
2010	698
2011	711
2012	684
2013	639
2014	609

Source: SIPRI (2015)

and Iraqi Kurdistan. Iraq, he reported back to Paris, is in a state of 'total decay'. The French word he used was *'décomposition'*. I suspect that applies to most of the Middle East. (Fisk 2015)

The scale of lethal intervention overseas on the part of the USA is reflected in its military spending (Table 2.1). The country spends more on defence than the next seven countries combined, namely China, Russia, Saudi Arabia, France, the United Kingdom, India and Germany (SIPRI 2015), and from 2001 to 2011 profits in the US defence industry profits nearly quadrupled (Robinson 2014: 148–9).

STRUCTURAL VIOLENCE

When dealing with the violence of capitalism, we need to take into account the violence and suffering caused by the inequalities and other injustices that are so characteristic of this system, which is sometimes referred to as structural, or society-related, violence (after Galtung

(1969)), as opposed to agent-related violence. With agent-related violence, the immediate perpetrator of violence is clear, whether it be (taking just three examples) one family member murdering another, a soldier killing other soldiers or a government waging war. By contrast with agent-related violence, structural violence refers to suffering experienced as a result of particular living or working conditions such as poor housing, poor air quality, sub-standard diet or a dangerous or unhealthy work environment, and perhaps resulting in premature death, ongoing pain or illness. There is often a strong correlation between people's relative wealth on the one hand and the degree of structural violence they experience on the other; individuals are more likely to die young and/ or suffer long-term ill health if they are poorer. In other words, a great deal of harm is done as a result of uneven distribution of resources both within particular societies and between societies.

Some of the clearest examples of the correlation between relative wealth and health are illustrated by way of comparison of life expectancy between countries, as shown in Table 2.2. That average life expectancy varies so much from one country to another, from forty-six years in Sierra Leone (where 70 per cent of the population live in poverty) to eighty-four years in Japan, is often quite simply accepted as a reflection of the way the world is, where no-one is to blame for the glaring variations from one country to another. But decisions are made daily and at many levels of international, national and local government and administration, not to mention in private firms, which affect this. These decisions have a direct influence on distribution of life and death, well-being and ill health, freedom from suffering and obligation to endure suffering. Civil and inter-state wars have an effect on life expectancy as well, of course, and in 2015 the conflicts in the Middle East created the largest refugee crisis since the Second World War, alongside the tragedy of many refugees drowning after boats that were supposed to bring them safely to Europe capsized. Global climate change is another clear example of actions (and inaction) by the richer nations threatening the livelihoods and lives of people living in poorer parts of the world.

Other general statistics are highly informative in this respect as well. For example, the likelihood of a child dying before their fifth birthday is almost four times higher in Bangladesh than in Belgium and more than ten times more likely in Uganda than in the UK (World Bank 2015).

Table 2.2 Life expectancy, selected countries, 2013

Country	Life expectancy, years (male and female)
Japan	84
Spain	83
Canada	82
United Kingdom	81
Chile	80
Cuba	79
USA	79
Czech Republic	78
Suriname	77
Vietnam	76
Saudi Arabia	76
China	75
Brazil	74
Iran	74
Nicaragua	73
Algeria	72
Indonesia	71
Bangladesh	70
Russian Federation	69
Nepal	68
Namibia	67
India	66
Rwanda	65
Yemen	64
Eritrea	63
Haiti	62
Kenya	61
Afghanistan	60
South Africa	59
Guinea	58
Uganda	57
Cameroon	56
South Sudan	55
Swaziland	54
Mozambique	53
Dem. Rep. Congo	52
Chad	51
Lesotho	50
Sierra Leone	46

Source: World Health Organization (2013)

Appallingly bad conditions of work and working practices, including child labour, are still common in many countries of the world, despite work by trade unions and local and international campaigns to improve conditions. Garment workers, many of them women or children, are often among the worst off in this respect. Taking one example of neglect of a working environment that led to a serious accident, on 24 April 2013, the Rana Plaza factory complex in the outskirts of Dacca collapsed, leaving 1,134 workers dead and 1,500 wounded. By April 2015, according to Human Rights Watch (HRW), about ten companies that occupied the building had still not made compensation payments as they should have done and HRW made the point that if there had been union representation the workers' fears regarding cracks in the building before the collapse would have been reported and taken seriously, and the catastrophe would not have taken place. Although since April 2013 there have been reforms designed to enable the establishment of trade unions at the factory, some of those attempting to set them up have been physically attacked and others threatened with serious injury. Only 10 per cent of textile factories in Bangladesh, which employ 80 per cent women, are unionised (*Libération*, 2015). The garments sector has indeed become, in the words of War on Want Executive Director John Hilary (2013: 100), 'the defining example of how the process of globalisation has enabled capital to drive down wage costs and labour standards while evading all prospects of binding legislation'. The direct result of this is a great deal of suffering in the countries that produce these low-cost clothes.

There are, of course, many other recent examples of such appalling and avoidable industrial accidents, which will continue to take place until trade unions, governments and other organisations bring enough ongoing pressure to bear on companies regarding health, safety and working conditions. But more broadly and less obviously, dangerous and unhealthy working and living conditions for people who produce the enormous quantities of traded items (mainly to richer countries), from food to children's toys, mobile phones to car components, contribute to the disparity in health and life expectancy between poorer and richer countries.

Within advanced capitalist countries, meanwhile, we also see high levels of structural violence, with significant variations in life experience according to such factors as class, ethnicity and gender. Examining London in 2011, Therborn (2013: 82) describes how male life expectancy in prosperous Kensington and Chelsea was seventeen years longer than in far poorer Tottenham Green. If one travels east on the London Underground Jubilee Line, life expectancy of the residents near each stop declines by half a year per stop, and, since 1980, inequalities in the heartlands of capitalism have indeed been growing, including in terms of life expectancy. But behind these bald statistics lie millions of people in the heartlands of capitalism living in poor conditions because of the way in which society is organised, not because the resources are not there to provide properly for everybody. The situation has become substantially worse since the beginning of the crisis in 2008 and, for example, the number of people in homeless shelters in New York doubled from approximately 30,000 in 2005 to about 60,000 in 2015 (*The Economist* 2015b: 37). A similar pattern is seen regarding child poverty in the UK, where from 2010 to 2014, the number of children living in poverty rose by approximately half a million to something in the region of 3.7 million (CPAG 2015).

Barbara Chasin (2004: 45) confirms that inequality leads to structural violence, as we have seen, but also points out that structural violence in turn often leads to interpersonal violence of various kinds, including domestic violence, violent street crime and scapegoating weaker and more vulnerable members of society as a result of anger and frustration. This then leads to police violence against those committing these acts and the growth and consolidation of ghettoised communities (including gated communities for the affluent), which in turn reinforces inequalities. In other words, there is a vicious circle of inequality and violence of various kinds that becomes even worse when the national and international economy is doing less well.

LATE CAPITALISM AND ITS FUTURES

On the day I am writing these particular lines, 2 July 2015, there are long queues forming at cashpoints in Greece as people try to withdraw dwindling reserves of cash; withdrawals are limited to 60 Euros per person per day. The fear is that the struggle over further austerity measures between the Greek people and the Greek government on the one hand and the European Union (EU), European Central Bank (ECB) and the International Monetary Fund (IMF) on the other will provoke a Greek exit from the EU, a return to the Drachma, a freeze on banks' assets, restrictions on the movement of capital, an investment 'strike' and, most important of all, still greater hardship for many Greeks. This is just one – particularly graphic – result of the Great Recession that started in 2008, arguably the most recent serious crisis of international capitalism since the 1930s.

Since its inception, capitalism has been in a constant state of flux. It is characterised by profound internal contradictions that generate regular economic crises, a fact that even some of its staunchest defenders now recognise; boom and bust, the rise and fall of different production techniques and modes of working, the emergence and disappearance of whole sub-sectors of the workforce, and mass, forced or quasi-forced displacement of labour (people) are just part of what is taken for granted in the package that capitalism offers. One moment there is galloping inflation and the next deflation, interest rates soar for a number of years and then plummet, a period of steadily rising living standards and near-full employment is quickly followed by high unemployment with hundreds of thousands of workers thrown into poverty, growth is followed by stagnation or recession, unexpected stock market crashes in one part of the world have repercussions in other parts that have serious effects on individuals and speculation in one area (including housing) can similarly wreak havoc with many people's lives. Over the longer term, the capitalist system evolves, reacts and adjusts, and has so far survived the many internal crises it has suffered in the relentless pursuit of profit, in the process wrecking many lives and making some people very wealthy. It also of course survived the long period of competition from systems claiming to be communist, a contest that began in earnest in 1917 and continued for many decades, with capitalism emerging triumphant in the early 1990s – the notable vestiges of twentieth-century communism being communist-capitalist China, tyrannical and deeply oppressive North Korea and isolated and impoverished Cuba.

In previous sections of this chapter we looked at some of the violence associated with the capitalist system. We now need to ask the question as to whether capitalism may evolve in such a way as to generate still greater levels of violence, including in the late capitalist heartlands of Western Europe and the USA, where there is for the moment a combination of capitalism and liberal democracy. A brief glance back over the past half-century or so in advanced capitalist countries will help put the present state of capitalism in its proper context.

In the post-1945 era, up to the early to mid-1970s, there were various developments that improved the lot of ordinary working people;

substantial portions of the fruits of capitalist economic success were won by salaried workers, capital made significant concessions to labour in terms of trade union rights and the state set up a welfare infrastructure that helped provide a degree of material security and well-being. Each of these characteristics has been eroded since the mid-1970s, but none has yet been entirely eliminated; material inequalities have risen greatly, with a small but significant layer of the very rich at one extreme and a permanent and substantial layer of impoverished people at the other, and a significant level of permanent unemployment in a number of countries. Socio-political concessions made by capital in the post-1945 period such as increased trade union rights have been partially retracted via new legislation, or have been eroded due to unemployment, fragmentation of the labour force through 'restructuring' of the economy and consequent decline in trade union membership. The role of the state in terms of material protection of ordinary people has diminished, with parts of welfare systems scaled down and/or privatised. To put developments in the capitalist labour process since the mid-1970s in the terms of the Regulation School, Fordist production based on traditional manufacturing, epitomised by a production line in a large factory employing many workers, gave way to a post-Fordist system where there was greater reliance on information technology, far fewer employees and increasingly 'flexible' working patterns. This was partly a response to the rise of manufacturing in lower-income countries and brought a declining influence of trade unions. Meanwhile, the service sector grew, but was characterised by low levels of unionisation and often by lower pay. All of these developments meant that well before the beginning of the Great Recession in 2008, capital was far more dominant over labour than it had been during the post-war era.

Although most analysts agree that capitalism is prone to cyclical crisis – in other words that it has a strong tendency to suffer damaging episodes that are beyond the control either of governments or of those who benefit from the system most – the international financial, fiscal and economic crisis that began in 2008 took almost all economists by surprise. According to Marx, and to many generations of Marxists after him, such structural crises were likely eventually to bring about the downfall of capitalism, as long as the political action of many ordinary people supported such a development as well (that seemed very likely). Communism, with all the redistribution, reduction of waste and broader justice that would go with it, would then become a possibility; the basis for the peaceful flourishing of human beings would at last be established once class conflict stopped destroying so much of their potential. Today, some of the most insightful political economists are still influenced by Marx, but many now have a view of the future that is more open-ended than was Marx's own, and indeed one that is considerably less optimistic. None of the authors discussed below rule out a brighter, more egalitarian future, but each believes that a bleaker, even more violent capitalism or post-capitalism is a real possibility in the medium term.

Wolfgang Streeck (2014b) argues that various recent developments are likely to have dramatic consequences, although these consequences are not predictable in their detail. First, there has been a slow but steady breakdown of the post-war order, or what he describes as an erosion of 'social capitalism' (xvi). After 1968, the approaches of capital on the one hand and labour on the other were so divergent that the post-war order characterised by liberal democracy and capitalism was bound to break down, as capitalism had diminishing room for manoeuvre. Capital's response was to emerge from its previous state of passivity and pull out of the post-war contract. Streeck argues that many economists underestimate the extent to which capital has become a political – as opposed to a purely economic – actor and that there has been a 'revolt of capital against the postwar mixed economy' (3). Many firms, industries and business associations have joined forces to fight for a more neo-liberal capitalism. Government support for this process was led primarily by Margaret Thatcher in Britain and Ronald Reagan in the USA, and it involved crushing the trade unions, mass unemployment, the decline of the welfare state, greater income inequality and high levels of both public and private indebtedness (26–30). Streeck's story so far is familiar, particularly for those with experience of the heartlands of the neoliberal reaction.

However, he goes on to argue that the logic of all this is something that a majority of analysts do not anticipate, namely the end of mass liberal democracy in the medium term. Electoral participation is already in steady decline and '[t]he political resignation of the underclasses consolidates the neoliberal turn from which it derives, further shielding capitalism from democracy' (55). Moreover, neoliberalism needs a strong state in order to thrive and ultimately this is incompatible with a liberal democratic state, because the tendency of a democratic state is always to redistribute profits generated by the market economy to the less well-off.

Ultimately, according to Streeck, there is limited compatibility between capitalism and liberal democracy, and the relatively brief coexistence there has been was the result of a high level of intervention and regulation and he concludes, rather chillingly, that if things carry on like this, 'the time will come when the paths of capitalism and democracy must part' (172). The crisis that began in 2008 is, according to Streeck, the 'end point' of the transformation of the capitalist economy from its more distributive, post-war incarnation into its current neoliberal form. Inflation, public debt and private debt allowed capitalism to continue to 'buy time' and to appear to act in the interests of all, or at least of many people. Each measure became too costly, however, and there are now no other options left; the capitalist class is itself at a loss to know what to do, but what seems certain is that 'the clock is ticking for democracy as we have come to know it [and it will be] reduced to a combination of the rule of law and public entertainment' (5). In addition to confusion among the capitalist class about where to turn now, voters are growing weary of conventional, liberal-democratic political parties who seem ever-less effectual and voters are attracted in increasing numbers to parties that are breaking the post-war mould, including fascist, far-right and nationalist-populist parties, but also Green and far-left-leaning parties like Syriza in Greece and Podemos in Spain.

Immanuel Wallerstein, meanwhile, takes several observational steps back compared with Streeck and argues that all systems come to an end, including capitalism, which is already about 500 years old. Capitalism, like all systems, went through a 'normal' stage, but this normal stage is now over and capitalism is now in its 'terminal' stage, which is likely to last another twenty to forty years (Wallerstein 2013: 9–10). He explains that the dominant characteristic of a capitalist system is 'the persistent search for the *endless* accumulation of capital – the accumulation of capital in order to accumulate more capital', which is nothing short of 'a thoroughly irrational objective' and its ability to do this is now over (10–11; emphasis in the original). In geopolitical terms, during more stable periods, hegemonic powers dominate either in particular regions or globally, without using excessive force, but as the weak begin to rebel the hegemonic powers engage in repression and often military activities, which are not wholly successful, which in turn encourages the rebellious to resist further. All this is costly in both human and financial terms as the hegemonic powers and their ability to dominate globally is undermined, while other states recover somewhat and are emboldened in terms of influence beyond their own borders. By this point, gradual decline of the hegemonic power is inevitable (16).

Moreover, the costs of production have, Wallerstein argues, increased steadily if we factor in not only relatively recently increased expenditure relating to climate change, but also more general costs of transportation, communications and welfare, much of which is borne by the state. Various strategies for recovery that have been used for several hundred years are no longer effective and accumulation of capital without end is no longer plausible (24), while recourse to the financial sector as in previous cycles in response to a slow rate of capital accumulation had disastrous consequences (29). The rise of the BRICS (Brazil, Russia, India, China and South Africa) and other emergent countries paradoxically reduces the potential for the accumulation of capital, because there are now more people mopping up the surplus value produced by a globalised system, and also because widespread austerity measures undermine the ability of consumers to buy products from the BRICS (31).

Things cannot, then, stay broadly the way they have been for decades – and even centuries in some respects – and over the next half century a new politico-economic system will have to be created:

> The question before the world today is not in what ways governments can reform the capitalist system such that it can renew its ability to pursue effectively the endless accumulation of capital. There is no way it can do this. The question therefore has become what will replace this system. And this is a question both for the 1% and the 99%, in the language used since 2011. Of course, not everyone agrees, or phrases it in this way. Indeed, most people still assume that the system is continuing, using the old rules, perhaps after amending the rules. This is not wrong. It is just that, in the present situation, using the old rules actually intensifies the structural crisis. (Wallerstein 2013: 32–3)

Ideologically, there has been an offensive by the neo-liberal right and political stability has been undermined by the decline of centre-oriented liberalism, which promised that things would get ever better for everyone, as long as they all, or almost all, toed the line (28). One result of all this is the rise of the extremes of right and left, together with more repressive governments (32). The new political-economic systems that must be created could either be far more repressive than the regimes we are used to in the West, or they could be more egalitarian and democratic (33), but the compromise between these two approaches that many advanced capitalist countries have got to know since the end of the Second World War is no longer viable.

William Robinson addresses the relationship between capitalism, war and violence more generally in his book *Global Capitalism and the Crisis of Humanity* (2014). Drawing on his earlier *A Theory of Global Capitalism* (2004), he argues that the current crisis is not simply a repeat of the 1930s or the 1970s, because this time there is a truly global system, there is a properly transnational capitalist class and transnational state and there are new types of inequality, domination and exploitation, including the increasing importance of the North–South divide (2). Contra David Harvey, Robinson argues that US military intervention post-9/11 is not a new imperialism, but a reaction to the latest crisis of global capitalism and an attempt to force certain regions into the system of global capitalism and to respond to stagnation via militarised accumulation (4). At the level of the nation state, political, social and economic elites risk substantial crises of legitimacy as they fail to respond adequately to discontent on the part of many people who are downwardly mobile, unemployed or who experience greater fear and insecurity in their day-to-day lives. The threat of ecological catastrophe is one of these fears, and a real one. All this is already translating into types of party politics that are quite different to the centre-oriented political tendencies of much of the period since the Second World War. Mapping all this onto the world stage, Robinson warns of a 'crisis that is approaching systemic proportions, [which] threatens the ability of billions of people to survive, and raises the specter of a collapse of world civilization and degeneration into a new "Dark Ages"' (5).

He argues that there have already been indicators of what such a crisis of humanity may look like, including the Israeli invasions of Gaza and their disproportionate brutality, genocide in the Congo, the criminalisation of immigrant workers, and the rise of the far right and neo-Nazi parties in Europe, the US, Colombo, Mexico and Honduras. Other indicators include extreme masculinisation, racism, scapegoating and militarisation of cities and cultures in the US and Israel, which is closely connected to these countries' military involvement in other countries, together with the global war economy. Robinson suggests that 'fascism is a response to capitalist crisis that seeks to contain any challenge to the system that may come from subordinate groups' (164–5). A future fascism would not be a repeat of twentieth-century fascism, but one that would allow political parties to function within a framework of a written constitution and regular elections, but anything that threatened transnational capitalism would be rendered useless or abolished. Moreover, this state of affairs could develop slowly, without a sudden takeover and would be a dictatorship of transnational capital, not of national capitalism as was fascism in the twentieth century. Indeed, as the economic crisis has deepened in the past few years, international capital has already become more coercive in order to defend the march of neoliberalism (169–70).

We need not enter into a debate about who among these political economists is more convincing, particularly given that they agree in important respects. But we should note that they all point convincingly to a capitalism that is running out of ideas and more importantly running out of options. It is therefore becoming more violent and potentially becoming hugely more so in the medium term, while at the same time restricting further the already very thin forms of democracy that currently exist. The reason I provide an extended summary of their work is that the sort of capitalism combined with liberal democracy found in large parts of Europe and in North America in particular is not necessarily an accurate picture of the future, either in these regions themselves or elsewhere. It is important to reiterate that neither Wallerstein, nor Streeck, nor Robinson believes that a more just and egalitarian society will inevitably follow the demise of capitalism. There are various ways in which currently capitalist societies could develop in the post-capitalist period, perhaps for the better or even considerably better, but the other possibility is a much worse scenario with far greater inequalities and many dire injustices, including widespread slavery. What they are sure about, however, is that capitalism itself cannot survive for very much longer. We may therefore be forced into a choice between on the one hand deeply authoritarian regimes that will stop at nothing in order to maintain their rule, and on the other a far more egalitarian and democratic society. Arguably the 'socialism or barbarism' dichotomy is at least as valid as when Rosa Luxembourg put it forward in 1915, and perhaps more so.

*   *   *

The purpose of this chapter has been three-fold. First, it was necessary to remind ourselves of the violent nature of capitalism, a violence that is ongoing and is integral to the way in which the system operates, even when it puts on its best face by joining forces with liberal democracy. Capitalism was born using a great deal of violence and it has perpetrated a great deal in its relentless pursuit of profit. In addition to the often brutal and dangerous conditions in which workers have extracted raw materials, produced goods and provided services, countless wars have been fought in order to defend this state of affairs. Many uprisings that have been broadly anti-capitalist in nature have been brutally put down. Structural violence, which is closely connected with the vast inequalities on which capitalism depends, has also been prevalent since the dawn of capitalism and is easy to identify. This is the other side of modernity, a side that is far from the one characterised by a peaceful and non-violent dynamic that I examined in Chapter 1. Each side of this coin is an accurate picture of modernity, but an important question is which side will be allowed to dominate as time goes by?

Second, it was necessary to look at the violence of historical communism, which, in the name of profound equality and the liberation of humanity from oppression, perpetrated some of the most appalling crimes against humanity. This is not only a tragedy in itself, in other words for all the people who suffered or died in the name of communism. It also presents a major obstacle for those – like me – arguing that a profoundly egalitarian future is the only possible way that we can avoid moving towards its opposite, namely even more rampant and perhaps out-of-control capitalism and the political dictatorship and the inequalities – combining with virtually unbridled violence – that will doubtless accompany it. Anti-communist historians have written a great many words in an effort to suggest that violence and injustice were the inevitable result of an attempt in Russia and elsewhere to overthrow capitalism once and for all. We need to listen to what they say and read what they write, and not dismiss every word. But we also need to analyse the failure of the Soviet Union and other countries claiming to be communist from a point of view of historians who allow themselves greater optimism regarding the idea of communism and to begin to think about communism again in concrete terms. In other words, we need to continue to attempt to understand the failures of historical communism without simply jumping into the anti-communist camp and arguing that there is now no alternative to capitalism, with all the (perhaps increasing) injustices and violence that it brings.

Finally, I wished to suggest in this chapter that the future of capitalism even in the advanced capitalist countries may indeed be more violent and far less 'tolerant' than we have come to expect. Capitalism as a system evolves constantly and has always been prone to serious crises. These crises will continue and they may well become more acute, as the various, formerly somewhat more independent, parts of the world become increasingly interconnected and the dangers of climate change increase. The search for alternatives, then, is as necessary, and more so, as it has ever been.

Chapter 3

CASTRO, HUMANISM AND REVOLUTION

We hope that you will stay with us and fight against the master who so ill-used you. If you decide to refuse this invitation – and I am not going to repeat it – you will be delivered to the custody of the Cuban Red Cross tomorrow. Once you are under Batista's orders again, we hope that you will not take arms against us. But if you do, remember this: We took you this time. We can take you again. And when we do, we will not frighten or torture or kill you . . . If you are captured a second time or even a third . . . we will again return you exactly as we are doing now.

Fidel Castro cited in Walzer ([1977] 2006a: 181)

In Chapter 1, I made a case for putting peace and non-violence at the heart of any struggle for a better world and argued that there exist important elements of a peace dynamic in the world we live in. In Chapter 2, I pointed out that the capitalist system – but also historical communism – has a ruthless and very violent side to it, and that in all likelihood this tendency in capitalism will get worse. These are divergent or contradictory aspects of modernity and capitalism that are deep-rooted and are unlikely to be resolved easily; in other words, these contradictions may well become more acute. It is by no means clear which one of these tendencies – violent or peaceful – will gain the upper hand; to take a firm position on this would be both unrealistic and perhaps unnecessarily fatalistic. We can be sure, however, that actions by sections of society with particular interests will determine which of these tendencies will prevail and that the outcome will also depend – even more so than in the past – upon events in various, disparate parts of the world and on the way in which these events affect one another. Thus, the future is open; it is for human actors to determine which direction it goes in, whether this be one that is far more egalitarian and that offers emancipation, or one that is less equal and less just and even more violent than in the past. In many countries of the world, individuals and groups have made decisions regarding taking up arms in pursuit of a particular cause. I am not by any means claiming to be able to offer guidance for all such situations, as pacifists or Just War theorists may do. My argument is that, sooner or later, people in various types of countries – richer, poorer, more advanced capitalist and less advanced capitalist – are likely to be confronted with the question of whether or not it is possible and fruitful to engage in some form of armed uprising. This is a question of tactics that many people have considered in the past and that is indeed posed in various places across the world today. There is never an easy way of resolving this dilemma and each case will require a different type of answer. However, while bearing in mind the discussions of the previous two chapters, in this chapter I begin by examining one particular case of violence in revolt that I believe sheds light on the question of bloodshed in pursuit of emancipation in a more general way.

HISTORY WILL ABSOLVE ME

On 16 October 1953, Fidel Castro delivered a speech that has gone down in history as one of the greatest statements of defiant humanism of the twentieth century. Alongside Martin Luther King's 'I have a Dream' of August 1963 and Nelson Mandela's 'I am Prepared to Die' of April 1964, it displayed a readiness to make the ultimate personal sacrifice for a just cause, but also made clear that emancipation would come about only as a process of collective struggle. Delivered at the end of a trial where he was accused of organising an armed uprising against the Batista dictatorship, Castro's speech reflected on an abortive attack and its gruesome aftermath. He and 160 comrades had stormed the Moncada Barracks in Santiago de Cuba on 26 July 1952 with the primary aim of seizing arms for use in subsequent insurgency, as well as attacking a powerful symbol of repression. The assault was easily repulsed by the regime's soldiers and it was very quickly apparent that in practical terms it had failed, although Castro's fighters killed fifteen soldiers and three policemen stationed at the barracks, whereas only three of their own people died in the attack. The dictator Fulgencio Batista demanded that ten insurgents be killed for every one of his own men who had died; on his direct orders, sixty-eight imprisoned Castro-ites were subjected to an orgy of sadistic, protracted torture that was followed by death in almost all cases. The lives of Castro and the twenty-eight other defendants at the Moncada trial were saved following a public outcry about the atrocities – the magazine *Bohemia* published photographs of the tortured rebels' mutilated corpses –and by the intervention of the Archbishop of Santiago, Enrique Pérez Serantes (Merle 1965). The attack, the trial and the speech took on huge symbolic significance, in large part because of the contrasting attitude towards violence displayed by Batista on the one hand and by Castro and his men on the other, a contrast that Castro described in his speech in some detail and to great effect.

A lawyer by trade, Castro mounted his defence on the basis of the right to revolt against a regime that had come to power illegally by coup d'état in March 1952 and that embodied cruelty, tyranny and despotism. Not only did he and his fighters have a moral right and a duty to revolt, but Batista's regime was illegal and unconstitutional, which in itself gave the defendants the legal right to revolt against it. 'You are well aware', he argued, 'that resistance to despots is legitimate. This is a universally-recognised principle and our 1940 constitution expressly makes it a sacred right' (Castro [1953] 1987: 141). In terms of general law, he explained, the right of insurrection against tyranny is well-established by people of varying beliefs, from theocratic monarchies in remote antiquity to the heroes of the struggle for Cuban independence from Spain, via Thomas Aquinas, Martin Luther, John Knox, John Milton, Rousseau and many others. He invoked the memory and influence of José Martí, the hero of the struggle for independence from Spain, saying that

> [i]t looked as if his memory would be extinguished for ever. But he lives. He has not died . . . Young men, in a magnificent gesture of reparation, have come to give their blood and to die in the hearts of his countrymen. O Cuba! What would have become of you if you had let the memory of your apostle die! (Castro [1953] 1987: 153)

He then closed the speech by suggesting that 'imprisonment will be harder for me than it has been for anyone, filled with cowardly threats and hideous cruelty' and by uttering the now-immortal words: '[b]ut I do not fear prison, as I do not fear the fury of the miserable tyrant who took the lives of seventy of my comrades. Condemn me. It does not matter. History will absolve me' (ibid.).

The further significance of the speech for our purposes is that on the one hand Castro goes out of his way to give graphic details of the cruelty and blood lust of the counter-insurgent soldiers and in particular their commanders, devoting a large portion of the speech to a description of the 'horrible, repulsive crimes they had practised on the prisoners'. While Cubans were 'suffering the cruelest, the most inhuman oppression of their history' and

> [w]hile the long-cherished hopes of freeing our people lay in ruins about us, we heard those hopes gloated over by a tyrant more vicious, more arrogant than ever. The endless stream of lies and slanders, poured forth in his crude, odious, repulsive language, may only be compared to the endless stream of young blood which had flowed since the previous night – with his knowledge, consent, complicity, and approval – being spilled by the most inhuman gang of assassins it is possible to imagine. (Castro [1953] 1987: 84–93)

Castro then contrasts the enemy's behaviour with that of his own fighters, speaking of the 'humane and generous treatment [with which] we had at all times treated our adversaries', and insisting:

> Everyone had instruction, first of all, to be humane in the struggle. Never was a group of armed men more generous to the adversary. From the beginning we took numerous prisoners – nearly twenty – and there was one moment when three of our men . . . managed to enter a barracks and hold nearly fifty prisoners for a short time. These soldiers testified before the court and without exception they all acknowledged that we treated them with absolute respect, that we didn't even subject them to one scoffing remark. (Castro [1953] 1987: 94–5)

Castro also made full reference to what we may now call the widespread structural violence in Cuba and the insouciance of the Cuban regime regarding this suffering. For example, he argued:

Ninety per cent of the children in the countryside are consumed by parasites which filter through their bare feet from the ground they walk on. Society is moved to compassion when it hears of the kidnapping or murder of one child, but it is criminally indifferent to the mass murder of so many thousands of children who die every year from lack of facilities, agonizing with pain . . . Public hospitals, which are always full, accept only patients recommended by some powerful politician who, in turn, demands the electoral votes of the unfortunate [patient] and his family so that Cuba may continue forever in the same or worse condition. (Castro [1953] 1987: 111)

He speaks of 600,000 Cubans who are unemployed, but do not wish to emigrate to find work; 500,000 farm labourers who live in miserable dwellings, paid only four months a year, and whose children suffer even more; 400,000 industrial workers and labourers whose pensions have been embezzled; 100,000 small farmers who 'live and die working land that is not theirs . . . who like feudal serfs have to pay for the use of their parcel of land by giving up a portion of its produce' (106).

He pays tribute to under-paid teachers, frustrated professionals such as doctors, engineers and lawyers, and small businessmen who are heavily indebted, with no prospects, and 'harangued by a plague of grafting and venal officials'. This structural violence and humiliation will enlist its victims to the cause of revolution: 'These are the people, the ones who know misfortune and, therefore, are capable of fighting with limitless courage!' From this, Castro goes on to outline the five revolutionary laws that would have been proclaimed if the revolutionary assault had been successful: a return to the 1940 constitution until the people decided to reform or replace it; transferring ownership of land to all tenant and subtenant farmers, as well as lessees, sharecroppers and squatters who hold parcels of five *caballerias* of land or less; granting employees the right to 30 per cent of the profits of all large industrial, mercantile and mining enterprises, including sugar mills; allowing all sugar planters to share 55 per cent of sugar production; and finally the confiscation of all property and 'ill-gotten gains' of those (and their heirs) who had committed fraud under previous regimes (106–8).

The manuscript of the remarkable speech, known from the start simply as *History will Absolve Me*, was destroyed at the end of the trial, but the imprisoned Castro re-wrote it from memory and had it smuggled out of gaol in small portions. It was then typeset, printed and distributed widely by his supporters who made sure that it became well known. In this way, an abortive attack by 160 poorly armed men and women, with little support among the broader population and none from established political parties, became a defining moment in the struggle against Batista, indeed the founding act on which the revolutionary movement – henceforth named 26 July Movement – was built and from which people drew ever-greater inspiration. In Badiouian language, this was the Event in relation to which increasing numbers of people acted in fidelity; as a result of this commitment Batista was eventually driven out of Cuba forever.

CUBA'S HISTORY OF VIOLENCE

Castro's humanist speech in response to the bloody aftermath of the Moncada attack, then the ethically informed approach to guerilla warfare by the 26 July Movement in the countryside in the late 1950s, the almost-bloodless final uprising against Batista in 1959, and thereafter for many years Castro's frequently declared ethically informed approach to the question of violence in combat, together with great emphasis on healthcare, literacy, education and land reform – all these aspects of Castroism and the Cuban revolution were in dramatic contrast to the endemically violent and ruthlessly exploitative history of Cuba up until 1959. The island had for centuries been marked by particularly intense violence, even compared with other countries in the region, which themselves had often been far from peaceful (Gott 2004; Languepin 2007; Thomas 1971). During the colonisation of Cuba in the sixteenth century, the Spanish virtually wiped out the indigenous population, who numbered about 150,000 before the arrival of the *conquistadores* and only 5,000 half a century later. Many died in massacres and tens of thousands of others died from over-work in forced labour – often in gold mines and plantations – and still others from smallpox or yellow fever. From 1517 to 1886, more than a million slaves were shipped from Africa to Cuba with perhaps even worse prospects than the indigenous people. Cuba's long war of independence from Spain was particularly bloody, with 400,000 Cubans, a fifth of the total population, dying as a direct result. From 1868 to the time of formal independence in 1898 (later than for many other Spanish colonies),

Spain sent almost 350,000 men to Cuba, which Languepin suggests was 'a considerable transfer of troops for the time, a sort of Vietnam before its time' (Languepin 2007: 21). In the course of this struggle, the merciless Captain-General Weyler designed a counter-guerilla strategy that relocated half a million civilians into army-controlled camps. He was later deemed to be the inventor of the concentration camp and some 150,000 to 170,000, or 10 per cent of the population, died in this process (Tone 2006: 223).

After the Spanish finally withdrew from Cuba, the US occupied the country for four years until 1902 and again from 1906 to 1908. But direct occupation was only a slightly more explicit version of the approach taken by the US for much of the sixty years between the end of Spanish rule and the revolution. The Platt Amendment of 1901 in effect made Cuba a colony of the US, ruling out any treaty or military relationship with other countries, allowing close scrutiny of public finances by the US, the right to intervene directly whenever it chose to do so and the right to maintain permanent military bases, including at Guantánamo Bay. Economically, US dominance was overwhelming and by 1958, 90 per cent of mining concessions were in US hands and 50 per cent of land was owned by the US, which controlled three-quarters of exports and imports. Sugar accounted for 80 per cent of all exports, in a classic colonial and neo-colonial distortion of the rural economy that had its roots in previous centuries during the Spanish occupation (Languepin 2007: 25).

As the twentieth century wore on, the US came to regard Cuba not only as a source of easy profits and a pleasant holiday destination for hundreds of thousands of North Americans each year, but also as a conveniently located playground for the rich, the seedy, the corrupt and the criminal. By the mid-1950s many of Havana's businesses were controlled by members of the US underworld, who were running the numerous casinos and brothels in the capital, together with the highly profitable drug trade. Officers in the Cuban police and army relaxed in the casinos and nightclubs and made extra money by running protection rackets. Batista himself was closely involved in this world of high profits and low morals, making millions from business transactions run by organised crime, whose key figures were among his personal friends, including Meyer Lansky and Lucky Luciano. At the same time, much of the Cuban population was falling into even greater poverty, and about a quarter of the adult population was unemployed. While illiteracy in Havana was relatively low, at 10 per cent, it was more than 40 per cent in rural areas and healthcare for the rural poor was almost non-existent (Languepin 2007: 26–34). To some extent, this was also the situation in much of the rest of Latin America, as the young Ernesto (later 'Che') Guevara had found during the road trip with his friend Alberto Granado, as described in his *Motorcycle Diaries* ([1952] 2004): illness, illiteracy and abject poverty were everywhere.

In Cuba, violence had gone hand in hand with politics for many years, almost as much under the less-obviously repressive regimes of Grau San Martín (1944–8) and Prío Socarrás (1948–52) as during the Batista dictatorship from 1952. Since the 1930s, the word *'gangsterismo'* had been used to describe the way in which government at all levels, from local town halls to national ministries and everything in between, was infused with intrigue and corruption, with state employees bribing, blackmailing and using public money to build themselves houses and make large donations to friends and relations. Most vividly, *gangsterismo* involved back-street killings followed by escape in a speeding car, and assassination was the fate of various national politicians and trade union leaders killed by government-hired gunmen, including the leader of the sugar workers' union, Jesús Menéndez, killed in 1948. Shady businesses, government corruption, murders for political ends and routine low-level violence were already well established even when Batista came to power for the first time in 1933 as part of the Revolt of the Sergeants, but in these later years he made things far worse and, as John F. Kennedy put it, 'murdered 20,000 Cubans in seven years – a greater proportion of the Cuban population than the proportion of Americans who died in both World Wars' (Kennedy 1960). The army became a crucial player, its power and presence overshadowing every area of life, and often death as well. All of this led the veteran *New York Times* journalist Herbert Matthews to comment in the late 1960s:

> I remember thinking, on visits to Cuba in the 1950s, that of all the countries around the world in which I had worked during my career, there was none where human life was so cheap as it was in Cuba. (Matthews 1969: 56)

Castro's revolutionary struggle thus took place against a backdrop of structural violence on the one hand, where the needs of the poor and deprived were ignored in the interests of lining the pockets of the rich and corrupt, and on the other regime-perpetrated violence, where politics was infused with threats of violence and many actual killings, and where politicians and high-ranking soldiers rubbed shoulders with the mafia. Castro and the other surviving Moncado Barracks attackers were released from jail in an amnesty in May 1955 and later that year he met Che Guevara in Mexico. In late 1956 they sailed from Mexico with eighty other rebels on the *Granma* and landed on the south-east coast of Cuba, quickly taking to the hills. It took just over two years of guerilla fighting against Batista's army and much work with local people in the countryside to reach the tipping point where they had sufficient support, where they were strong enough militarily and where support for Batista was sufficiently eroded for the *barbudos*, as they were now known, to march on Havana, where they met virtually no resistance and indeed received a hero's welcome. Batista fled the island on 1 January 1959 and Castro slowly made his way across the country, feted as he went; he arrived in Havana on 8 January and became Prime Minister on 16 February.

The moment of seizure of power in the capital was thus virtually bloodless, and as Hugh Thomas (1971: 1,033) puts it, the insurgents 'did not drink, did not loot, conducted themselves as if they were saints. No army had ever behaved like this in Havana.' The British journalist Edwin Tetlow commented similarly that Castro's men and women 'were one of the best behaved armies you could imagine . . . To a man they behaved impeccably' (cited in Skierka 2004: 70). A strict ethical code governed Castro's approach to guerilla warfare and his brother Raúl's words in the epigraph at the beginning of this chapter sum it up. Captives were treated with respect and were not harmed. They were fed, given water and had their wounds tended by rebel medics. Where possible, prisoners were handed to the Red Cross and where this was not possible they were given medical attention and medical supplies as necessary and were left where they could be located by their own men or by the Red Cross. Of course, this was not entirely altruistic, for prisoners are a burden to a guerilla army and a drain on often slim resources, and holding prisoners means that stealthy movement from one place to another is more difficult. Just as importantly, humane treatment of captured enemy soldiers weakened morale among enemy soldiers because this behaviour contrasted so strongly with the brutality of Batista's officers and men. Castro's ethically informed approach was sending a clear message, as he explained in the course of the fighting in the Sierra Maestra:

Since January 1957 . . . some six hundred members of the armed
forces have passed into our hands . . . none has been killed . . .
while torture and death has been the certain fate awaiting every
rebel, every sympathizer, even every suspect who fell into enemy
hands. In many cases poor unfortunate peasants have been assassinated to add to the number of bodies with which to justify the
false news of the chief of staff . . . more than six hundred defense-
less citizens, in many cases far from any revolutionary activity,
have been assassinated [by the army]. In these twenty months of
campaign, killing has made nobody stronger. Killing has made
them weak; refusing to kill has made *us* strong . . . only cowards
and thugs murder an enemy when he has surrendered . . . the
rebel army cannot carry out the same tactics as the tyranny which
we fight. (Castro cited in Thomas 1971: 998–9; emphasis in the
original)

But there was a broader point of principle that reflected an overall philosophy, as we shall see.

Castro and his fellow soldiers did of course engage in battle and
they did kill. They were in no doubt that it was necessary to do so in
order to free Cuba from the oppression, violence and corruption that
had plagued it for so long, Batista's regime being just one among many
examples over the years and centuries of ruthlessness and greed, with
the USA ever present either as occupier or in the immediate background. As we have seen, the Moncada Barracks attack of 1953 had
begun with the killing of fifteen of Batista's soldiers. In the engage-
ments in the Sierra Maestra and elsewhere, soldiers on both sides
were killed or seriously wounded. In this respect Castro's approach to
violence was quite conventional; killing the enemy together with loss
of insurgents' lives were a regrettable but necessary means to an end.
There were even exceptional cases where captives were executed, in
the few instances where guerrillas were discovered working for Batista.
One of the best-known cases of this was of Eutimio Guerra, whom
Castro's men discovered providing information to the enemy and planning to assassinate Castro himself. He was shot on 17 February 1957.

Revolutions and other dramatic changes of regime are known for
their tendency to perpetrate or at least tolerate periods of violent
vengeance or violent attempts to consolidate the new order, and
often a mixture of the two; the French Terror of 1793–4 is the classic

example, but there are many others, including the Red Terror after the Russian Revolution, atrocities committed by both sides in the Chinese Civil War and extra-judicial purges against alleged Nazi collaborators in France in summer 1944 followed by state-organised purges. This semi-formal blood-letting arguably serves several constructive or relatively constructive purposes: it channels resentment into organised or quasi-organised trials and punishment, instead of allowing a more random process of revenge; it secures and consolidates the legitimacy of the new regime, preventing a return to the old order; and it begins to allow a process of greater order to replace disorder. The argument can be made that if formal trials, imprisonment and executions take place, lives are in fact saved, and certainly fewer innocent lives are lost. After the revolution in Cuba, Revolutionary Tribunals were set up in order to put on trial the most cruel and repressive among Batista's men. As a result, in the first few months of 1959, there were several hundred executions of Batista collaborators who were convicted of having tortured and murdered under the old regime, together with some executions of members of the 26 July Movement convicted of betraying their comrades. Che Guevara was put in charge of La Cabaña prison in the fortified entrance to Havana Harbour, where many of the executions took place of military men found guilty of war crimes, torture of civilians or of soldiers taken prisoner; there were 164 executions, according to Alain Foix (2015: 22). Three of Batista's most notorious officers were tried in a public sports stadium in Havana, and in his autobiography Castro suggests that exposing the accused to public humiliation was an error. However, he argues that

> this may have been the only revolution in which the main war criminals were tried and brought to justice, the only revolution that didn't rob or steal, didn't drag people through the streets, didn't take revenge, didn't take justice into their own hands . . . And if there were no lynchings, no bloodbaths it was because of our insistence and our promise: 'War criminals will be brought to justice and punished, as examples.' (Castro cited in Ramonet 2007: 221)

He also commented nearer the time: 'We have shot no child, we have shot no woman, we have shot no old people . . . We are shooting the assassins so that they will not kill our children tomorrow' (cited in

Skierka 2004: 78). Influenced by the Nuremburg Trials, the tribunals certainly both limited and formalised the post-revolutionary bloodshed, making it less arbitrary, although according to most accounts Guevara was considerably more in favour of purging by killing than was Castro.

In relative terms, that is compared with the vicious behaviour of Batista, not to mention countless predecessors in positions of authority in Cuba, the comportment of the 26 July Movement was impeccable. Compared with the bloodletting during and after other revolutions, including the French, Mexican, Russian and Chinese revolutions, it was also exemplary. Castro's influence in this respect – an influence beginning in earnest with his speech from the dock in October 1953 – was central to this; his humane and reflective approach in relation to violence was explicit from the start. But it was also the case that, compared with other revolutions, the rebels were pushing at an almost entirely open door; Castro and his comrades became heroes with tremendous authority because their aim – ridding Cuba of a reviled tyrant – was relatively uncontentious. Opposition to the rebels was fairly weak and in the end Batista left quite easily. In terms of international reaction, even the USA at first recognised the new government led by Castro and endorsed the overthrow of Batista, although the friendly gestures were to prove short-lived. The difference, in terms of both internal and external opposition to the revolution, with the revolution of 1789 and especially that of 1917, could hardly have been greater, when there were in both cases enormous vested interests, both within the country and abroad, which opposed the revolution tooth and nail. In Cuba, it was no doubt the longer-term matter of lasting peace, equality and broader emancipation that was to be more difficult to achieve, a question to which we will return.

CASTRO'S ETHICS OF VIOLENCE

Let us pause for a moment in the examination of the history of Cuba's revolution in order to begin to place Castro's ethics of violence within other theories of emancipatory violence. The most influential literature relating to the ethics of violence in revolt can be divided, broadly speaking, into three main categories. First, there are works that can be described as pacifist, that is they argue that no violence is justified in struggles for transition from one type of regime to another and that violence is bound to have a dehumanising effect on those who perpetrate it, and therefore also on any political arrangement emerging from a violent struggle. Gandhi is the best-known and most significant exponent of this approach, arguably putting peaceful protest into practice with great effect in the campaign for independence in India in the first half of the twentieth century. But we may also mention Martin Luther King, who was an admirer of Gandhi and who in the 1950s and 1960s brought this approach to bear on the civil rights movement in the USA. Furthermore, certain authors have written about the question of peace and violence from a feminist perspective that takes on board elements of pacifism, including Sara Ruddick, whom I discussed in Chapter 1.

The second major category of work on violence in revolt is characterised by an argument that violence in defence of (broadly speaking) liberal-democratic values, goals and achievements is justified under certain conditions, because liberal democracy and the values that tend to go with it (freedom of speech, freedom of association, individual liberties and so on) are legitimate and should be defended vigorously. By the same token, this means that violence against regimes purporting to be liberal democratic may be judged illegitimate. This sort of approach has been articulated most fully in recent times by Michael Walzer in his book *Just and Unjust Wars* ([1977] 2006a), and according to some analysts by Hannah Arendt (1969), although Arendt's theory of violence arguably crosses some of the boundaries between the three approaches under discussion here. Albert Camus ([1951] 1971) is more fully part of this second category of thinkers, when he argues in favour of rebellion against injustice, but against revolution; the main difference between the two activities, he argues, is the degree of violence employed. He was, in particular, highly critical of the Algerian Front de Libération Nationale's use of violence against civilians in pursuit of independence from France, although he supported their overall objectives.

A third group of writers is usually thought to take as read the idea that violence against extreme oppression is wholly and necessarily justified, an approach often described as incorporating the idea that the (violent) means justify the (just) ends, sometimes described simply as the 'just ends' approach. Those who are often placed in this category include Georges Sorel ([1908] 1999), Frantz Fanon ([1961] 2001) and Jean-Paul Sartre ([1961] 2001), and more recently Slavoj Žižek (2008). Marx and Engels's writing is generally thought to fit into this final category, together with that of Lenin and Trotsky, and this perhaps explains in part why, among analysts of Marx, Engels, Lenin and Trotsky, there is little discussion of their work in relation to violence. (Chapter 4 is largely devoted to an examination of Marx and Engels.)

A great deal of discussion has taken place regarding the contributions of Fanon and Sartre regarding the role of violence in liberation or in revolutionary struggles. They amply make the case for the legitimacy of violence in the course of a just struggle. Fanon also explores in a particularly humane way the effect on the oppressor of violence perpetrated by the oppressor. But they are both, nevertheless, primarily concerned with the legitimation of violence against the oppressor. Fanon and Sartre were writing at the height of a particularly acute and bloody conflict, when Algerian liberation fighters were being subjected to greatly disproportionate numbers of deaths in battle compared with the French, alongside widespread torture (itself often leading to death), assassination and routine harassment and intimidation. In a new Introduction to Fanon's *Les Damnés de la Terre*, which still includes Sartre's Preface, Alice Cherki (2002: 11–12) suggests that Sartre goes too far in his justification of violence, and that Sartre 'diverts' (*détourne*) Fanon's preoccupations and tone, justifying violence and presenting it as obligatory, whereas Fanon's intention is to analyse rather than justify violence. When Sartre famously argues that 'to kill a European, you kill two birds with one stone, killing an oppressor and an oppressed person at the same time – the result being a dead man and a free man', according to Cherki these sorts of remarks reduce the impact and scope of Fanon's words because they seem to justify not just violence but also individual murder.

Cherki's comments have the effect of breaking a taboo in the study of Fanon and Sartre, questioning as they do the – until now – almost obligatory reading of a strong complementarity between what Fanon writes in his main text and what Sartre writes in his Preface. To endorse Fanon had previously been necessarily to endorse Sartre. Cherki goes as far as saying that Sartre misrepresents Fanon's work, with Sartre suggesting that violence is not only a justified means to an end but also a good and beneficial thing in itself. Violence has, he argues, an in-itself emancipating effect on the oppressed perpetrator quite apart from helping to achieve the next staging point in the struggle for emancipation. This view is reminiscent of Sorel's argument that political violence has a 'cleansing' effect. Fanon is indeed far more humanist in his text than Sartre and is at great pains, for example, to discuss the psychological effects on the perpetrator of committing violence, as mentioned above.

This is very much about means and end, then, and in particular about whether violent means are justified by a particular – let us assume emancipated and peaceful – end. Various authors have suggested that there is a far more complex relationship between violent means and their consequences than this question seems to imply, and that one way of taking this matter forward is to scrutinise means in isolation, in other words independently of the end. Walter Benjamin ([1921] 1978: 277–8) raises the question of 'whether violence, as a principle, could be a moral means even to just ends. To resolve this question a more exact criterion is needed, which would discriminate within the sphere of means themselves, without regard for the ends they serve.' It is not the case, according to Benjamin, that violence is simply 'a raw material, the use of which is in no way problematical, unless force is misused for unjust ends'.

It is also worth mentioning a pamphlet written in 1938 by Leon Trotsky, entitled *Their Morals and Ours* ([1938] 1969). The circumstances in which it was written were dramatic: Trotsky was in exile in Mexico; it was becoming clear that Franco was gaining the upper hand in the civil war in Spain; the Second World War was becoming increasingly likely; and the Moscow show trials had recently sentenced the author of the pamphlet to death in absentia. This context may explain the particularly biting and disdainful tone of some of the pamphlet. But the core message deserves far more attention than it has received to date in scholarship on violence in revolt. While maintaining that there is no such thing as 'eternally-valid morality' or a 'supra-class moral principle', Trotsky argues that to say '*any* means . . . was permissible if only it led to the "end" . . . [is] an internally contradictory and absurd doctrine' ([1938] 1969: 12; emphasis in the original). This is because 'the principle, the end justifies the means, naturally raises the question: And what justifies the end? In practical life as in the historical movement the end and the means constantly change places' (14–15). This is an important point and in order to reinforce it he quotes Ferdinand Lassalle, who writes:

Point not the goal, unless you plot the course,
For ends and means to man are tangled so
That different means quite different ends enforce;
Conceive the means as ends in embryo. ([1938] 1969: 37–8)

Trotsky is not against liberating violence where he believes it is necessary, of course. He was, after all, not only one of the leaders of the Russian Revolution, but also founder and leader of the Red Army in the immediate aftermath of the Revolution. Regarding the situation in Europe in 1938, he makes the point that although to combat Franco necessitates taking up arms 'with its wake of horrors and crimes. Nevertheless, . . . violence "in [itself]" warrant[s] condemnation . . . as does the class society which generates them' (27). There is a 'dialectic interdependence of means and ends' and '[a] means can only be justified by its end. But the end in its turn needs to be justified'. Ultimately, '[t]hat is permissible . . . which *really* leads to the liberation of mankind' (37; emphasis in the original).

Thus, Trotsky did not, as many have claimed, simply assert that 'anything goes' in terms of revolutionary violence as long as it led to revolution or a consolidation of the revolution. He was clear that the means had an influence on the end, and similarly to Benjamin believed that the means itself needed to be examined independently of the end and from an ethical point of view. Indeed there was often no clear distinction between means and ends, and at the very least there existed a dialectical relationship between them. He was also clear that, although violence in itself is a terrible thing – 'history chooses cruel pathways' – at times recourse to violence was necessary and was the more morally responsible path to take, as in the case of the war against Franco 'with its wake of horrors and crimes'. He is clear that revolutionaries need to be wary of violence but that violence is unavoidable at times if a more humane future is to be constructed.

If we return to the Cuba of the years 1956–9, the immediate goal, or end, was the overthrow of Batista, but this soon became the means to a further end, or series of ends, including a very substantial literacy campaign, land reform, improved healthcare and sending doctors, teachers, engineers and soldiers to help in other countries. These further ends, in turn, were quickly to become means to greater emancipation and the primary goal thus quickly became the means to the next goal, or as Trotsky puts it, 'the immediate end becomes the means for a further end' (38). Castro and his comrades took the view that – quite apart from their wanting to compare favourably with Batista – if the overthrow had been unscrupulously violent, this would have had an effect on the way in which the post-revolutionary process would have taken place. The transition had to be handled very carefully if the post-revolutionary period was to be successful. In this sense, Trotsky's pamphlet sheds light on Castro's approach, although Castro had not – as far as I am aware – read Trotsky's argument. Nevertheless, Trotsky's position lacks the more developed and explicit humanism of Castro's, which goes out of its way to emphasise the need for the revolution to contrast with the barbarity of much of what went before in Cuba and, moreover, to be ethically justifiable in broader terms. Hindsight and a different context are luxuries, of course, but one cannot help feeling that more explicit humanity on Trotsky's and Lenin's – not to mention Stalin's – part in the Russian Revolution and its aftermath might have helped create a Soviet Union less prone to regime-perpetrated violent crime.

Castro, then, introduces a strong ethical and moral dimension to the practice of insurgent violence, arguing not only that the end should be a worthy one, but that the means of achieving this end must itself be subjected to ethical scrutiny. More specifically, insurgents should never use violence against unarmed civilians, should never use torture, never execute prisoners and avoid execution within the revolutionary organisation (although there were exceptions to this, as we know). Arguably, Castro's approach to emancipatory violence is superior to others in that it combines ethics with a discourse and practice of freedom fighting, together with a deeply egalitarian logic.

Castro is often at great pains to emphasise the ethically upstanding nature both of the struggle for Cuban independence and of the Cuban revolution since 1959. In *My Life* (Ramonet 2007), he looks back over forty-plus years of the Cuban revolution and has a great deal to say about ethics, violence, defence of the island from attack, treatment of prisoners and Cuban army activities abroad. Indeed he is very unusual among either rebel leaders or Western politicians in his explicitly ethical stance. For Castro, as far as guerilla war is concerned, revolutionary fighters engage the enemy in combat in the normal way, but outside of that there is no killing, no torture and no humiliation and, above all, innocent people are never killed. Physical violence 'simply does not work in the long run' (208) and rebel leaders made clear that brutality was not on the agenda: 'without that philosophy, combatants might have shot prisoners left and right – heaven only knows what might've been done . . . For us it was a philosophy, a principle, that innocent people must not be sacrificed. It was always a principle – practically dogma' (210–11). Moreover, they did not use terrorism that killed innocent people in explosions, or assassination, and chose not to target Batista himself, as the enemy would simply have installed someone else in his place. Asked about terrorism in the early twenty-first century, Castro replies: 'I say to you that no war is ever won through terrorism. It's that simple. Because [if you employ terrorism] you earn the opposition, hatred and rejection of those whom you need in order to win the war' (211).

INFLUENCES ON CASTRO'S THOUGHT

Cuba as a whole and Castro in particular reveres and seeks inspiration from the nineteenth-century intellectual José Martí – writer, orator, organiser and above all hero of the struggle for independence from Spain. It is busts and statues of Martí that tend to feature in Cuba's public buildings and public squares, rather than representations of Marx, Lenin or even Che Guevara (although there are some of these). In various ways, Castro modelled himself on the figure of Martí, in terms of both his life and thought. Much of Martí's life was spent in the struggle for Cuban independence and he died for that cause in the 1895 Battle of Dos Ríos, aged forty-two. Although he lived for many years in the US leading Cuban exiles, he believed deeply not only that Cuba should gain independence from Spain, but also that any union with the USA – a potential trajectory supported by many members of the Cuban elite at the time – would offer nothing but continued exploitation. He was, moreover, passionately in favour of racial equality and consistently condemned discrimination on the grounds of ethnicity, a form of oppression that was clear to see in many domains, both in Cuba and the US. In particular, he spoke in defence of the plight of indigenous peoples, again both in Cuba and the US, and he had a special concern for education. As far as political economy was concerned, although he was far from being a Marxist, he was vehemently anti-capitalist and was a supporter of the early trade union movement. In 1892 he set up the Cuban Revolutionary Party, believing that independence from Spain would be achieved via armed struggle, but a struggle that would be ethically informed; he promised a 'civilised war' in which civilian Spaniards would not be harmed. He insisted that 'anyone is a criminal who promotes an avoidable war; and so is he who does not promote an inevitable civil war' (cited in Thomas 1971: 863). As regards religion, his views are not clear, but in his best-known poem, 'The White Rose', he writes of 'turning the other cheek', a clear biblical reference. Had he survived independence from Spain, there is no doubt that Martí would have become the first president of an independent Cuba.

The similarities between Martí and Castro, and the influences of Martí on Castro, are plain to see: Castro built the movement for liberation – this time liberation not from Spain but from the US-supported Cuban government – and fought a 'civilised war' against Batista; they were both strongly egalitarian, both defended minority groups and both were passionate about universal education, although Castro was increasingly influenced by Marx, unlike Martí; they were both accomplished orators and writers, as well as men of action; and they abhorred injustice and declared very publicly that they were prepared to die fighting it in the struggle for Cuban emancipation. Martí did die for his cause and Castro did not, despite the countless attempts on his life. Concerning religion, as I have suggested, it is not clear what Martí's beliefs were, but more importantly, Castro is insistent that '[Martí's] philosophy contains a certain amount of Christian ethics. He was a man of great ethical conviction. The highest Christian ethics had exerted great influence on him' (Ramonet 2007: 154). At the end of Castro's trial in 1953, the judge asked Castro who had inspired the attack on the Moncada Barracks. His answer was simple: José Martí.

It is also clear that Castro is also influenced in some important ways by Christianity, although he insists that he has never had any spiritual religious belief. His views on religion are revealed in a book of conversations between himself and Frei Betto, a Brazilian Dominican friar and liberation theologian, entitled *Castro and Religion* (1985). Castro attended a Jesuit school and college that taught self-sacrifice and austerity, he insists, and there was an environment where, despite the teachers' unshakable right-wing views, there was a strong ethical code that instilled in Castro a strong sense of right and wrong, fairness and unfairness, and a sense of 'personal honour, . . . honesty, courage and the ability to make sacrifices' (110). For his Jesuit teachers, he explains, the profit motive counted for nothing and although the Church has in some respects been part of capitalist and other forms of domination for a long time, '[w]ith the teachings of Christ you can formulate a radical socialist programme, whether you're a believer or not' (Castro with Ramonet 2007: 156). Defence of the poor, for example, is a common theme between radical egalitarians and the Christian Church, and as far as Castro is concerned communists and Christians can struggle together for a world where the lot of the poor is vastly improved.

Christian and revolutionary thought are highly compatible, he argues, and at the heart of Christ's teaching is identification with the needs of the oppressed. The idea of sacrifice is another element in common and Castro points out that just as particularly committed Christians devote their lives to spirituality and spreading the word of the Bible, militant socialists give up their lives for the revolution, even though many of them do not believe in life after death.

With regard to persecution of the Church, Castro suggests that the Cuban revolution was exceptional in that priests were not mistreated and certainly not executed, and no churches were closed, in contrast with the 1789 French Revolution, the Mexican Revolution of 1910 and Russia after 1917, where in each case many religious people were killed and imprisoned, not to mention the Spanish Civil War, where priests were killed by both sides. Political and ethical principles and ideas explain this more tolerant attitude in Cuba, he argues (240). Castro met three different Popes in Cuba, in January 1998, March 2012 and September 2015, and Pope Francis played an important role in negotiations between the US and Cuba regarding a certain thawing of relations, including opening embassies on each other's soil.

It will now be clear that there is a strong ethical dimension to Castro's thought, which he is pleased to acknowledge and discuss. This is relatively rare among modern leaders of revolutions and other dramatic regime changes, although Nelson Mandela is a clear exception to this general rule. Mandela was indeed a great admirer of Castro, not least because of Cuba's extensive fighting in Africa in the 1970s and 1980s, especially at the Battle of Cuito Cuanavale in south-eastern Angola in 1987–8, which contributed to the downfall of the apartheid regime a few years later. But beyond that, they share a concern to examine the ethics relating to liberation and other struggles (see Mandela 1970; Mandela 1995).

MODERN CUBA AND THE USA

From the standpoint of the early twenty-first century, it is clear that Cuba's revolution has been shaped greatly by its relationship with the USA. The island has maintained its political and ideological independence from the capitalist world and against all odds it has managed to create and maintain world-class benefits such as healthcare, education (including higher education) and welfare systems, all of which are free at the point of use. Full employment, housing for all and the right to free water, electricity and telephone are other significant achievements. In 2014 the rate of infant mortality was lower than in the US, at five per thousand births, and significantly better than the Latin American average. Similarly, life expectancy in Cuba rose from seventy-four to seventy-eight years in the 1990s, although the worst years of profound hardship after the fall of communism saw a slight rise in mortality for certain sectors of the population (Morris 2014: 6–7). It has achieved all of this in the face of constant aggression from its neighbour 90 miles across the sea, aggression that has taken an enormous toll on the population and has certainly made the revolution harder to sustain than it would otherwise have been; this was of course the intention. The most damaging aspect of the US onslaught has been the trade embargo, first imposed in 1962 and increased steadily until it became a de facto blockade. From 1963, under the terms of the Trading with the Enemy Act of 1917, President Kennedy extended the ban to cover all unlicensed commercial and financial transactions between the Cuba and US citizens, also covering transactions into third countries and trade with third countries where materials originated in Cuba. Travel to Cuba from the US was also outlawed. These developments were taking place against the backdrop of the Cuban missile crisis and its wake, and rapprochement between Cuba and the Soviet Union, a new departure that was both partial cause and partial effect of deteriorating relations between the US and its diminutive neighbour.

The USSR brought Cuba practical help from the early 1960s up until its collapse in 1991, both in terms of military protection and close economic relations; for example, the Soviet Union guaranteed imports to the Eastern bloc of an annual quota of sugar with a purchase price of $0.42 per pound in the early 1990s, compared with a world market price of $0.09, and imports from Comecon accounted for 40 per cent of Cuba's gross domestic product (GDP), including 50 per cent of Cuba's food and 90 per cent of its oil. A hefty trade deficit was also subsidised by the USSR (Morris 2014: 15). After the demise of the Soviet Union, the US blockade continued, and indeed was reinforced when in 1992 trade was banned between Cuba and US-owned subsidiaries in third countries, trade that was substantial by the early 1990s and that mainly consisted of food and medical supplies. Moreover, ships that had docked in Cuba were now banned from entering a US harbour for six months. In short, the Soviet lifeline had disappeared and the US went further in its attempts to isolate Cuba economically from the rest of the world. This certainly had part of the desired effect, and Cuba entered what it described as its Special Period, a war economy in peace-time that left many Cubans short of essential goods, or, put more bluntly, destitute, with the usual attendant dangers to health and well-being. As recently as September 2015 the US renewed the Trading with the Enemy Act despite the UN, for the twenty-third year running, passing a resolution calling on the US to lift the embargo, with only the US and Israel voting against and the other 191 states voting in favour. Only with the movement to the left of governments in various countries in Latin America, especially Venezuela, Argentina and Brazil, was the economic plight of Cuba somewhat alleviated, but the island nevertheless continued to live essentially in a state of siege in relation to much of the outside world, despite successful attempts to increase tourism. President Obama's declared aim in late 2015 of approaching Congress with proposals to relax the embargo remains unfulfilled as this book goes to press, despite restoration of diplomatic relations and freer travel.

The CIA has also, of course, made numerous attempts over the years not only on Castro's life – including poison-contaminated wetsuits, exploding cigars and a cyanide pill in a chocolate milkshake – but also on ordinary Cubans' lives, which in some cases were successful. Swine fever was introduced in 1971 and dengue fever in 1981, which killed more than 100 people; hundreds of covert operations in rural areas destroyed thousands of tons of sugarcane; there were arson attacks on warehouses; and bombs were planted at power stations and in hotels (Skierka 2004: 101). The most notorious assault was the invasion at the Bay of Pigs in April 1961, which was designed to provoke a wider uprising against the regime, but that quickly became a fiasco with lasting consequences for the US. About 1,500 Cuban exiles, trained by the CIA, landed at the Bay in the south-west of the island, the intention being to defeat the soldiers they met initially and then go on to organise a wholesale counter-revolution in alliance with those on the island who were hostile towards the regime. The invasion was strongly supported and wholly financed by the US government under John F. Kennedy, but there were no US soldiers involved in the landing party. It was extremely badly organised, with one ship full of weapons sinking just before reaching shore and about thirty invaders drowning before they had set foot on the island. Indeed this set the tone for the rest of the operation. Castro himself quickly took control of the response against the attackers, who were ill-equipped and had very little training. He personally manned the forward command post and drove a tank in the thick of the battle. After three days the combat was over, with more than a hundred deaths among the assailants and many more among those defending the revolution. More than 1,000 prisoners were taken and Castro insists that '[n]ot one was even hit with a rifle butt, because that has always been our principle' (Ramonet 2007: 260). They were, however, put on public trial and among the defendants there were five who had been violent henchmen for Batista, and who were later executed. Nine others were sentenced to thirty years' imprisonment for their activities under Batista. The rest of the prisoners were held while the Cubans negotiated with the US government and were finally exchanged for many million dollars' worth of medical supplies.

Many of the invaders had a material interest in defeating the revolution in its early years and according to Thomas (1971: 1,360–1) the 1,500 invaders had once owned a million acres of Cuban land, together with 10,000 houses, seventy factories, five mines, two banks and ten sugar mills. But Castro took the opportunity to show to the world that Cuba's revolution was humane, treating the enemy well and severely punishing only those with an appalling record of brutality under Batista. The effect of the defeat of the invasion and the treatment of the captured men was both to consolidate the revolution and to increase the hostility of the US regarding Cuba, but also its wariness. The dénouement of the Bay of Pigs invasion was one of the many turning points in the history of US–Cuba relations, and one that was closely bound up with ethics and revolution; in the eyes of much of the world (and especially much of Latin America), the US was both ruthless and incompetent, whereas Cuba heroically defended its territory and after the defeat treated prisoners correctly.

During the Cold War, Cuba – more than any other developing country – played an important role well beyond its own borders and sent soldiers to fight alongside anti-colonial and liberationist armies in many sites of conflict, particularly in Africa. Some 36,000 Cuban soldiers were fighting in Angola in 1976 and 55,000 by 1988 (Gleijeses 2010: 327). Castro comments:

we were in Angola for fifteen years, from 1975 to 1990; we were at the decisive battle of Cuito Cuanvale. You can go ask the South African army whether any of its men who were taken prisoner by us there were mistreated by Cuban troops, or beaten or struck in any way. They felt safe in our hands . . . We fought in Ethiopia, pushing back the aggression launched by Siad Barre against the revolution there. I'll tell you, our soldiers have never executed a prisoner, and have never mistreated one . . . More than half a million Cubans have gone on internationalist missions as technicians [doctors, teachers, and so on] and as combatants. (Castro with Ramonet 2007: 261, 572–3)

WITH AND BEYOND CASTRO

In terms of the practice of revolutionary uprising, there is little doubt that – unless one takes an entirely pacifist line of argument – Castro's minimal use of violence and explicit and reflective humanism is exemplary. In an insightful study, Dayan Jayatilleka (2007) examines Castro's ethics of violence, suggesting that the Cuban leader resolved the disagreement between Sartre and Camus regarding violence and morality, namely where Sartre was critical of Camus for Camus's disapproval of the violence of the oppressed. Castro's main contribution to Marxism, Jayatilleka argues, is the way in which he introduces an ethical and moral dimension. Jayatilleka suggests that there are three possible approaches to violence: by those who contend that violence is always wrong; by those who defend it if it is in pursuit of a just end; and by those who argue that not only should the end be a worthy one but that the means of achieving this end must be subjected to ethical scrutiny. It is this last position that he argues is the correct one and the one that Castro embraces (13). Jayatilleka argues convincingly that neither Sorel nor Fanon nor Sartre

> went beyond the understanding of the effect of dehumanization of the violence of the oppressor on the oppressed and the effect of *humanization* on the oppressed of the exercise of counter-violence, to an understanding of the effect of *dehumanization* of violence on the oppressed (which the Gandhians and other pacifists understood), when used by them without limits. *There is no dialectical understanding of the violence of the oppressed, encompassing its contradictory aspects, both liberating and dehumanizing.* This, however, was a concern of Camus, though his attempt to resolve the contradiction was unsatisfactory. (Jayatilleka 2007: 26; emphasis in the original)

These are thought-provoking interpretations of Castro's approach. But we need to ask ourselves two questions that follow from this and indeed highlight possible limitations regarding Castro's ethics of violence. First, to what extent is the Cuban revolution of 1959 comparable with other armed struggles for emancipation? In other words, to what extent can we generalise from the Cuban example? If we compare it with the Russian Revolution, it is true that there was little explicitly humane about the attitude of Bolshevik leaders, at least in the short term; their considerations were entirely ones of defending the revolution and humanist considerations were barely considered, it seems. The stakes were arguably far higher in Russia, and the revolution was under attack from other countries' armies, alongside the White Army within Russia. As I have pointed out above, the guerilla fighting of the late 1950s in Cuba, followed by the overthrow of Batista in late 1958 and the beginning of 1959, were in many ways a nationalist revolt against a despot who had strong connections with the USA, rather than a socialist revolution. The revolutionary moment of 1958–9 combined elements of social revolution with national liberation, and the overthrow of the US-backed dictator was certainly the primary aim. Explicit socialism, or communism, came later, and became particularly clear after the Bay of Pigs invasion and the decision to ally closely with the Soviet Union. Nevertheless, the ethics and the sparing use of violence on the part of the 26 July Movement, and Castro's well worked-out position on these questions in particular, compared very favourably with the approach towards violence on the part of insurgents in many other revolutions, as we have seen. This does not by any means, as some historians have argued especially since the fall of communism, imply that these other revolutions should be condemned in every regard, but it does mean that in the respect that primarily concerns us here – the ethics of violence in emancipatory struggles – they fell short compared with the Cuban revolution.

The second question that arises is: how did Cuba fare in the longer term in relation to the questions of emancipation and greater humanity? Thinking back to Trotsky's discussion of the dialectical relationship between means and ends, we can begin to assess the contribution of Castro and of Castro's Cuba to our overall discussion regarding violence for emancipation. We have seen that Trotsky suggests that ends often in turn become means to further ends, and so on. I suggested above that in the case of Cuba the revolutionary means up to 1959, which were on the whole humane, were intended to lead to the ends of land reform, better working conditions, greatly improved systems of healthcare, education and welfare, and much else beyond. These improvements, or ends, then became further means to further ends, that is, to further emancipation. In the early 1960s, Che Guevara in particular was explicit in his belief that the leaders of the revolution were aiming for a higher stage of the revolution where one would see the emergence of what he called the New Man, enjoying 'full realization as a human being, having broken the chains of alienation'; the New Man – and we should of course add the New Woman – would be more fulfilled because they were freer, and freer because they were more fulfilled, as he put it (Guevara [1964] 1968: 393, 399). Now it is clear that such a stage has not been reached in the Cuba of the early twenty-first century. Certainly, there have been some remarkable achievements in Cuba, a country that in some respects now compares favourably with the richest nations on Earth in terms of alleviation of poverty, housing provision, education, healthcare and welfare. Moreover, Cuban doctors, nurses and care workers have been and continue to be sent all over the world where their help is needed. These are very considerable achievements and were unthinkable under Batista, and since 1959 they have been achieved against the odds, given the ongoing assault Cuba has experienced at the hands of the US.

Gender equality was one of the priorities for the revolution from the start and the position of women has indeed improved greatly; for example, contraception and abortion are now widely available, women's health has improved greatly and childbirth is now safer than in numerous places even in the developed world. Many women now go out to work, although no doubt still shoulder far greater responsibility for child rearing than men. Racial equality was another priority from the beginning and, again, much has improved in this domain, although – similar to the situation in richer countries – there are, for example, far more arrests of young black men than of young white men. The process of gay liberation was far slower to begin and to take root properly, and homosexual sex was a criminal offence until 1979. But since then, and particularly into the twenty-first century, movements defending gay rights organise openly. There is, however, no doubt a long way to go in this respect, especially in terms of rights and acceptance of lesbianism (Chomsky 2015: 110–25).

In other areas Cuba falls far short in respect of even minimal, liberal liberties. Freedom of expression is truncated in terms of rights of assembly, press freedom and access to the Internet, and criticism of the government is sometimes met with temporary or longer-term detention, house arrest, travel restrictions or surveillance; Amnesty International (2015) suggests that there were nearly 9,000 'politically-motivated short term detentions' in 2014, a 27 per cent increase over 2013. There have also been many restrictions on travel abroad, although these have been relaxed since 2013. The Catholic Church, which was never outlawed but was restricted in its activities, can now operate almost entirely freely, and there have been three papal visits to Cuba. Capital punishment still exists in Cuba, and although it is used relatively infrequently, the fact that it still exists is certainly an indictment of the regime more generally and an indication that the revolution has at least partially failed.

Castro and other leaders have long argued that the formal political process in Cuba is more democratic and fairer than its counterparts in richer, liberal democratic countries, in part because all candidates have access to exactly the same, highly minimal, resources, by stark contrast with the situation in richer countries where unequal amounts of money behind different campaigns makes a very substantial difference to their success or failure. Since the Cuban constitution was reformed in 1992, there have been direct elections to the National Assembly, as well as to Provincial and Municipal Assemblies. The Communist Party does not select candidates (selection takes place in the local community), the Party cannot campaign for its candidates and candidates do not have to be members of the Party. However, there is only one candidate per seat and the Communist Party is the only party allowed to exist, so its members have a significant advantage over independent candidates in terms of selection and therefore election. The logic of this, according to the Cuban government, is that if other parties were allowed to exist some of them would no doubt be backed heavily, both financially and ideologically, by the US, and this is undoubtedly true. There is no campaigning, so money does not play a role. This may all seem odd, and no doubt undemocratic, when compared with procedures in a liberal democracy, but turnout, which is not compulsory, has been consistently high in the three national elections up to 2013: in 2003, 97.2 per cent of those eligible to vote actually voted; in 2008, 96.9 per cent voted; and in 2013, 90.9 per cent voted. Blank and spoiled ballots (the way in which people protest against this system) amounted to only 3.9

per cent in 2003, 4.8 per cent in 2008 and 5.8 per cent in 2013 (August 2013: 178).

In many liberal democracies, the positive aspects of the political process include formal rules that are on the whole adhered to, regarding freedom of political expression, freedom of competition between candidates of various hues and the right to belong to any of the various parties, and composition of governments that reflect the expression of preferences by the electorate, although certain voting systems do skew this considerably and deny representation of smaller parties, for example. However, in liberal democracies there is little acknowledgement that without social equality there can be no political equality, and that greater equality regarding education, income and leisure time are needed for a more democratic society. Neither is there acknowledgement that deeper democracy requires greater control over places of work by their employees and greater say in local matters by inhabitants of a particular area. More generally, the capitalist economy often operates in a fashion that is virtually autonomous from the needs and desires of a particular electorate and cannot be constrained even if it is desirable to do so; the 'law of the market' is above politics and must be obeyed. This is confirmed on a daily basis in myriad ways and the imposition of severe austerity measures on the people of Greece from 2010 is a particularly graphic example of the way in which the international economy and in particular the financial system has tight and unaccountable hold over nations' economies, which makes forging a path that is independent of this system extremely difficult, and soon encounters enormous obstacles. The Greek electorate found that an anti-austerity government could do very little to resist draconian austerity measures imposed by the European Commission, the European Central Bank and the International Monetary Fund. The major political parties often have very similar positions on the important matters of the day and particularly on economic policy, and therefore offer little real choice, which explains in part why participation in elections is often so low. In liberal democracies the people are not in fact sovereign by any means and there are huge and unaccountable vested interests that have a great deal of influence over the political system. Certainly, the formal political system appears to many to be properly democratic, but in fact it allows the powerful to rule and prevents many of the less powerful from taking part in processes that would transform their lives and make them immeasurably better. The formal political system is thus in part simply a way of generating consent.

There are certainly indefensible restrictions on freedom of expression in Cuba. But again, the 'freedoms' practised in many liberal democracies are partially illusory, because – to take just one example – the enormously powerful, major media outlets are owned by virtual monopolies that publish and broadcast what they would themselves no doubt brand propaganda in a non-capitalist country. Moreover, however one makes the comparison, big business combined with wealthy individuals in the US and other major capitalist countries put far more resources into political manipulation of elections than does the Cuban regime in its elections. The fact that any party hopeful of winning a general election in Britain feels obliged to attract the support of Rupert Murdoch and his media empire is indeed a severe indictment of the current system and gives the lie to any idea that it is truly democratic. Commenting on the way private financing affects whose views are allowed to appear most forcefully in richer countries' media, Castro insists that

> our system is a thousand times more democratic than the capitalist, imperialist system of the developed countries – including the NATO [North Atlantic Treaty Organization] countries, which plunder our world and ruthlessly exploit us. I believe that our system is really much fairer and much more democratic. (Castro and Betto 1985: 249–50)

While this may be a greatly exaggerated view of the situation, it does point to the highly undemocratic nature of politics in many richer countries and remind us that Cuba's political system attempts – ultimately unsuccessfully – to forge an alternative approach in extremely difficult circumstances.

It should also be said that in addition to the electoral process in Cuba, there is an extensive deliberative framework that becomes particularly active in times of hardship or crisis. For example, in 1994, there were some 80,000 meetings, or 'workers' parliaments', held in places of work in order to discuss what to do as a result of the USSR disappearing and thus the island's principal lifeline being cut off (Saney 2004: 52). Proposals finally accepted by these meetings, which involved a total of three million workers, included the removal of government subsidies to state-owned factories that meant some job losses; confiscation of goods obtained through the black market; increasing prices for rum and cigarettes; and the introduction of a small charge for participation in sporting and cultural activities, which had previously been entirely free of charge. These and various other measures were discussed and voted upon by the workers' parliaments and the resulting proposals were put to the National Assembly, and many were adopted.

There are certainly contextual explanations for the negative aspects of modern Cuba – characteristics that can only mean that socialism has so far, at least, failed to materialise properly – including most obviously the appalling treatment meted out by the US, and indeed the collusion of much of the rest of the world with this treatment, despite UN condemnation of the US embargo each year. Being forced to ally with the Soviet Union of course did nothing to push Cuba in a more socialist-democratic direction or to encourage greater freedom of expression and movement. The cult of leadership that grew up around Castro also had a negative effect, although Castro did not indulge in high living and personal enrichment in the way that the leaders of many other communist countries did; in that respect, as in many others, he largely led by example. Perhaps most of all, the fact that other countries in the region failed to become, or to remain, socialist – in many cases due to the intervention of the US – meant that Cuba was very isolated in the region and has for many years led an existence that may be described as siege socialism.

Given the renewal of diplomatic and the probable development of at least some trading relations between the US and Cuba, what may the future bring? Certainly, in some ways the US blockade, given that it did not destroy Cuba as a state with a distinctly egalitarian and egalitarian orientation and identity, has helped keep the country united in common cause against a cruel enemy and neighbour. So relaxation of the blockade may itself generate more criticism among Cubans of the socialist or quasi-socialist system. Also, any substantial relaxation of the embargo is likely to be accompanied by demands that US companies are allowed to trade and operate widely in Cuba, with all the negative consequences that that may bring with it. Moreover, if this and more broadly the free (or freer) market is adopted, the appeal of consumer items and foreign travel may also introduce a taste for the capitalist way of life that is barely seen in Cuba at present. The potential love of consumer items is not necessarily in itself destructive, but it is possible that it will be accompanied by privatisation and economic liberalisation that may well roll back many of the enormous social gains made since the revolution of 1959; the introduction of the market into education and healthcare, for example, could result in substantial deterioration of provision for large numbers of people, as indeed it has both in the former Eastern bloc and in other countries where neo-liberal economic policy has prevailed. On the other hand, by contrast with the situation that prevailed for many years, there are numerous countries in Latin America that are – or have recently been – friendly to Cuba, including Venezuela, Brazil, Argentina, Uruguay, Nicaragua, Panama, Haiti, Ecuador and Bolivia. If Cuba is able to maintain and consolidate good trading and diplomatic relations with some or all of these countries there is a greater likelihood that many of the gains of the revolution will be maintained.

*   *   *

The detail of the Cuban revolution, and particularly of Castro's ethics of violence in revolt, is highly relevant to our discussion, and it helps us address some of the central ideas of this book. Insofar as the revolution represented Castro's humanism, it was against violence and was conducted in pursuit of peace. Decisions were taken carefully regarding how violent the day-to-day practice of revolutionaries could be in the name of peace and anti-violence. It was fought against a murderously violent, corrupt regime that favoured an unscrupulous elite that acted systematically and in many and glaring ways against the interests of the mass of ordinary people. The new regime ended the age-old violence in Cuba and it brought literacy, wider education, excellent healthcare, greatly improved welfare and much employment. There was no period of Terror after the revolution in Cuba, although there were trials of former sadistic associates of Batista that took the form of vengeance of the island's people and that were no doubt unjustifiable in broader ethical terms, convenient and practical though they were at the time.

The Castro regime was obliged to contend with various forms of violence, together with relentless negative propaganda from the USA, which would stop at nothing in order to attempt to restore capitalism in Cuba. Cuba's response was to turn to the Soviet Union for military protection, financial help and trade, which the USSR offered in large amounts. But this also led to the establishment of a repressive state in Cuba in order to attempt to consolidate the achievements of the revolution; very real progress and greater equality were enabled by an authoritarian state and the cult of the – certainly very remarkable – individual, in the form of the *Lider Maximo* rather than wider and deeper democracy. Severe restrictions were placed upon foreign travel, freedom of expression and assembly, dissidents were imprisoned and the death penalty was used (albeit far less than in many countries, including the USA). This is not to say that these aforementioned, classically liberal lacunae were more important than the very real achievements of the revolution. It is also not to say that the revolution could have been sustained without at least some of the repressive measures. It is also the case that the onslaught by the US and to some extent by the rest of the capitalist world – that hardly raised a voice in complaint when Cuba was semi-starved, deprived of medical supplies and driven to the brink in terms of energy requirements by the US embargo – was largely to blame for the inability of the Cuban revolution to go further; no-one can say what would have happened if the US and the capitalist world at large had not driven Cuba to the point of collapse.

We can certainly say that the Castro regime – even if we call it a dictatorship – is the most humane regime that Cuba has ever known. In a previous chapter we examined the foreign relations of the USA since 1945 (we could have taken other countries as case studies) and saw that in the interests of defending its 'right' to exploit the resources of the world and to defend capitalist 'freedoms' across the globe, many people in developing countries have been killed, a great many more have endured ongoing suffering and the legacy is in many cases one of ongoing turmoil.

It is not necessary to endorse all of Castro's views and practices in order to recognise in his argument a most helpful contribution that moves a debate forward regarding the ethics of violence in revolt. At the very least, it offers highly concrete examples in an area where one is in danger of remaining either in a very general and abstract discourse, or within the individual pragmatics of cases as they arise, without a middle way that offers an ethics based both on principle and practice.

Certainly, if we make comparisons with the other major examples of 'actually existing' socialism – or historical communism – of the twentieth century that had a far worse record on political violence (not to mention capitalist violence from the most wealthy, resourceful and privileged nations on Earth who mainly wished to maintain the privileges of the elite), it should be noted that the Cuban revolution was not in as difficult a situation as were others. The old regime in Cuba was not defended as ferociously as it was in Russia or China, for example, and even the USA was obliged to recognise at first that the insurgents were fighting against a cruel dictator who was the enemy of the interests of most of the island's population. In addition, Cuba was a small island with a small population – about seven million in 1958 (and eleven million in 2015) – and it was assumed by many that the revolution would before long become unsustainable on this politically isolated island. Finally, although the USA tried hard to make Cuba collapse, it did not invade, in part due to the protective mantle of the Soviet Union. All this notwithstanding, it was no doubt in large part because of the support of a large section of the population for Castro's regime that prevented the USA from carrying out a wholesale invasion.

Most importantly, for our purposes, Castro is deeply reflective on the ethics of violence in revolt and offers the most developed morality in relation to violence in pursuit of emancipation of any revolutionary leader. We may say that Castro and the practice of the Cuban revolution offer the *spirit* with which we should approach the question of violence in revolt, which promotes the importance of the life and well-being of all human beings, with the regretful acknowledgement that fighting and loss of life in pursuit of a substantially more just and less exploitative society is sometimes necessary. This is, at the very least, a highly inspiring way to approach the question.

Chapter 4

MARX, ENGELS AND THE PLACE OF
VIOLENCE IN HISTORY

The proletariat created by the breaking up of the bands of feudal
retainers and by the forcible expropriation of the people from the
soil, this 'free' proletariat could not possibly be absorbed by the
nascent manufactures as fast as it was thrown upon the world. On
the other hand, these men, suddenly dragged from their wonted
mode of life, could not suddenly adapt themselves to the discipline
of their new condition. They were turned *en masse* into beggars,
robbers, vagabonds, partly from inclination, in most cases from
stress of circumstances. Hence at the end of the fifteenth century
and during the whole of the sixteenth century, throughout Western
Europe a bloody legislation against vagabondage. The fathers of
the present working class were chastised for their enforced transformation into vagabonds and paupers. Legislation treated them
as 'voluntary' criminals, and assumed that it depended on their
own good will to go on working under the old conditions that no
longer existed . . .

Elizabeth, 1572: Unlicensed beggars above 14 years of age are
to be severely flogged and branded on the left ear unless someone
will take them into service for two years; in case of a repetition
of the offence, if they are over 18, they are to be executed, unless
some one will take them into service for two years; but for the
third offence they are to be executed without mercy as felons.

Marx ([1867] 1954: 686–7)

Over the past hundred years or so, many uprisings and revolutions
employing violent means have been inspired – at least in part – by
the thought of Marx and Engels or by others in the Marxist tradition,
including Georges Sorel, Lenin and Frantz Fanon. More recently, both

111

Alain Badiou (2007) and Slavoj Žižek (2007a, 2008) have defended a broadly Marxist-Leninist approach to violence in revolt. However, by comparison with other aspects of their work, little has been written on a theory of violence that may be either explicit or implicit in the work of Marx and Engels. Indeed Marxism as a body of thought is not associated with a properly formed theory of violence, either regarding violence that takes place routinely in various forms under capitalism or regarding violence in revolt. The question of the ethics of violence in Marx and Engels has suffered from such neglect that classical Marxist thought is open to the allegation that it is at least partially responsible for the violence perpetuated in its name in the Gulag in the USSR, in the Cultural Revolution in China and in Cambodia under Pol Pot, to mention only the most infamous cases of mass violence under regimes claiming allegiance to Marxism.

The insistence or assumption made by many working in the Marxist tradition is that violence of the oppressed is necessarily justified because it is a legitimate – and probably decisive – weapon in struggles against the bourgeoisie and imperialism; indeed, the legacy of Marx and Engels regarding violence is often interpreted as justified violence against the profound and endemic injustices of capitalism. This is in part because of Marx and Engels's apparent readiness to condone and justify proletarian violence against the ongoing exploitation and other injustices of capitalism as long as it is tactically useful; one of the final few lines of their *Manifesto of the Communist Party* declares that Communist ends 'can be attained only by the forcible overthrow of all existing social conditions'. Any questioning of violence in revolt may be seen as a weakening of a resolve to achieve socialism and the end of exploitation, and the only limiting factor regarding violence in revolt, then, may be the question of when it is tactically counter-productive.

In this chapter I argue that it is important to explore in some depth what Marx and Engels say on the question of violence, to be mindful of the context of their treatment of violence and to examine the way in which this treatment was projected into the twentieth century by on-the-ground leader-interpreters. I argue that, without abandoning a broadly Marxist framework or advocating a pacifist stance, it is neces-sary to approach the question of violence in a nuanced fashion, which goes beyond the traditional 'just ends' – or justified violence – argument and suggests a framework for the examination of the ethics of violence in revolt that puts the damaging nature of *any* violence centre stage.

I argue that because Marx and Engels's major theoretical contribution was historical materialism – or (mainly) the 'scientific' analysis of capitalism – the legacy has been to downplay more ethical (or, for that matter, utopian) aspects of their thought or even the potential for exploration in these areas. The emphasis was placed on the analysis of capitalism and the potential that capitalism offered for a transition to socialism, rather than on the ethical case for socialism.

In the discussion below (and following Galtung 1969), as in earlier chapters, I draw a distinction between two types of violence, both of which are addressed by Marxism taken as a whole. On the one hand, there is personal, or agent-generated, violence. This is a form of violence where there is deliberate intent to cause physical harm to one or more people on the part of one or more people with a particular end in mind. On the other hand, the notion of structural, or society-related, violence refers to harm inflicted, for example, as a result of particular conditions of work (perhaps resulting in ongoing pain, illness or death), or harm as a result of uneven distribution of resources in society. In what follows I am primarily concerned with personal violence, but argue that in order to make use of Marx and Engels's profounder theory of violence it is important to take structural violence into account as well.

My intention in this chapter is not to accept or defend the inevitability of – still less to advocate systematic – violence in revolt, as Marx and Engels have often been interpreted as doing. Rather, it is to explore an interpretation of Marx and Engels that allows for a framework for discussion of violence in revolt that fully acknowledges the horror of all violence, whoever the perpetrator may be. In fact, my intention is to distance myself from the notion that Marx and Engels are predominantly 'pro-violence'.

ENGELS'S THEORY OF *GEWALT*

The only attempt at an explicit theory of personal violence from Marx and Engels comes from Engels as sole author. This is found in his *Anti-Dühring* and takes the form of three short chapters collectively entitled *Gewalttheorie*, or Theory of Violence (the German word *Gewalt* means both 'violence' and 'force', but here will be translated here as the former). The more general form and context of the *Anti-Dühring* is important; the book is a lengthy polemic against Eugen von Dühring, who had recently published popular works based on a philosophical-scientific framework that offered proposals for harmony between the rich and the poor. In Engels's lengthy riposte he accuses Dühring of inverting the real relationship between the economy and politics by arguing that the political sphere is the driving force of history and that the economic sphere is determined by the political. The chapters entitled *Gewalttheorie* were written more specifically in opposition to what Engels saw as Dühring's fundamental error of locating *Gewalt* at the heart of human history and against Dühring's argument that domination in human societies was best understood by reference to slavery, a notion that in Dühring's work plays a crucial role.

Dühring illustrates his own theory of violence, then, by referring to the Robinson Crusoe story and suggesting that the act of enslaving Friday was both a political act and an act of violence that resulted in a particular economic situation. Thus politics and violence give rise to a particular economic relationship. Engels, however, argues that the exact opposite is true and that slavery is the result of economic development:

> Crusoe, 'sword in hand', makes Friday his slave. But in order to pull this off, Crusoe needs something else besides his sword. Not everyone can make use of a slave. In order to be able to make use of a slave, one must possess two kinds of things: first, the instruments and material for his slave's labour; and secondly, the means of bare subsistence for him. Therefore, before slavery becomes possible, a certain level of production must already have been reached and a certain inequality of distribution must already have appeared. And for slave-labour to become the dominant mode of production in the whole of a society, an even far higher increase in production, trade and accumulation of wealth was essential. (Engels [1878] 1975: 192–3)

In this highly deterministic version of the relationship between the economic and (political) violence, then, violence is treated by Engels as a decidedly subordinate phenomenon that is not to be treated independently from other spheres; violence is indeed 'completely subordinate to the economic situation' (207) and the Theory of Violence is located in a sub-section of the book entitled Political Economy. The theory is mainly created by inverting Dühring's own deterministic schema rather than establishing a more sophisticated theory that is properly distinct from Dühring. Certainly, the immediate intellectual context is important. Engels sought to fend off any further advance of Dühring's ideas that were so markedly different from those of Marx and himself, and the *Anti-Dühring* was a polemical work that no doubt bent the stick in the other direction more than may otherwise have been the case.

Nevertheless, in terms of any ethics of violence, Engels's text suggests that we should view violence as inevitable, accept past violence and presumably not fret unduly about present violence, but assume that it will pass eventually. We should also be reassured by the fact that bourgeois militarism contains the seeds of its own destruction, for there comes a point when 'the armies of the princes become transformed into armies of the people; the machine refuses to work, and militarism collapses by the dialectics of its own evolution. What the bourgeois democracy of 1848 could not accomplish ... socialism will infallibly secure' (204–5).

Thus Engels's concern is to establish a causal relationship between economics and violence rather than dwell on any morality of the use of force. In fact, even the violence of slavery is something to be accepted and – historically, at least – to be thankful for:

Without slavery, no Greek state, no Greek art and science; without slavery, no Roman Empire. But without the basis laid by Grecian culture, and the Roman Empire, also no modern Europe. We should never forget that our whole economic, political, and intellectual development presupposes a state of things in which slavery was as necessary as it was universally recognized. In this sense we are entitled to say: Without the slavery of antiquity no modern socialism. (Engels [1878] 1975: 216)

We must, then, simply accept slavery as a historical stage, for however 'heretical' it may seem, 'the introduction of slavery under the conditions prevailing at the time was a great step forward' (217). Violence is a historical fact that will be superseded because of the inevitable overthrow of the current order of things and indeed violence plays a revolutionary role such that

in the words of Marx, it is the midwife of every old society pregnant with the new one, [and] it is the instrument with the aid of

which social movement forces its way through and shatters the
dead, fossilized political forms. (Engels [1878] 1975: 220)

If, as Engels argues, particular manifestations of violence inevitably
occur in association with different phases of economic development,
presumably the same applies to the violence of capitalism, and the
implication is that we do not have to worry about it too much as it will
inevitably disappear with the demise of capitalism. Similarly, violence
in revolt is simply a necessary stage, a tool to be used in order to move
forward and not to be dwelled on for too long. In short, violence is not
really an object worthy of study in itself. Perhaps this implication is
in part a consequence of the polemical nature of Engels's work, but it
should also be seen as part of an attempt to establish a truly scientific
approach to socialism and related matters, a project on which Engels
expended a great deal of energy in his later years. One of the consequences of this approach – and that is reinforced by circumstances, as
we shall see – is that classical Marxism is rather unquestioning about
violence.

A more general point should be made regarding Engels's work
before we move on. There is of course a considerable debate as to what
extent we should view Marx and Engels's thought as a unified whole
and in particular the extent to which Engels 'distorted' Marx's thought
with an over-emphasis on the scientific basis of Marxism, especially
in his later works, and thus exaggerated its economic determinism.
Certainly, Engels places a great deal more emphasis than did Marx
on a scientific reading of capitalism and the transition to socialism,
in particular in *Anti-Dühring* and including the sections of this work
that became 'Socialism: Utopian and scientific' (Engels [1880] 1968a).
Engels has, to say the least, a particular interest in the scientific, ration-
alist, perhaps almost positivist approach to questions of human behaviour and historical change, summed up in his famous speech at Marx's
graveside where he asserts that '[j]ust as Darwin discovered the law of
nature of organic matter, so Marx discovered the law of development
of human history: the simple fact, hitherto concealed by an overgrowth
of ideology, that mankind must first of all eat, drink, have shelter and
clothing, before it can pursue politics, science, art, religion, etc.' and
that 'the production of the immediate material means of subsistence
and consequently the degree of economic development attained by
a given people' determines the nature of state institutions, the law of

the land, art and ideas about religion (Engels ([1883] 1968b: 429–30). Having said that, it is worth pointing out that Marxism's real originality does lie precisely in a materialist view of history and the way in which such a materialist view suggests the potential for change, based not on aspirations for an idealised socialist society dreamed up by intellectuals but on a detailed understanding of the actual nature of capitalism and on the identification of the revolutionary potential of the proletariat. As we have seen, in the jointly written *Communist Manifesto* Marx and Engels are withering about the utopian socialists (especially Saint-Simon, Fourier and Owen), condemning their ideas as mere products of their imagination and criticising the utopians because they 'reject all political, and especially all revolutionary, action; they wish to attain their ends by peaceful means, and endeavour, by small experiments, necessarily doomed to failure, and by the force of example, to pave the way for the new social Gospel' (Marx and Engels [1848] 1968: 60).

Perhaps most importantly for us, Engels's late works introduced many readers to Marxism in both communist and anti-communist spheres, putting a particularly 'scientific' slant on it. Terrell Carver (1989: 249–50) is categorical about this, arguing that 'Socialism: Utopian and Scientific' was widely translated, quickly went into several editions and in fact formed:

> the *Communist Manifesto* of its time, but arguably it was even more influential, and it went out under Engels's name alone. 'Socialism: Utopian and Scientific' was the work from which millions of conversions to Marxism were made . . . through it Engels decisively influenced the way that socialists perceived Marx and read his works, and hence the way that socialism and communism were subsequently developed throughout the world.

Engels cannot, of course (and this is not the suggestion that Carver is making), be held responsible for all of the consequences of the many ways in which Marxism has been interpreted since the late nineteenth century. I am, however, arguing that the legacy of Engels's approach to the question of violence in *Anti-Dühring* was to tend to legitimise all violence on the part of the socialist movement and militate against restraint and against any attempt to demonstrate in practice that socialists were more humane than their enemy. One of the consequences of

Engels's approach to violence is that the ethics of violence in revolt, uprising and revolution is not addressed – or barely – because violence is treated as part of the superstructure that will soon disappear anyway and be overtaken by an entirely new reality.

The context in which Marx and Engels wrote is of course important. Compared with today, capitalism was youthful and its alleged fragility was plausible. The *Manifesto* was published less than sixty years after the French Revolution of 1789 had so convincingly disposed of the *ancien régime* and the socio-economic order that went with it. It was now, it seemed, the turn of the proletariat in the post-feudal, rapidly industrialising countries to dispose of the new order and in several countries the labouring classes were indeed frequently experiment-ing with armed insurrection; the Europe-wide revolutions of 1848 and the 1871 Paris Commune are the clearest examples of the insurgent populace bringing about changes in regime with relative ease, despite the ferocity of the counter-revolution. In short, revolution ushering in a form of communism was thought of as being close at hand, as Marx and Engels often made clear, including in their address to the Communist League in March 1850 when they took the view that '[t]he whole proletariat must be armed at once with muskets, rifles, cannon and ammunition' (Marx and Engels [1850] 2010). The other point of context worth mentioning is the fact that death, injury and violence were very obviously part of nineteenth-century European society, for example in the domains of war, high levels of infant mortality, frequent epidemics of infectious diseases such as cholera, punishments by the state, domestic violence and accidents of various kinds at work (a point to which I return below). This no doubt made revolution seem more urgent and consideration of the means – violent or otherwise – from an ethical point of view less important, given that violence and death was all around in any case.

All this is relevant to the way in which Marx and Engels have often been interpreted as suggesting that violence in revolt is wholly justi-fied because the status quo is even more violent than revolution, and revolution will – so the argument goes – bring peace. Even if the status quo is not particularly violent, violence in revolt is sometimes seen as legitimate defence of particular goals. But this particular interpretation, if left unqualified at least, is not a fruitful source for a developed ethics of violence in revolt. For a more subtle analysis, we must approach Marx and Engels somewhat differently.

LENIN AND THE OCTOBER REVOLUTION

Before moving on to argue that in some other aspects of both Engels's and Marx's work there are more helpful pointers to an ethics of violence in revolt, I will dwell briefly on one particular interpretation of the Engels-Marx approach towards violence that has passed into the orthodoxy of the twentieth century. The approach to violence in revolt that became associated with Marxism was one that made the October 1917 Bolshevik revolution a key point of reference, or what Eric Hobsbawm (1994: 56) describes as 'the special house-style it imposed on its successors'. There is little doubt that Lenin and the other leaders of the October Revolution were more ruthless and violent than can be justified in retrospect. Most controversially, they were convinced that coercion and in some cases extreme violence against natural allies was justified in the circumstances, as was infamously demonstrated in the suppression of the uprising of the Kronstadt sailors in March 1921. However, several points should be made about the context of October 1917. First, the Russian revolution took place within living memory of the massacre of tens of thousands of Parisians at the end of the Paris Commune in the *semaine sanglante* of May 1871. Lenin and his fellow Bolsheviks were therefore even more determined to consolidate the revolution and defend it with much violence against its enemies if necessary, enemies who themselves had so recently been shown to be without mercy. Lenin, following Marx, argued in 1908 that the Communards had not taken the question of military action seriously enough, with Lenin ([1908] 1972: 476) identifying 'excessive magnanimity on the part of the proletariat' as one source of their defeat and adding that 'there are times when the interests of the proletariat call for ruthless extermination of its enemies in open armed clashes'.

Second, the enemies of the October Revolution were not only very much on the offensive, but were themselves also ruthless. The potential threat to the ruling interests of the dominant countries not only of Europe but of the entire world was enormous. In 1917 Russia had a population of more than 150 million and was a major European power, and the Bolsheviks had every intention (plausibly) of helping spread the revolution to the rest of the world. So the stakes were, to say the least, high and the Bolsheviks fought to defend the revolution against combined attacks not only within Russia but from outside as well. The Allies not only funded counter-revolutionary (White) armies against the Bolsheviks but sent British, French, American, Japanese, Polish, Serb, Greek and Rumanian soldiers to fight in these armies, and millions of Russians (men, women and children) died defending the revolution in the civil war. Finally, the First World War formed the hugely violent backdrop to 1917, providing further evidence that international capitalism was prepared to sacrifice millions of young men of largely working-class origin. Thus both Lenin and perhaps in particular Trotsky (as founder and leader of the Red Army) were in no doubt that the might of conventional warfare needed to be fought with the same weapons and the same tactics.

Lenin's *State and Revolution* places particular emphasis on the violent nature of capitalism and very much promotes the importance of its violent overthrow; citing Engels in *Anti-Dühring* where he asserts (quoting Marx) that force is the 'midwife of every old society pregnant with the new one', Lenin adds that Engels's analysis of the role of the bourgeois state is a 'veritable panegyric on violent revolution'. Moreover: 'The necessity of systematically imbuing the masses with *this* and precisely this view of violent revolution lies at the root of the *entire* theory of Marx and Engels . . . The suppression of the bourgeois state by the proletarian state is impossible without a violent revolution' ([1917] 2008: 276–7; emphasis in the original). Given the context, as discussed above, and given that Lenin wrote this work on the very eve of the revolution (August–September 1917), such words are perhaps hardly surprising. However, these are texts that have – often in far-removed contexts – dominated the interpretation of the Marxist theory of violence, or at least what stands in for one, perhaps reaching its theoretical apogee in Merleau-Ponty's ([1947] 1969) *Humanism and Terror*, where he goes further than any other non-Soviet or Eastern bloc intellectual in the post-war period in arguing that systematic violence on the part of the Soviet state is – or at least may be – justified. Combined with the (late-) Engels-inflected view of the role of violence, this legacy bestowed on twentieth-century Marxism an approach that viewed it with a certain inevitability, and even allowed violence to be a hallmark of a serious revolution, and indeed of serious revolutionaries.

THE STRUCTURAL VIOLENCE OF MODERNITY

Despite what I argue above, and although neither Marx nor Engels (nor Marx and Engels as co-authors) have a fully formed theory of violence, I suggest they do provide a useful starting point for a theory of the ethics of violence in revolt. Paradoxically, we need to look for this starting point *not* in Engels's explicit theory of *Gewalt* but elsewhere. Both Marx and Engels frequently refer to the inhumanity, hardship and actual violence that is an integral part of capitalist society, and this becomes an important part of their case against the status quo and therefore their argument for socialism. Potentially, this sets such an ethics off in two directions. First, such references serve to establish a stark contrast between the violence of capitalism and the (often implicit) peace and humanity of communism, thus suggesting the moral superiority of communism and more generally the importance of humane (non-violent) treatment of one human being by another. Second, however, this also suggests – again rather paradoxically – that violence in revolt is at least to a certain extent justified and to be expected. Ultimately, it is this justification (that I mention above), this balance between the intrinsic injustice of violence and violence as a sometimes necessary instrument of transition, that is so crucial to the elaboration of any ethics of violence in revolt.

I wish to dwell, then, on aspects of the way in which Marx and Engels describe and analyse the nature of modernity and will refer to three instances in their works where the structural violence of modernity takes centre stage. First, Engels describes at great length the often appalling conditions of the labouring classes in *The Condition of the Working Class in England*. First published in 1844, the book is a remarkable record of the poverty, illness, atrocious living and working conditions and premature death that were characteristic of large parts of English cities in the mid-nineteenth century. Referring to his observations in London, where – as in Manchester, Liverpool, Nottingham and elsewhere – the rapid growth in manufacturing had produced such widespread misery, Engels ([1844] 1999: 109) describes 'these pale, lank, narrow-chested, hollowed-eyed ghosts, whom one passes at every step, these languid, flabby faces incapable of the slightest energetic expression'. Both empathy and a sense of profound injustice are evident throughout this work and Engels points to the collective responsibility of the bourgeoisie for the miserable conditions of the working class:

When one individual inflicts bodily injury upon another, such injury that death results, we call the deed manslaughter; when the assailant knew in advance that the injury would be fatal, we call his deed murder. But when society places hundreds of proletarians in such a position that they inevitably meet a too early and an unnatural death, one which is quite as much a death by violence as that by the sword or bullet; when it deprives thousands of the necessities of life, places them in conditions in which they *cannot* live – forces them, through the strong arm of the law, to remain in such conditions until that death ensues which is the inevitable consequence – knows that these thousands of victims must perish, and yet permits these conditions to remain, its deed is murder just as surely as the deed of the single individual. (Engels [1844] 1999: 106; emphasis in the original)

Both the general tone and the content of this work amount to a very different (and more subtle) approach to violence than that found in the Theory of Violence written more than thirty years later and *The Condition of the Working Class in England* reads as a thorough condemnation of the structural violence of industrialisation.

Accounts of the violence of modernity are found in various other places in Marx and Engels's writings, but nowhere more powerfully than in the famous first part of the *Communist Manifesto*. Here we have a description of a ruthless bourgeoisie whose entire modernising project is imbued with violence and the language is replete with references both to violence against people and other types of physical destruction. We read that the bourgeoisie

has pitilessly torn asunder the motley feudal ties ... and has left remaining no other nexus between man and man than naked self-interest ... It has drowned the most heavenly ecstasies of religious fervour ... in the icy water of egotistical calculation ... In one word, for exploitation, veiled by religious and political illusions, it has substituted naked, shameless, direct, brutal exploitation. (Marx and Engels [1848] 1968: 38)

The portrayal of violence is extended to inanimate, socio-economic forms, and '[a]ll old-established national industries have been destroyed or are daily being destroyed. They are dislodged by new industries, whose introduction becomes a life and death question for all civilized nations' (39).

There is nothing cold and calculating (or unduly economic-determinist) about any of this. Page after page of the *Manifesto* seeks to persuade its readers to join the Communists by insisting how brutal and immoral the capitalist system is – a system in which '[t]he bourgeoisie . . . compels all nations, on pain of extinction, to adopt the bourgeois mode of production' (Marx and Engels [1848] 1968: 39) and to join the havoc that is modern capitalism, a force that is 'like the sorcerer who is no longer able to control the powers of the nether world whom he has called up by his spells' (40). Indeed these spells and this violence and destruction bring with them the conditions of the bourgeoisie's own – immanent – destruction, for '[t]he weapons with which the bourgeoisie felled feudalism to the ground are now turned against the bourgeoisie itself . . . But not only has the bourgeoisie forged the weapons that bring death to itself; it has also called into existence the men who are to wield those weapons' (41). These men are the proletarians, of course, who wish to revolt in part because they are the 'slaves of the bourgeois class . . . [and] are daily and hourly enslaved by the machine, by the overlooker' (43).

Perhaps better in this respect than any other interpreter of Marx, Marshall Berman, in *All that is Solid Melts into Air: The Experience of Modernity* (1982), analyses the paradoxes, tensions and creative destruction that Marx and Engels describe in the *Manifesto* and that they argue are so characteristic of capitalist modernity. Capitalism is, then, highly destructive in the ways we have explored and many more, but it is at the same time so creative that it invents the pre-conditions not only for its own destruction but also for its replacement with a communist society that brings with it the end of exploitation, injustice and want. It allows for the proper flourishing of the human race at last. Moreover, the bourgeoisie is so revolutionary that it not only overthrows feudalism in order to establish its own rule, but gives birth to the ultimate revolutionary class – the proletariat – that is so revolutionary because it has nothing to lose and everything to gain, and, what is more, it significantly outnumbers its enemies.

Where, then, does this leave us in relation to an ethics of violence in revolt? Again, there appear to be two messages. On the one hand, there is a profoundly humanitarian message that rages against the inhumanity and cruelty of the ruling class and seeks to end this rule because such suffering is wrong in itself. On the other hand, the proletariat is enjoined to take up arms against the bourgeoisie, in other words to create further pain and suffering, but this time with a worthy goal in mind. The simple message of the *Manifesto* is that, to quote a slogan current among parts of the European left in the late twentieth century, 'a year of revolution is less bloody than a week of capitalism'. What is missing from Marx and Engels's account, as Finlay (2006: 390) points out, is any indication of limits that may be put on violence in revolt, although this is perhaps not surprising given the context in which they were writing, but from the point of view of the twenty-first century this does seem a serious lacuna.

If we turn now to Marx's account in *Capital* entitled 'Bloody Legislation against the Expropriated, from the End of the Fifteenth Century', we once again see a revulsion against the cruelty of capitalism, reminiscent of Engels's description of the conditions of the English working class in his book published many years earlier. In a perhaps rather romanticised view of pre-capitalist society, Marx ([1867] 1954: 686) suggests (as quoted in the epigraph to this chapter) that the proletariat was formed through 'the forcible expropriation of the people from the soil . . . [and] these men, suddenly dragged from their wanted mode of life . . . were turned *en masse* into beggars [and] robbers'. He describes how in the fifteenth and sixteenth centuries laws against vagabondage in many places in Western Europe permitted systematic, physical cruelty; under Henry VIII, for example, beggars could be 'tied to the cart tail and whipped until the blood stream[ed] from their bodies' (686). In this way 'were the agricultural folk first forcibly expropriated from the soil, driven from their homes, turned into vagabonds, and then whipped, branded, and tortured by grotesquely terroristic laws into accepting the discipline necessary for the system of wage-labour' (688).

A little later in the same work, Marx describes the inhumanity of the process of petty accumulation of capital in relation to the indigenous populations of America, India and Africa. This involves widespread enslavement, death in accidents in the pursuit of natural resources, murder and 'the commercial hunting of black skins', all acts performed by the nascent bourgeoisie in the course of looting other regions of the world in order to turn the plundered goods and substances into capital in Europe. In the new industries of England, meanwhile, Marx describes the 'vast, Herod-like slaughter of the innocents', where children as young as seven were flogged, fettered and tortured in order to make them work longer and harder, children who were often severely malnourished and in some cases driven to suicide. Marx goes out of his way, then, to draw attention to the profound inhumanity and cruelty of capitalist modernity.

(RE-)INTERPRETING AND COMPLEMENTING MARX AND ENGELS'S ETHICS OF VIOLENCE

My argument, then, is for a re-examination of the legacy of Marx and Engels in this domain in a way that includes more centrally an emphasis on the humanising aspects of their work, on the core ideas of freedom, transcendence of exploitation and moving beyond dehumanisation and alienation, all of which addresses the notion of moving beyond violence. Taken as a whole – which is, I believe, how Marx's works in particular should be taken – their writings place great emphasis on the idea of an as-yet unrealised, free, 'socialist man'. As Brenkert (1983: 165) argues, the notion of freedom that lies at the heart of Marx's ethics 'entails the removal of force, violence, and coercion from the lives of humans'. Rather than transferring what Marx and in particular Engels say specifically on violence directly to the twenty-first century and developing an ethics of violence in revolt based on that, I suggest a framework that maintains the humane spirit of the more general Marxist approach to structural violence, but that allows us to build an ethics of violence in revolt that is suitable for today, rather than a time when it seemed capitalism was about to implode almost of its own accord. Such an ethics could retain the critique of the dehumanising and profoundly violent nature of class society and this is an aspect of classical Marxism I believe we should dwell upon. If we place emphasis on the profoundly humanising aspects of Marx and Engels's ethics and read them in light of human history since 1917, we may reach different – and ultimately more useful – conclusions from those reached by Sorel, Lenin, Fanon and others. This would not a priori rule out a defence of violence in revolt and Castro's approach is a very concrete example of precisely this, as we have seen in Chapter 3.

Another source of inspiration for further development of such an ethics should be Ernst Bloch in his work *The Principle of Hope*, where he places emphasis on what he sees as the more utopian aspects of Marxism (Bloch [1938–47] 1986). Certainly, Bloch argues that Marx and Engels understandably avoided description of a future communist society and that it was very important for them to contrast their own approach to the 'imagined phalanstères or New Harmonies' of the utopian socialists who were Marx's contemporaries. But Marx and Engels's virtual silence on the precise nature of a society where freedom would come at last was according to Bloch 'essentially a *keeping open*' to perhaps unforeseen ways in which a communist future would be built, so that 'this omission occurred solely for the sake of the future'. Marx's thought was thus a *'unity of hope and knowledge of process*, in short, realism', rather than anti-utopian (621–2; emphasis in original). Bloch goes on to argue for a '[c]oncrete utopia [which] is therefore concerned to understand the dream of its object exactly, a dream which lies in the historical trend itself . . . a utopia mediated with process' (623). Asserting that Marxism is in essence 'humanity in action', he explains:

> Precisely humanity itself is the born enemy of dehumanization, indeed because Marxism in general is absolutely nothing but the struggle against the dehumanization which culminates in capitalism until it is completely cancelled out, it follows *e contrario* that genuine Marxism in its impetus, its class struggle and its goal-content is, can be, will be nothing but the promotion of humanity. (Bloch [1938–47] (1986): 1,358)

Bloch reminds us that in the *Critique of the Gotha Programme* (written in 1875) Marx does look to a higher phase of communist society where (quoting Marx) 'the antithesis between physical and intellectual work has disappeared' and where the 'all-round development of individuals' productive forces has grown as well' (21), but Bloch is far from being a simple dreamer and insists that his 'warm stream', utopia-inspired Marxism must be accompanied by the 'cold stream' of what we more commonly think of as Marxist analysis, with particular emphasis on a careful dissection and meticulous examination of the nature of capitalism. My own argument is that in the mainstream discussion of violence in revolt that is influenced by Marxism, the tactical violence of the 'cold stream' is dominant and the goal of freedom and the crucial end of non-violence is almost entirely lost. This has unfortunate consequences.

Bloch insists in *Atheism in Christianity* ([1968] 2009), in a way that is reminiscent of Castro on religion, that Christianity and in particular the Bible contain an important core both of truth about the world as we know it and inspiration regarding a possible future, both of which are of great relevance when thinking about communism. Certainly,

Christianity has been and continues to be used to great effect by the oppressors, but if it is stripped of its metaphysical trappings it becomes a source of hope. Christ the rebel and some of the Christian teachings about equality, the worth of ordinary people and the need to treat all humans equally may have been conveniently sidelined by Christians allied with the ruling class, but a close reading of the Bible – 'detective work' (57) – allows it to become a source of atheist hope, which Bloch calls utopia, and that allies Christian optimism with a belief in a future communism. He thus suggests that

> [w]here there is hope there is religion, but where there is religion there is not always hope: not the hope built up from beneath, undisturbed by ideology . . . hope is able to inherit those features of religion which do not perish with the death of God. (Bloch [1968] 2009: 50)

Vulgar Marxists, he suggests, only see religion as the 'opium of the people', but if the passage regarding religion from Marx's *Critique of Hegel's 'Philosophy of Right'* is quoted at greater length, it takes on a far more subtle hue and does not by any means depict religion as wholly bad: 'Religious misery is at once the *expression* of man's real misery and the *protest* against it. Religion is the sigh of the oppressed creature, the heart of a heartless world, and the soul of soulless conditions. It is the opium of the people' (50). This approach forms part of what, as we have seen, Bloch describes as the 'warm current', but he insists that this warm current also needs a scientific approach in order to transform the utopian vision into reality.

In the context of a general discussion about utopias, Panitch and Gindin (1999: 21–2) appeal for what they describe as 'rekindling the socialist imagination' and, drawing on Bloch, they go on to argue that while Marx created a more effective social science, where the oppressed work for a profoundly better society, proper discussion of the potential that human beings have to work with is still missing. What is needed, they argue, is 'a new conceptual layer to Marxism, a dimension formerly missing or underdeveloped' and among other areas this new layer would explore ideas regarding capacities and potentials. Norman Geras (1999: 41), meanwhile, argues that socialism is and has always been utopian, despite Marx and Engels's emphasis on scientific socialism and a sociology of the present that points to the potential for a different future. This leads to an interesting discussion of the relevance of the relationship between the present and the future and the idea that we should embrace utopia because of the moral intolerability of the realities of our time. Thus a vision of a better future may be one where disputes were resolved peacefully and without policing, but perhaps most importantly for this present discussion, Geras suggests that '[e]mbracing utopia means embracing an alternative ethics', far more so than the Marxist tradition is accustomed to do, in its preoccupation above all with politics and economics (52).

Returning to the question of an ethics of violence in revolt, a more utopia-influenced – or warm stream – Marx may allow us to move beyond a view of the present as an (eternal?) preparation for a hoped-for but largely undefined future. There could in this way be an ethics of the now that may well be partially informed by a utopian vision of the future, which would be influenced by Marx and Engels but would add to their thought as well. Various writers and revolutionaries working in the Marxist tradition, including Benjamin, Trotsky, Luxemburg and Victor Serge take the position that it is necessary to use humane means as well as ethically upstanding ends. Serge perhaps goes furthest in this direction and, in reaction to the increasingly ruthless nature of Stalinist rule in the Soviet Union of the mid-1930s, he argues that some con-siderations 'take precedence before all tactical considerations' and that

[m]an must be given his rights, his security, his value. Without these, there is no Socialism. Without these, all is false, bankrupt and spoiled. I mean: man whoever he is, be he the meanest of men – 'class enemy', son or grandson of a bourgeois, I do not care. It must never be forgotten that a human being is a human being. Every day, everywhere, before my very eyes this is being forgot-ten and it is the most revolting and anti-Socialist thing that could happen. (Serge [1942–3] 1963: 282–3)

In the wake of the 1917 Russian Revolution there were intense – and at times vitriolic – debates among Marxists regarding the legitimacy and role of violence on the part of people struggling for a better world, dwelling on the strategy of the immediate post-revolutionary situation but also relating to broader questions of ethics in a uniquely revealing way. Rosa Luxemburg, in *The Russian Revolution*, which was written from prison in Germany and published in 1918, expressed her full support not only for the revolution but also for the Bolsheviks, whom she believed supplied both the leaders and foot soldiers who could be trusted with the communist future of Russia and the knock-on effects internationally that would no doubt be experienced before long. She was clear that the Bolshevik party displayed 'political farsightedness and firmness of principle' (Luxemburg [1918] 1961: 28), that the Bolsheviks were the only party in Russia to understand the real interests of the people and that the revolution was doing reasonably well in extremely difficult circumstances. Moreover, she was under no illusions that the aftermath of the 1917 Revolution could possibly be straightforward and was entirely convinced that '[d]ealing as we are with the very first experiment in proletarian dictatorship in world history (and one taking place at that under the hardest conceivable conditions, in the midst of the world-wide conflagration and chaos of the imperialist mass slaughter, caught in the coils of the most reactionary military power in Europe)' (28), a model proletarian revolution would be nothing short of a miracle. But although she accepted that short-term, emergency measures that punished the resisting bourgeoisie were necessary, she objected to the way in which the Bolshelvik leaders appeared to be generalising from these and making timeless principles out of what should have been steps taken only in a time of emergency and for a very short period of time. She objected to suspending voting rights for large swathes of Russians, closing down newspapers hostile to the new regime, and preventing people opposed to the Soviet system from organising politically. Luxemburg also opposed 'dictatorial force of the factory overseer, draconian penalties, rule by terror', 'the use of terror to so wide an extent by the Soviet government' and the premise of the 'Lenin-Trotsky theory of the dictatorship' that the Party knew best regarding the next step in the socialist transformation of Russia (71). The remedy for this increasingly violent and dictatorial situation – 'not the dictatorship of the proletariat, however, but only the dictatorship of a handful of politicians' (73) – was the broadest and most active political involvement possible of the Russian people that would in time come to replace force and decree with a democratic decision-making process with increasingly widespread involvement of ordinary people.

Luxemburg was doubtless somewhat naïve in identifying intense political participation of the mass of ordinary people as the alternative to the use of terror and force and as a way of attempting to save the very life of the revolution from enormous and powerful opposition from both within and beyond Russia. The reality of the situation was that emergency measures had to be taken in order to address an urgent state of affairs where the life of the new regime was hanging by a thread. Mass political action, while no doubt laudable, was on its own inadequate and probably in any case unrealistic in such dire circumstances, and without some violence and other authoritarian measures would have done nothing to save the new order from its many (themselves ruthless) opponents and embed the revolution in the longer term. However, such criticism from someone so sympathetic to the goals and to many of the methods of the October Revolution was no doubt an alarm bell of some significance and at the very least went to the heart of questions regarding the effects of violent means on the further communist end. These were precisely questions that Castro was to address in such explicit and persuasive terms forty years later in Cuba. Although the situation in Russia after 1917 was radically different from that of Cuba in the late 1950s, as we have seen, and although Batista and later the USA were ruthless in their use of violence, it was on a quite different scale and the stakes were far lower than they had been in Russia. Nevertheless, Lenin ([1918] 2015) was no doubt wrong to argue, in sharp contrast to Luxemburg, in his Speech at the First Congress of Economic Councils in 1918 that the dictatorship of the pro-letariat not only was crucial at this point but also implied 'power based directly on force and unrestricted by any laws' and 'rule won and main-tained by the use of violence by the proletariat against the bourgeoisie, a rule that is unconstrained by any laws'.

Karl Kautsky, in *Terrorism and Communism*, written in 1918–19, and in some of his subsequent publications, argued forcefully against many of the methods of the Bolsheviks and held the view that the dictatorship of the proletariat was un-Marxist, and indeed un-socialist. The Russian Revolution, he maintained, had turned into the opposite of what it had once stood for, because it was riding roughshod over democracy, and routinely using violence – including torture – in order to pursue its aims. Forced labour, he declared, was an 'infernal state of such slavery [that] can only be compared with the most horrible excesses that capitalism has ever shown' (Kautsky [1919] 1920: 200). By contrast with Luxemburg, it was not mass political activity that would offer a remedy to the excesses and wrong turnings of the revolution, but a parliamen-tary road; in other words the revolution had been a mistaken adventure in the first place and it was necessary to wait until calmer times and the appropriate level of economic development before embarking on a transformation to socialism. Trotsky's rejoinder to Kautsky, also entitled *Terrorism and Communism* ([1920] 2007) and published in 1920, was dismissive of Kautsky's advocacy of a parliamentary road to socialism, arguing that the times were entirely unsuited to such a course. He insisted that 'violent revolution has become a necessity precisely because the imminent requirements of history are helpless to find a road through the apparatus of parliamentary democracy' (38). Large numbers of countries had sent soldiers to support the cause of counter-revolution in Russia and the transfer of ruthless violence of the World War to Russia meant that in 'a country throttled by a blockade and strangled by hunger, there are conspiracies, risings, terrorist acts and destruction of roads and bridges' (51). Trotsky is convinced that 'we are fighting a life and death struggle' and it was sometimes necessary to 'shoot landlords, capitalists and generals who are striving to restore the capitalist order' (59); 'Red Terror is a weapon utilized against a class, doomed to destruction, which does not wish to perish' and without the Terror 'the Russian bourgeoisie, together with the world bourgeoisie, would throttle us long before the coming of the revolution in Europe' (63). There was no doubt in Trotsky's mind:

> Who aims at the end cannot reject the means. The struggle must be carried on with such intensity as actually to guarantee the supremacy of the proletariat. If the socialist revolution requires dictatorship . . . it follows that the dictatorship must be guaranteed at all cost. (Trotsky [1920] 2007: 25)

In Trotsky's *Terrorism and Communism*, then, written quite literally in the heat of the battle, he does not mince his words. If they wish to defend the revolution, the Bolsheviks have no choice but to use the state in a dictatorial way. Violence must be employed against the enemies of the revolution because the alternative is to accept not only the violence of the enemy (the White Terror and no doubt more) but also defeat of the revolution with all that it will entail. As a text removed from its context, Trotsky's *Terrorism and Communism* certainly lacks the subtlety of his later work, *Their Morals and Ours* ([1938] 1969), where he insists (as we saw in Chapter 3) that to argue '*any* means . . . was permissible if only it led to the "end" . . . [is] an internally contradictory and absurd doctrine' (12; emphasis in the original) and that, quoting

Ferdinand Lassalle, we need to '[c]onceive the means as ends in embryo' (37–8). In other words, the later text takes a far more humanist approach than the one written in reaction to Kautsky's wholesale attack on the revolution while the revolution was fighting for its life. In broader, ethical terms, I do not believe that Trotsky's positions in the earlier text (reflecting those of Lenin and numerous other Bolshevik leaders) can be justified. But at least he addresses in a remarkably honest way the question of violence in the midst of an extraordinarily difficult situation, and the question of violent means and just ends, without obfuscation. There is no doubt that there were many excesses even at this early stage of Russian communism, which we may even compare with the Allied terror bombing of German cities during the Second World War; the bombing of Dresden, Hamburg and other cities was doubtless unjustifiable in ethical terms given the large numbers of non-combatants who died in the raids, together with the fact that the attacks did not even achieve their declared objective of hastening the end of the war and saving lives in the longer term. In neither case – thinking in deontological terms – could the violent acts be justified ethically, and in both cases the argument at the time was that the end justified the means. Certainly, if the revolution had been more successful than it was eventually and history had been written by those schooled in its inherited values well beyond the twentieth century, the Red Terror would not have become the preoccupation – bordering on obsession – it has become for the current generation of historians of Russia. By the same token, the terror bombings of the Second World War are today often glossed over, or explained in highly favourable terms, by many historians of the Second World War.

This defence of the Red Terror also raises questions about the relationship between Leninist-Trotskyist methods employed in the immediate wake of 1917 and the cruelty of Stalinism after the death of Lenin in the late 1920s and beyond. It would certainly fly in the face of historical fact to deny any connection between the violence of the period of the civil war on the one hand and on the other the violence of Stalinism once Soviet communism was established as a viable and ongoing system of government and organisation of society; the practice of repression and elimination of opponents for the good of the longer-term success of communism was to some extent transferred from violence against what were deemed to be genuine counter-revolutionaries to those who were seen as political opponents of Stalin, especially in

the great purges of the 1930s. Certainly, Trotsky's and Lenin's practice and published defence of the Red Terror cannot be held directly
responsible for the brutality of the (on the whole) less fragile situation
of the Soviet Union in the Stalinist era. But the notion that any means
are justified – for this is the drift of Trotsky's argument in *Terrorism
and Communism* – in the pursuit of longer-term proletarian rule can
credibly be seen to suggest that such an approach can legitimately be
developed and applied over the longer term to communism in a more
stable period. I am not suggesting that there is a direct and inevitable
connection between the approach to violence in the two periods, as do
many historians now, but that to abandon ethics at a time of emergency
is a highly dangerous path to tread.

BALIBAR'S CRITIQUE OF MARX ON VIOLENCE

Etienne Balibar (2010: 251–304) makes a significant contribution to
the debate regarding Marx and Engels and their treatment of violence
and argues that Marx has a paradoxical relationship with the role and
notion of violence. He argues that Marx's thinking on this contrib-
utes in important ways to our understanding of the place of violence
in history, especially regarding the relationship between forms of
domination and exploitation under capitalism, the inevitability of class
struggle and the role and nature of revolution. In this way, according
to Balibar, Marx's conception of the role of violence in history enables
a better understanding and definition of modern politics. However, he
also suggests that Marxism is not able to offer a full explanation of the
relationship between politics and violence, and a major reason for this
is that in Marxist theory there is an absolute emphasis on a particular
form of domination, namely the exploitation of labour, and the other
forms of domination are simply 'epiphenomena' of the exploitation of
labour. Other types of exploitation are therefore disregarded or under-
explored in discussions of violence.

Another reason Balibar gives for Marx's inability to address fully
the relationship between politics and violence is the 'anthropological
optimism' that characterises his notion of progress, found in the idea of
the development of human productive forces that is critical to Marx's
idea of the history of social formations. Third, Balibar points to Marx's
metaphysics of history, which, he argues, with the ultimate overcoming of alienation, borrows from both theology and philosophy in order

to convert violence into justice. For Balibar, this acknowledgement of
the social role of violence but failure to fully take on board the political
role it plays has had unfortunate effects on the nature of some ongoing
struggles and revolutions that draw inspiration from Marx. An exploration of both the contribution that Marx's theory can make to our understanding of violence and its limitations is important for any discussion
regarding possible egalitarian futures and the means to achieve them.

In addition to examining Marx's own – according to him limited –
theory of violence, Balibar considers the work of Engels, Lenin, Fanon
and Luxembourg, all of whom deal with the role of violence in struggles
to overcome oppression and in pursuit of emancipation. He does this
against a background of the periods of intense class struggle, revolution,
anti-imperialist struggles and postcolonial conflicts of the twentieth
century. He points out that among the many catastrophes of the twentieth century, there were a number where people acting in the name of
Marxism were either perpetrators or victims, and in some cases both.
One major conclusion he draws from this exercise is that it is necessary
for the left to reconsider the contribution that Marxism can make to the
struggle for a better world and he argues that this should take the form
of a 'civilising of revolution' (*Zivilisierung der Revolution*) and indeed
a 'civilising' of politics more generally; the latter is dependent on the
former. Balibar believes that rethinking the domain of political violence
and the notion of revolution are not only *the* fundamental questions
for politics in the early twenty-first century, but also the way to make
Marxism as an approach to politics fully useful in the longer term.

Balibar suggests that Marx moves between various different
approaches to violence, including an 'ultra-Jacobin' one, which almost
glorifies violence in moments of revolutionary transformation and that
Lenin developed still further with his own conception of the dictatorship of the proletariat. But Balibar contends that there are in Marx
approaches to violence that are of greater contemporary relevance.
First, he points to the extreme exploitation and violence that is part and
parcel of the capitalist mode of production and in particular capitalist
modernisation, which includes the violent suppression of pre-capitalist
ways of life and culture; I have discussed this aspect of both Marx and
Engels at some length above. But Balibar also argues that Marx suggests in *Capital* that a violent conflict between the proletariat and the
bourgeoisie is not the only possible path that an ultimate struggle
between capital and labour will take:

[T]he work [i.e. *Capital*] had opened up other possibilities, which it will always be possible to turn to without abandoning the 'Marxist' reference: namely a process of reforms imposed on society by the state under pressure from increasingly powerful and organized workers' struggles, which would oblige capital to 'civilise' its methods of exploitation, or to innovate constantly in order to overcome resistance from 'variable capital'; also the exporting of overexploitation to the periphery of the capitalist mode of production, in such a way that the effects of 'primitive accumulation' are prolonged . . . In these scenarios the proletariat no longer appears as the predetermined subject of history, and the *Gewalt* [violence and force combined] which it either suffers or wields does not lead 'naturally' to the final goal. The subjectivization of the working class, that is its transformation into revolutionary proletariat, then appears as an indefinitely distant horizon, an improbable counter-tendency, or even miraculous exception to the course of history. (Balibar 2010: 281)

Balibar argues, then, that debates and disagreements among Marxists about reform versus revolution have been framed in the wrong way and besides this the important question with regard to discussions about transition from one type of regime and society to another is how to 'civilise' revolution, as mentioned above.

There are certainly shades, here, of debates within the European left in the second half of the twentieth century regarding reform versus revolution as a means of transition from a status quo characterised by the capitalist mode of production to one where socialism would be the order of the day. Balibar himself was a member of the French Communist Party for many years. But the idea of 'civilising the revolution' also has some echoes of what I am arguing in this book, namely that in any struggle for socialism the ultimate goal of peace and non-violence, alongside radical equality and broader social justice, must be to the fore. For me – perhaps by contrast with Balibar – this does not rule out some violence in the course of transition from one type of society to another, although the goal would no doubt be ever-present in the methods of struggle. In other words, Luxemburg and the later Trotsky (in *Their Morals and Ours*) would be there as influences, but the earlier Trotsky (of *Terrorism and Communism*) and Leninist-Trotskyist practice would be far less so.

Balibar defines the present as an 'era of global violence' and posits that the level of actual violence or the threat of violence, worldwide, is so high that there is a risk that the practice of politics itself will become impossible. Contrasting this with the idea of civility, defined here as the 'circumstances where the practice of politics is made possible', he argues that globally extreme violence and mass insecurity is employed as a type of 'preventative counterrevolution or counterinsurrection' against emancipatory movements and is also the result of the tendency in the West for supposedly consensual and certainly conflict-averse forms of government. These forms of government, according to Balibar, approach politics as if it were just superstructure and real conflict is circumvented whenever possible, denying the crucial 'insurrectionary element' and widespread popular participation so important for proper politics and its renewal (Balibar 2004: 115–19). If anything, this would seem to suggest that extensive 'civilising of revolution' (if we interpret this as limiting us to nonviolent reform only) is highly unlikely.

Balibar also puts forward the perhaps surprising idea that a reconciliation of the thought of Lenin and Gandhi may be possible, suggesting that they are the two most important 'revolutionary activist-theorists' of the first half of the twentieth century (Balibar 2010: 305–22). He maintains that there are two important areas that Lenin and Gandhi share in terms of their theory and practice. First, they both highlight the central role of popular mass movements, which must be able to weather both successful and less successful periods and must in any case be able to endure over the longer term. Second, both activist-theorists take a confrontational approach towards the state and both therefore advocate breaking its laws in an ongoing way; for Lenin the interests of the revolutionary class are placed above the law of the capitalist state and for Gandhi the tactic of civil disobedience is deployed in order to push the state towards significant reform. This potential reconciliation is a thought-provoking idea, but when Balibar gets into the detail of a comparison between Lenin's and Gandhi's approaches to the tactics and strategy of transition from one regime to another – what we may call the process of emancipation – it begins to appear less plausible. Balibar points out that in Lenin's theory of revolution violence plays a central, and indeed decisive, role in his description of state power as class dictatorship, his call from 1914 onwards for 'turning the imperialist war into a revolutionary civil war' and, moreover, his concept of the dictatorship of the proletariat (Balibar 2010: 315). Gandhi, on the other hand, campaigned for what he described as a need to go beyond a hatred of the enemy and to engage in 'aggressive' but 'constructive and non-violent, albeit law-breaking, acts'. He held – reminiscent of Benjamin and perhaps Fanon as well – that the nature of the struggle (the means) has a strong effect on the nature of the outcome (the end), whereas this was almost entirely absent from Lenin's approach to violence. Gandhi's theory of 'dialogism', which involves mass movements making tactical concessions to their opponents, thus controlling the process of transformation and limiting the degree of violence involved, also seems to fly in the face of Lenin's approach.

Like the notion of 'civilising revolution', a juxtaposition of Lenin's and Gandhi's approaches to violence and struggle is a thought-provoking idea. But both of Balibar's propositions suffer, ultimately, from an attempt to reconcile the irreconcilable. It would be comforting to believe that revolt could always be peaceful and at the same time that it could be combined with a hard-nosed theory-cum-strategy for a transition to a communism. But this is probably as unrealistic as believing that a world driven by an insatiable thirst for profit could be transformed using persuasion alone and in particular carefully constructed arguments for the laying down of the considerable arsenal of weapons of destruction that are at present used to pursue the interests of capital.

*   *   *

My contention, then, is that it is worth returning to Marx and Engels and viewing (and reviewing) some of their writing on violence in a somewhat different light; I suggest that their writings may be a source of inspiration for a more subtle – and indeed more peace-oriented – approach to the question of violence than that with which they are usually associated. Indeed, certain aspects of classical Marxism provide a useful basis for a framework within which to develop an ethics of violence in revolt that is appropriate for the twenty-first century. However, rather than drawing on Engels's *Gewalttheorie* as expounded in his *Anti-Dühring*, and interpreting the Marxist legacy in this domain via this and similar works, we should look more closely at Marx and Engels's frequently expressed revulsion at violence in various other places. This, I argue, is part of the ethics of freedom that is at the core of classical Marxism but that tends to receive far less attention than Marx and Engels's critique of the economics and politics of capitalism or their writings on strategies for overthrowing the bourgeoisie. This is not an argument for pacifism, but it does conceive of all violence as ultimately antithetical to the notion of progress and freedom, tragically necessary though violence might be in certain circumstances.

The more conventional interpretation of Marx and Engels's approach to violence concludes that violence in revolt is inevitable and necessary and that therefore it is a mere tool that is not worthy of study in itself; this is the classic line of argument where the ends justify the means without apparent need for further reflection. This approach should be complemented at least in equal measure with one that expresses the view that any violence is in contradiction with the goal of moving beyond exploitation, oppression and alienation and that either non-violence or the use of minimum necessary violence in any situation is a goal in itself. This sort of approach to the works of Marx and Engels may be termed, following Bloch's discussions, 'warm stream' and may include a certain amount of utopian thought in order to help elaborate an ethics of the now as well as of the future.

It should be said that Marx, Engels and those working in the Marxist tradition such as Lenin, Trotsky and Benjamin have, in their different ways, displayed an acute understanding of the vexed question of the relationship between means and ends, which is often in sharp contrast to the way in which liberals approach this question. Many are prepared to be frank in a way that Western liberals are not. We have discussed the hypocrisy of the West at some length in other chapters and will discuss the terror bombing of German cities during the Second World War in the next chapter, but let us also mention the case of Allied bombing of cities in northern France in the later stages of the Second World War when the civilian death toll was high, in the course of a carefully calculated attempt to weaken Germany's position by killing non-combatant French people (see Dodd and Knapp 2008). Bearing in mind that these are not only civilian deaths, but Allied civilian deaths, this is a very clear example of the means justifying the end, which is often glossed over in liberal approaches to philosophy and history while liberalism attacks Marxism for being unduly ruthless in this respect.

I do argue, notwithstanding the above remarks, that when constructing a framework for discussion of the ethics of violence in revolt it is useful to look at concrete examples of revolt in order to bring to bear some of the realism that is necessary to temper a more idealised approach – thus my close scrutiny of aspects of Cuba and Castroism elsewhere in this book. In the above discussion I have attempted to take a nuanced approach to the legacy of Marxism as it was played out during and in the aftermath of the Russian Revolution. To argue, as do various historians today, that the early Bolshevik leaders were so violent as to merit being characterised as bloodthirsty individuals who elevated violence to a level comparable only with fascism is both incorrect and simplistic. There were many excesses in the few years following 1917, as Luxemburg pointed out at the time and as Deutscher (1972: 87) did later, commenting that the early Communist leaders including Lenin and Trotsky 'participated in this glorification of violence as a self-defense mechanism'. These were truly extraordinary circumstances, where the legacy of Tsarism and the reality of world war combined not only with counter-revolution but with civil war and with foreign intervention as well, and they were bound to lead to more violence than would have been necessary if the revolution had been less besieged.

The question remains, however, how much more violent the Bolsheviks were than they needed to be, even given the circumstances. James Ryan, in his measured study of *Lenin's Terror*, suggests that

[t]hough Marxists were certainly not averse to using violence, Lenin was the first and most significant Marxist theorist to dramatically elevate the role of violence as revolutionary instrument and function of the ambivalent Marxian concept of the dictatorship of the proletariat. (Ryan 2012: 3)

Certainly,

[t]he Bolsheviks faced a life-and-death struggle for survival in a brutal civil war, and needed to mobilize an often reluctant, even hostile populace in conditions of desperate privation. Politicians and military commanders have typically condoned and advocated various forms of violence and brutality during exceptional times – the Bolsheviks did not invent terror. (Ryan 2012: 7)

But he also suggests that they 'made certain choices that often intensified socio-political conflicts and resulted in the large-scale application of violence, whereas less abrasive choices were often possible' (8). When attempting to pick one's way through the enormous questions

raised by the legacy of Marx and Engels's writings that are of relevance
to violence in pursuit of emancipation, combined with their first major
application in practice – in Russia – this approach would seem well
worth bearing in mind.

Chapter 5

TERROR AND TERRORISM

Ask an Arab how he responds to the thousands of innocent deaths [on 11 September 2001], and he or she will respond as decent people should, that it is an unspeakable crime. But they will ask why we did not use such words about the sanctions that have destroyed the lives of perhaps half a million children in Iraq, why we did not rage about the 17,500 civilians killed in Israel's 1982 invasion of Lebanon. And those basic reasons why the Middle East caught fire last September – the Israeli occupation of Arab land, the dispossession of Palestinians, the bombardments and state-sponsored executions – all these must be obscured lest they provide the smallest fractional reason for the mass savagery on September 11 . . . Eight years ago, I helped make a television series that tried to explain why so many Muslims had come to hate the West. Now I remember some of those Muslims in that film, their families burnt by American-made bombs and weapons. They talked about how no one would help them but God. Theology versus technology, the suicide bomber against the nuclear power. Now we have learned what this means.

Robert Fisk (2001)

In everyday – including mainstream media – parlance, 'terrorism' describes non-state actors attacking others for political ends. In other words, terrorists are those who are committed to a particular cause and decide to use violence that is outside the law, directed against soldiers, police or other public employees, or alternatively against people who are entirely 'innocent', meaning people who do not directly represent or work for the entities the attackers are opposing. It will be clear from what I have said in preceding chapters that I would in almost all cases condemn these sorts of attacks for a variety of reasons, but the question of terrorism does raise some very important questions. Many struggles in the past that we may deem to be in pursuit of emancipation, including wars of national liberation, resistance against foreign occupation and revolutions of various kinds, have used these sorts of tactics. Many of those who are described as terrorists today, including, no doubt, members of Islamic State, believe that they are using legitimate tactics in pursuit of emancipation.

At the beginning of the twenty-first century these sorts of attacks are highly prevalent and at the time of writing they are hardly ever out of the news; attacks on non-combatants in poorer countries account for by far the highest number of deaths by these means, but suicide bombings and other politically motivated attacks on ordinary people on public transport, in shopping malls, at sports events and in the street also take place in richer countries and gain a great deal of press and media coverage. The media plays a crucial role in determining which incidents become widely known about and how they are portrayed, and of course much of the point of such attacks is to gain publicity for certain groups that would otherwise be almost unknown. On 11 September 2001, the destruction of the Twin Towers in New York, the similar attack on the Pentagon and the fourth hijacked plane that crashed, killing more than 3,000 people in total, has become one of the most-debated terrorist attacks of all time and will no doubt be seen as one of the turning points in modern political history. The subsequent 'War on Terror' by the USA and its allies and the enormous repercussions of the ensuing military offensives have defined much of the world's international relations since 9/11. The killing of twelve people at the *Charlie Hebdo* premises in Paris and five more in related attacks in January 2015 is also a significant moment in the history of terrorism, particularly as one response to it was a demonstration of up to a million people in Paris, including political leaders from around the world, some of whom could themselves be accused of using terror tactics while in power. The killing of 130 people in Paris on 13 November the same year was yet another watershed moment in the history of modern terrorism, particularly as the victims were chosen because they were 'soft' targets, that is to say non-combatants and not operating in a capacity that was defending or representing the state.

In order to reflect on these sorts of attacks and their relationship with struggles for emancipation, we need first to think in broad terms about the nature of terrorism.

DEFINING TERRORISM

Defining terrorism is in one sense fairly straightforward. It is always a pejorative term; in other words terrorism is always an act to be condemned in the eyes of the person using the word. Terrorists are always blameworthy, do not deserve any airing of their views, let alone negotiation, and there is no such thing as a terrorist who is viewed positively except perhaps in the deliberately oxymoronic title of Doris Lessing's (1985) novel *The Good Terrorist*. The term is used to mean an immoral and incorrect use of violence, which implies that terrorism should be stopped – often using supposedly legitimate counter-violence, sometimes called 'counter-terrorism', and often accompanied by increased surveillance – and terrorists should be punished for their illegitimate and illegal activities.

If we look a little closer, however, it becomes clear that defining terrorism is more complex than this. For example, a person some describe as a terrorist will almost certainly be thought by others to be acting in a legitimate and ultimately constructive manner (for example, in pursuit of liberation from foreign occupation) and will typically be described by their supporters not as a terrorist but as a freedom fighter (or a soldier in an army of liberation), and they are thus deemed to be acting in a heroic, often selfless manner, especially if they die fighting for their cause. Terrorist acts are often used – or at least have been in the past – to achieve ends that are widely recognised in the longer term as legitimate and it has become almost clichéd to point out that 'yesterday's terrorist is today's statesman'. There are indeed many who fit this description, including: Menachem Begin and Yitzhak Shamir, whom the British once described as terrorists and who later both became Prime Ministers of Israel; Ben Bella, leader of the National Liberation Front in Algeria that fought against the French for national liberation and who became the country's first Prime Minister after independence; Nelson Mandela, leader of the African National Congress that fought the Apartheid regime in South Africa, who became the country's President; and Gerry Adams, who was closely associated with the Irish Republican Army and was subsequently a major player as a leading politician in the Peace Process in the North of Ireland.

The term is thus almost always shorthand for illegitimate, unscrupulous and debased, and is often little more accurate in its descriptive qualities than any other simple term of abuse. The terms 'terror', 'terrorism' and 'terrorist' are so loaded and emotionally charged that they often do little more than assert the view that the violent actions in question are wrong and that counter-measures must be taken in order to attack the perpetrators and to defend the status quo. Perhaps most importantly, to use the term 'terrorist' is often to state that the terrorist act should not only be condemned but that it should be condemned without further discussion of what brought the violence about or of the causes being fought for, or discussion of the demands or goals of the people pursuing the attack. No discussion of the issues involved or of the wider causes of the discontent is required; on the contrary, the discussion is closed in the process of expressing outrage at the violence, in describing it as terrorist. It is also often a way of legitimating a very violent response against the attackers and their perceived collaborators, and of clamping down via police or army activity, or surveillance of either individuals or the wider population. Examples of this include: *Berufsverbot* in West Germany in the 1970s, where supposedly as a response to Red Army Faction attacks those holding radical left-wing views were not allowed to work as civil servants; special courts in the North of Ireland, especially Diplock Courts that suspended trial by jury for alleged terrorist activities by Republican or Loyalist paramilitaries from 1973; and proposed surveillance of all Internet activity in Britain from 2016. I am not arguing that acts often described as terrorist are in fact generally legitimate – often quite the contrary – but that governments, with much help from the media, use such acts to defend or consolidate their own power, and to contrast what they call terrorist with their own violence and other forms of oppression, which they portray as regrettable but necessary and legitimate. The term is thus used as a way of separating the 'good' – us, the status quo and all that goes with it – from the 'bad' – them, the terrorists, and the causes they stand for.

In some approaches to the question of terrorism, it is described as the way the weak fight the strong and it is what those who lack power do in order to build their movement against the powerful. There is of course much to be said for this view of things and it may be argued that, for example, the prevalence of terrorist acts both in the Middle East and related to conflicts in the Middle East since the beginning of the twenty-first century is a result of the vast power and resource imbalance between the rulers and the ruled in that part of the world, not to mention the way in which the governments of more powerful, richer nations have intervened in the region militarily and politically, including in the Israel–Palestine conflict.

However, Noam Chomsky turns this idea of terrorism being the arm of the weak against the strong on its head and suggests that national governments practise far more terrorism than sub-national groups and individuals, and that 'like most deadly weapons, terrorism is above all the weapon of the powerful'. He goes on to argue that when the opposite claim is made it is 'only because the powerful also control ideological and cultural apparatuses which allows their terror to pass for other than terror' (Chomsky 2015: 68). Indeed, it may be argued that the word 'terrorism' is always employed as propaganda, or at least polemic, against political violence; it cannot be used as a value-free, neutral descriptor.

Certainly, according to the way in which the term 'terrorist' is usually used – that is, in common parlance – governments in liberal democracies cannot commit terrorist acts because what elected governments do is 'legitimate', given that they have a mandate from and the trust of their electorate, whereas terrorists are accountable only to themselves or to a very small group of people. However, I agree with those who argue that the notion of terrorism is meaningless unless it can be applied to both governments and other entities, and I will separate terrorism into what Charles Webel and others (Webel 2011: 42, footnote 6) describe as 'terror from above' and 'terror from below'. I am also adopting Webel's definition of terrorism as 'premeditated, usually politically motivated, use, or threatened use, of violence, in order to induce a state of terror in its immediate victims, usually for the purpose of influencing another, less reachable audience, such as a government' (2011: 32). I am including agents or employees of the state (politicians, soldiers, police officers and so on) as targets of terrorism, and also non-state targets. I would only add to Webel's definition that terrorism, in addition to being used as a means of influencing another audience, is also often used in order to draw attention to a cause or a group, in order to recruit new members to a group and more generally to attract support.

My argument, then, is that the word 'terrorism' as it is used in the contemporary media, by governments and by other entities seeking to reinforce the status quo, is closely related to the ideology of those using the word and can only be understood in that context. My own way of attempting to understand what are described as acts of terrorism is to examine them in relation to power and inequality. Terror from above is often a way of defending and consolidating the status quo in terms of power, distribution of wealth and other resources, and access to instruments of coercion and ideology. Terror from below often comes about as a result of oppression or persecution, which does not in itself justify it or mean that it is a useful tactic, but it does help explain it, and as Ted Honderich (2003c: 21) points out, 'the agents of [terrorist] violence are inevitably in the foreground' but 'not so with agents of inequality'. In many definitions of terrorism and when the word is used by government ministers and the media in particular, little notice is taken of the circumstances that may explain why people become terrorists, sometimes in large numbers. This is a necessary process, however, and we will be doing this in what follows.

TERRORISM FROM ABOVE, TERRORISM FROM BELOW

I argue throughout this book that a great deal of violence is perpetrated by the powerful against the less powerful, as a way of consolidating their own power and in order to prevent change. With clear precedents in the eras of mass slavery and colonial rule, terrorism from above may be conceived as a particularly intense version of violence by the powerful, although it is often an extension of normal power relations and must be combined with ideology in order for it to be effective. Antonio Gramsci famously argues that capitalism remains in place via a mixture of coercion and consent. If we apply this idea to terrorism from above in the modern world, there is a great deal of clear, physical coercion involved in this process, often at home in poorer countries and usually abroad in the case of liberal democracies. But much modern capitalist rule also requires the consent of the mass of people living in the countries whose governments are employing terrorist coercion, unless the government wishes to act without the consent of the majority of the people and take steps towards becoming in effect a fully fledged 'terror state', as in the case of Nazi Germany, for example. The consent that governments need in order to avoid this path (that is unstable in the longer term and dangerous for those in power) is sought both via political pronouncements of various kinds – government declarations, policy documents, speeches and press releases – and via the mass media and other ideological entities, including television, radio, newspapers and the Internet, but also feature films, novels and computer games. One goal of creating consent in this way is to persuade ordinary people that terrorism from above is legitimate, and in particular to persuade them that violence is being employed legitimately against illegitimate violence. This supposedly illegitimate violence is often described as 'terrorist'.

We have seen in previous chapters that countries that may be deemed to be highly successful in terms of the standard of living of their inhabitants and that are largely unthreatened militarily have engaged in a great deal of terrorist activity since 1945. There is no need to repeat the detail of that here, but broadly it includes: action against movements for national liberation in colonies; intervention in numerous countries – or support for deeply reactionary and violent forces in these countries – in order to prevent or stem the activities of (often democratically elected) left-leaning governments, especially in Central and Latin America during the Cold War; and, especially since the end of the Cold War, violent intervention in the Middle East.

The 'War against Terror' since 9/11 has of course involved a great deal of terrorism from above, in particular on the part of the US, but also by Britain and other supporters of the US. Drone warfare is one of the latest examples of state terrorism, where 'suspected terrorists' are killed in some cases without evidence that they have in fact engaged in violent acts, let alone been put on trial; moreover, unknown associates of those people are killed at the same time in what is euphemistically termed 'collateral damage', meaning deaths of – by any definition – innocent men, women and children. Not only is all of this terrorism from above, but it has greatly encouraged terrorism from below, violence that is often seen by the potential victims of state terrorism as the only way to combat state terrorism. As we shall see in the detail of our discussion of the terrorism in the early twenty-first century, the situation is often more complex than simple offensive and counter-offensive, but this core relationship nevertheless often holds true. Before moving on to an examination of the Middle East, I look at a major historical example of terrorism from above, which has set a precedent in terms of self-righteous mass killing of non-combatants by Western countries in pursuit of particular ends.

The terror bombing of German cities and then the terror bombing of Japanese cities – including nuclear bombing – during the Second World War is a clear case of terrorism from above, although its ultimate objective, the defeat of fascism, was a worthy one. Drawing on Igor Primoratz's (2013: 126–32) insightful treatment, we can summarise the episode as follows. In September 1939 Prime Minister Neville Chamberlain assured the House of Commons that '[w]hatever be the lengths to which others may go, His Majesty's government will never resort to deliberate attacks on women and children and other civilians for purposes of mere terrorism'. However, from spring 1940, there began a bombing campaign by the Royal Air Force (later joined by the United States Army Air Forces (USAAF)), whose objective was increasingly the targeting of the civilian population of German cities in order to break the morale of non-combatants; this was by no means a case of bombing primarily military targets and accepting civilian deaths as a side effect, and as the chief of the air staff, Sir Charles Portal, put it in a memo in February 1942: 'Ref the new bombing directive: I suppose it is clear that the aiming points are to be the built-up areas, *not*, for instance, the dockyards or aircraft factories . . . This must be made quite clear if it is not already understood' (emphasis in the original). In particular, working-class areas of numerous large cities were bombed and the techniques used were refined over successive months and years. In many raids, the aircraft would drop a mix of explosive and incendiary devices that created firestorms in the pursuit both of maximum possible loss of life and maximum possible destruction of buildings. In February 1945 came the most notorious instance of this technique when Dresden was destroyed in one night, with the loss of more than 20,000 lives, and although Churchill reacted by saying in a memo that he '[felt] the need for more precise concentration upon military objectives, such as oil and communications behind the immediate battle-zone, rather than on mere acts of terror and wanton destruction', the terror bombing continued until a matter of weeks before the end of the war. In all, during this particular campaign, in the region of 600,000 civilians died, approximately 800,000 were seriously injured and about thirteen million were made homeless. By the end of the war, Britain and the US had killed through bombing ten times as many civilians as had the Germans in air raids.

The terror bombing did not succeed in breaking the morale of the German population, nor did the fire-bombing of German and Japanese cities significantly contribute to persuading the German and Japanese governments to surrender, but instead had the effect of making the respective populations determined to fight with greater energy, just as the London Blitz and German bombing of other British cities had done. Neither did the atom bombs dropped on Hiroshima and Nagasaki make a significant difference to the course of the war in the Pacific, as the Japanese government had indicated that it was prepared to surrender before the bombs were dropped. In other words, there were millions of civilian casualties in the course of this terror campaign, without the aim of the operations being achieved.

Summing up the bombing of civilian targets, which he describes as an 'unmitigated atrocity', Primoratz suggests that

> it was a campaign of state terrorism – perhaps the longest such campaign in wartime, and the deadliest in terms of the number of victims. In terms of the spirit if not the letter of international law at the time, it was a war crime of immense proportions that deeply compromised the just cause for which the Allies were fighting. Viewed historically, it was a crucial stage in a process of ever-more comprehensive and systematic victimization of enemy civilians as a supplement to, or even a substitute for, fighting enemy soldiers. This process would soon lead to the conventional and then nuclear terror bombing of Japanese cities, and beyond. (Primoratz 2013: 147)

The example of bombing German cities is of course an extreme one in that very large numbers of people died, were seriously injured or were made homeless in a short period of time. There is a more plausible – although ultimately flawed – argument in favour of it compared with many other cases, in that the declared goal was to defeat fascism, itself an inherently brutal and murderous ideology and form of rule. But even if one accepts that deeply undesirable means are justified if the end is worthy, this is no defence, as it did not, in fact, hasten the end of the war. In the longer term, the bombing of German cities doubtless served to reinforce the idea that virtually unchecked violence abroad was legitimate as long as the end could be justified; in other words this was an extreme version of the argument that the end justifies the means. This approach and justification was employed by countries in the West subsequently in relation to many poorer parts of the world, from Indo-China starting in the 1940s to the Middle East at the beginning of the twenty-first century, with many millions of non-combatants dying as a result.

To begin our examination of terrorism from below, let us return to Antonio Gramsci's argument that capitalist rule is made up of both coercion and consent. Those who engage in insurgent violence, often described as terrorism, believe that their views are ignored by the established order and that their views are excluded from the dominant discourse of consent. In other words, exclusion from the dominant order, powerlessness and more generally oppression are clearly behind many attacks on either 'soft' (non-state-employed) targets or representatives of the state and may also be seen as a form of counter-coercion on the part of the oppressed. Ultimately, then, we can argue that it is at least in part absence of proper democracy – or in some cases any sort of democracy – and the absence of various forms of equality that explain the existence of terrorism from below. Again, this does not, in itself, imply that terrorism is legitimate, or indeed effective, but it does help explain it and puts the ultimate blame for terrorism over time squarely at the door of the powerful and the oppressors rather than at the door of the oppressed.

I will further illustrate the relationship between terrorism from below and terrorism from above (and more generally oppression) with reference to the Middle East.

THE MIDDLE EAST

Terrorism from below is almost always related to a history of profound injustice, and never springs from the deranged minds of a few evil master criminals, as the dominant political and media discourse often seems to suggest. The Middle East has become closely associated with terrorism from below, especially since 9/11, and if we look at some of the salient features of the history of the region since 1945, we gain a better understanding of some of the complex reasons why some of the countries of the Middle East have become associated with violence of various forms.

Let us begin by mentioning the rise and then the failure of Arab nationalism in the period when the Arab world was emerging from the long colonial era. In 1952, Gamal Abdel Nasser led the Free Officers movement in a successful national revolution against the British in Egypt. One of the largest Arab states in terms of habitable land mass and the largest in terms of population, Egypt's first properly independent regime was born, with its own foreign and security policy. Nasser's power in Egypt grew rapidly, and by 1956 he was both Prime Minister and President of the one-party state, which was characterised both by policies designed to improve the lot of the working class, including widespread nationalisation of industries, but also harsh repression against opponents. Later that year he nationalised the Anglo-French Suez Canal Company, a move that led to one of the most significant moments not only for much-desired independence of the Arab world from the West but also for the prospects of Pan-Arabism. This prompted military invasion by Israel, Britain and France, but the US refused to back the invasion, which became a fiasco for the invading countries and a watershed moment in the dying days of British and French colonialism. Indeed it seemed from this that Arab nationalism could be the ideology and practice that would lead much of the Middle East into greater unity, prosperity and – crucially – proper independence from the West.

The success of Arab nationalism was, however, short-lived. Certainly, well before the Suez triumph, Nasser was already emerging as a figure who seemed likely to bring greater cooperation and common vision across the region, and with the failed invasion by Israel, Britain and France that year he began to enjoy hero status among many people. In 1958 the United Arab Republic was formed from a merger of Egypt and Syria, and although it disintegrated when Syria withdrew from the alliance in 1961, pan-Arabism remained a dominant ideology in many countries. As the 1960s wore on, conflict between the Arab world and Israel became more intense and when Egypt cut off Israeli access to the Gulf of Aqaba in June 1967, the ensuing Six Day War became Arab nationalism's high noon – a conflict from which Egypt and many other countries were never properly to recover. Israel decisively defeated the various armies pitched against it and went on to occupy large areas of neighbouring Egypt, Syria and Jordan, namely (and respectively): the Sinai Peninsula, including the Gaza Strip; the Golan Heights; and the West Bank of the River Jordan and East Jerusalem. What became known as the Occupied Territories were populated by roughly a million Arab Palestinians and the conflicts stemming from this occupation have been at the heart of Middle East politics ever since. After the 1967 war both Arab nationalism and Nasser's personal reputation suffered a rapid decline, and in 1970 he died, aged 52, from a heart attack.

The second factor we must take into account in the modern history of the Middle East is the role of the Cold War. Various countries, including Egypt, Palestine, Lebanon, Syria and Iraq, had communist parties that enjoyed a degree of support and influence, especially on

matters of anti-imperialism and Arab nationalism, and indeed communist ideology had a strong influence on aspects of Nasser's politics.
The USSR sided strongly with Egypt after the invasion in 1956 and
threatened to intervene militarily. Access to vast reserves of cheap oil
became a major preoccupation for Western Europe and especially the
US, and Soviet influence in the region was seen as a major threat to
their longer-term energy concerns. From the 1967 Arab–Israeli war
onwards, when Soviet-backed and Soviet-armed Egypt and Syria
suffered such resounding defeats, American influence increased still
further, especially via US-armed Israel, but also Saudi Arabia, Kuwait
and Qatar, whom the US encouraged to foster Islamic fundamentalism in a bid to further counter the influence of the Soviet Union and
communism. In 1979, the USSR intervened in Afghanistan in order to
prop up a failing regime to which it was sympathetic and this became
a major theatre of the Cold War; the CIA supplied three billion dollars'
worth of arms and assistance to the *mujahideen* in Afghanistan and
persuaded Saudi Arabia to do the same. The USA was determined to
make Afghanistan the Soviet Union's Vietnam and in their bid to do so
they strongly backed, along with Pakistan, the Saudi insurgent leader
Osama bin Laden, who organised and trained many fighters against
the Soviet army.

Communism and anti-communism were thus influential in the
Middle East for a large part of the twentieth century and by the time
the Soviet Union collapsed in 1991, its demise compounded the failure
of Arab states in the Middle East to pursue anything like a common
cause or find a common ideology. From the perspective of the early
1990s, Paul Salem argues that, because of the multiple and far-reaching
problems suffered by the Middle East since the Second World War,
'the ideological movements that developed in the Arab world were not
effective in providing the legitimacy necessary for the stabilization of
Arab political systems'. He goes on to say:

> The problem in the 1990s is that whereas the old rules of the game
> have been more or less discredited, no new rules have been able to
> gain a stable ascendancy. Part of this is owing to the fact that ideo-
> logical movements in the Arab world have put forward competing
> sets of rules summarized in the three ideology types of liberal con-
> stitutionalism, secular one-party authoritarianism, and religious
> fundamentalist totalitarianism. None of these ideology types has

succeeded in completely eradicating the others and providing a comprehensive framework within which political life is conducted. Instead, the three ideology types often coexist uncomfortably in the same polity, contributing to high levels of disarray and instability within the system. With no widespread agreement about the basis of political life and the modalities of political interaction, political life is disorganised, volatile and highly conflictual and requires a significant dose of government coercion to keep under control. (Salem 1994: 262, 266)

By the 1990s, Arab nationalism had indeed largely failed. Communism had also failed to provide a unifying ideology or organising structure around which the Middle East could move forward. The US and Western Europe continued to assert their interests vigorously and were prepared to do so even when it involved significant loss of life. Indeed, a list of the major military defeats for Arab countries since 1945 serves to remind us of the way in which the Middle East was used for the pursuit of others' interests: in 1948, after Israel declared independence, various Arab armies attacked Israel but were repulsed, leading to the flight of most Palestinian Arabs; in 1956, the Israeli, French and British invasion forces were far superior to Egypt's army and it was the failure of the US to support them that meant the Suez affair could be presented as a victory for Nasser; the Six Day War in 1967 was an unmitigated disaster for the Arab world and a stunning military victory for Israel; in 1973, the October (or Yom Kippur) War was another decisive defeat for Egypt and other Arab states at the hands of Israel; and in 1982 Israel invaded southern Lebanon and Israeli forces stood by as Lebanese Christians killed about 1,700 mostly Palestinians and Lebanese Shiites in the Sabra neighbourhood and the Shatila refugee camp, a bloodbath that became known as the Sabra and Shatila massacre. In early 1991, the US led a large and highly destructive military coalition against Saddam Hussein's invasion of Kuwait, composed of both a huge air attack and a land war, which they called Operation Desert Storm.

When the Communist bloc collapsed in the early 1990s, the US was determined that the world should continue the process of globalisation according to a neo-liberal agenda devised primarily in North America, with a good deal of support from both Western Europe and the emerging new polities in the former Eastern bloc. Oil in the Middle East had brought huge riches to some in various countries, especially

Saudi Arabia, the United Arab Emirates, Iran, Iraq, Kuwait and Qatar. But economic development had in many respects been weak compared with that in Western Europe and the US, and the region's multiple other problems also made it less able to take up the neo-liberal gauntlet. Ali Laïdi (2006: 200–5) suggests that this marginal position in relation to the now quasi-global free market helps explain the rise in jihadi violence because, in a nutshell, the Arab world once again lost out. He points to conventional economic indicators that show that most of the Middle East had fared very badly for a long time, with a steady fall in GDP per inhabitant since 1970 and poor performance according to every conventional economic indicator compared with the Organisation for Economic Co-operation and Development (OECD) as a whole and with any of its member states. Even in the oil-producing sector most Arab countries had allowed key aspects of production to be taken over by foreign companies. As a result, apart from some leverage afforded by oil, many countries of the region fared badly compared with much of the rest of the world. Religion, Laïdi argues, was used to manipulate people frustrated by a modern history of failure in the Middle East, including severe economic under-performance, but religion is a vehicle of aggression, a way of mobilising people who are disadvantaged in various ways, and not its root cause.

The response of the USA and its allies to the 9/11 attacks is well known. The invasion and occupation of Afghanistan formed the first part of the War on Terror, the logic of the invasion (backed by many countries across the world) being support by the Afghan government for al-Qaeda. The second response, explained in the end by reference to fictitious reports (confirmed by the 2016 Chilcot report) of weapons of mass destruction in the hands of Saddam Hussein, was the invasion and occupation of Iraq by the US and Britain. The West had supported Saddam in its long war with Iran in the 1980s, when a million Iraqis had died. It had turned a blind eye when he used chemical weapons against Iranian soldiers, and very little was said when he did the same against his own population in Halabja in March 1988, killing in the region of 7,000 men, women and children. Now that the War on Terror had replaced the War against Communism, Saddam became public enemy number one, alongside bin Laden, both of whom were once supported by the West and both of whom were later executed by the West, or by its proxies. The invasions and occupations of Afghanistan, and especially of Iraq in 2003, made the situation much worse. Far from 'defeating terrorism' in the Middle East, the interventions by the US and its allies, coming close on the heels of highly destructive sanctions against Iraq, offered further proof, if proof were needed, that the West had only its own interests at heart. As President Jacques Chirac of France put it at the time, the US and British invasion of Iraq was 'likely to create many mini-bin Ladens' (cf. p. 154).

From the beginning of the war in Iraq it was the Iraqis themselves who were dying in large numbers from terrorist attacks and other causes. According to the website run by the independent organisation Iraq Body Count (2015), from 2003 to 2005 almost 25,000 civilians were killed and in the region of 42,500 wounded. In the year 2011, there were still more than 4,000 civilian deaths by violent means.

ISLAMIC STATE OF IRAQ AND THE LEVANT (ISIS)

In January 2014 the Islamic State of Iraq and the Levant took over Fallujah, one of the largest towns of the Al-Anbar province, only 60 kilometres from Baghdad, and the ISIS project began to take shape. The capture of the town was an important victory strategically, but it was also a symbolic triumph because of the bloody battle that had taken place when the American, British and Iraqi troops had taken it in November–December 2004; Fallujah was once again in the hands of anti-Americans. However, in the summer of 2014 ISIS won even more significant victories, bringing greater change to the geo-politics of the Middle East than had been seen since the establishment of the state of Israel in 1948, and arguably since the Sykes–Picot Agreement divided territories according to British and French interests after the First World War (Cockburn 2015; Luizard 2015; Lister 2015). In the space of a few months, ISIS fought its way along the Tigris and Euphrates rivers, conquering rural areas, towns and cities, including Mosul, Iraq's second largest city after Baghdad. By summer 2015 Islamic State had taken control of territory larger than Britain, covering parts of northwestern Iraq and northeastern Syria, and spanning an area from near Baghdad to Aleppo and from the Turkey–Syria border to the deserts in the west of Iraq, with a population of more than six million.

Among the most important – and certainly the most internationally renowned – characteristics of this group was its practice of extreme and much-publicised violence. But its greatest innovation was the declared aim of establishing an extensive territory across the Middle East, rather than attempting to influence the politics and religious practices of existing state structures, as its predecessors such as al-Qaeda had done. The aim of ISIS was to create an Islamic caliphate run by and for Sunni Arabs and based on Wahhabism, a fundamentalist form of Islam dating from the eighteenth century, which not only promotes sharia law but also stands for the lower status of women, and persecutes Shia and Sufi Muslims, Christians, Jews and homosexuals. In areas controlled by ISIS, men and women mixing in public is forbidden, women must be entirely covered when they go out and they need a permit from their male 'guardian' (their husband, father or brother, for example) to go out alone. Music, dance and of course alcohol are banned. Schooling is very selective and philosophy, history, art, sport and music have been removed from the curriculum.

ISIS has killed many thousands of non-combatants and caused acute suffering to countless others. In particular, many followers of minority religions have been executed, obliged to convert, obliged to pay a special 'tax' or enslaved. Women are particular targets for enslavement, including sexual servitude. This violence serves various purposes. First, it enables ISIS to govern with relative ease once it has seized control; either you toe the line or you die. If you are Sunni and you support ISIS, life will probably be better in many ways than it was before, particularly if you are a man. Second, extreme violence demonstrates the resolve of Islamic State to achieve its goals, a ruthless determination that again is appealing to many Sunnis who have themselves been persecuted since the 2003 invasion, and as Patrick Cockburn (2015: 39) puts it, ISIS 'has brought victory to a crushed and persecuted Sunni community'. Third, this extreme violence serves to shock the many enemies of ISIS, including the West, and to send the message that it does not need any sort of understanding or conciliation – let alone negotiation – from those who oppose it; victory will be achieved without any form of compromise.

ISIS has a slick, well-equipped and well-staffed media and communications operation, run by people who understand how to use modern communications technology effectively, and who generate carefully controlled news of ISIS via television, YouTube, Facebook and Twitter. The killing of US journalists has meant that most foreign journalists give ISIS a wide berth and that most information about ISIS and the caliphate comes from ISIS itself, and ISIS controls all communication with the outside world. Executions are often filmed and photographed and posted on social media precisely for the reasons given above: to terrify anyone thinking of fomenting dissent or even reporting dispassionately from the caliphate, to make divisions clear and to attract support. Destroying ancient archeological sites and works of art also attracts the world's attention and serves to set ISIS even further apart from what is perceived as Western ideology. Abu Bakr al-Baghdadi is the recognised leader, or caliph, and the caliphate has a large, well-equipped army and a great deal of military equipment, much of which originally belonged to the American army. Up to a third of its soldiers are foreign, including a large number from Chechnya, central Asia and numerous countries in the West. ISIS has an extensive bureaucracy and very significant financial resources, partly gained from local taxes and partly through oil revenue.

When attempting to understand the growth of ISIS, various related facts should be taken into consideration. First, the invasion of Iraq in 2003, the subsequent occupation and the circumstances of US withdrawal played an important role. Second, many Sunnis were drawn to or at least sought protection from ISIS, whether or not they believed in all aspects of the group's way of thinking and violent strategy. When the US pulled its last troops out of Iraq in 2011, it left neither a political system that was accountable to the general population, nor a proper civil service, and the US did not leave behind a well-trained and well-run army. After the overthrow of Saddam Hussein the Iraqi army not only dismissed many Sunnis, many of whom became unemployed, but it also became riddled with corruption at all levels; again, this served to bolster ISIS's ranks and crucially it provided highly trained soldiers to the new caliphate, whose military operations are very effective as a result. Many officers who once served in Saddam Hussein's army went on to join ISIS's troops in positions of authority.

Most importantly for what was to follow, the US left behind a country riven by ethnic and religious strife. The overthrow of Saddam Hussein had led to a state controlled by Shias who promoted Shia interests; the formation of the Nouri-Al-Maliki government was often seen as – and did in fact take the form of – a revenge of the Shia population over Sunnis, who became at best marginalised, both politically and economically, and more often second-class citizens or worse. Getting a job now depended far more on family, community and party ties than on merit, and Shia militias played their part in this process as well. Many Sunnis have therefore chosen to support ISIS, even if for some their allegiance is superficial and largely in the interest of their own survival.

In many respects, then, the birth and success of ISIS are the direct results of the USA's and its Western allies' activities in Iraq and Afghanistan. But interventions in Syria and Libya also played a significant role. In Syria, the war began as a popular uprising against a savage authoritarian regime, but then it became part of the battle of Sunni against Alawites and then the Shia–Sunni struggle in the broader region. There was also a squaring-up between the United States, Saudi Arabia and the Sunni states on the one hand and Iran, Iraq and the Lebanese Shia on the other. Moreover, Russia and the West were engaging in an echo of the Cold War, made worse by both the conflict in Libya and the situation in Ukraine. In Libya, Muammar Gaddafi was killed in 2011 after North Atlantic Treaty Organization (NATO) intervention against him and little was done to construct a viable governmental alternative. Moreover, the USA's close allies in the region have, over the years, played an important role in facilitating the rise of jihadism. Both Saudi Arabia and Qatar provided financial aid for jihadi groups and Saudi Arabia has done much generally to promote Wahhabism. Pakistan also supported fundamentalist insurgents. Turkey, meanwhile, has kept the 500-mile long border with Syria open.

We learn, from this brief look at aspects of the history of the Middle East since 1945 and the rise of jihadi violence, that the West has been and continues to be directly and deeply implicated in creating the conditions for the emergence of what is seen as quintessential terrorism. If anything, the West's actions since 9/11 have led to more violence born of desperation than in former years. Moreover, by contrast with the classic anti-imperialist struggles of the post-1945 period, much of the terrorism from below in the Middle East today seeks to replace one set of conditions of oppression and injustice with another set, where particular religious and community groups are oppressed and exploited in order to benefit others. In particular, women are often more oppressed than they had been previously, with regard to when, where and with whom they are allowed to go out, how they dress, how they are educated (if at all), where and if they go out to work and so on. But there are many other groups that are oppressed or persecuted, including Christians, Jews and homosexuals.

The case of ISIS is a particularly extreme form of this process, and is arguably the logical conclusion to many decades of, to say the least, clumsy and intensely self-interested intervention by the West. As mentioned above, the greatest innovation as far as ISIS is concerned is the establishment of a new state, or caliphate, based on extreme oppression of Shias, Christians, women, homosexuals and others. It is not clear whether this particular state will endure, but as an idea it is unlikely to disappear; as Cockburn (2015: 9–10) puts it, '[w]hat is happening in [Syria and Iraq], combined with the growing dominance of intolerant and exclusive Wahhabite beliefs within the worldwide Sunni community, means that all 1.6 billion Muslims, almost a quarter of the world's population, will be increasingly affected'. The violence practised by ISIS combines elements of both terrorism from below and, now that it is attempting to consolidate the caliphate, terrorism from above. This means that there are some similarities with fascism, where parties practise extreme forms of violence and enslavement in order to define clearly and ruthlessly who they are defending and who they are against, in order to eliminate or silence their opponents and rivals and in order to attract the loyal support of particular groups. The fact that ISIS was born largely out of the persecution of Sunni Muslims does not by any means imply that it will at some point look to create a more egalitarian society if the caliphate becomes properly established. On the contrary, although, like fascism, it draws on the disadvantaged to swell the ranks of its foot soldiers, it at the same time seeks to create not only a deeply divided society but also a successful capitalist economy. There is no doubt that, with time, the violence meted out by ISIS on its enemies will be turned against those low-ranking soldiers who are now doing the violent bidding of their leaders.

For the time being, however, the values that ISIS stands for and its celebration of violence are attracting young people in particular from a variety of countries, both in the Middle East and well beyond, who are deeply disillusioned with the country in which they live. Tens of thousands of volunteers who are swelling the ranks of ISIS see themselves as embarking on a life of adventure and in pursuit of a better world. They have even been compared with volunteers going to fight against Franco in Spain in the 1930s. But the differences between one phenomenon and the other are too clear to dwell on this more than very briefly. The volunteers in Spain went to fight for a more equal and less oppressive society and against a dictatorship representing very narrow interests; ISIS is seeking to replace one form of oppression and inequality with another, or else a consolidation of existing forms of oppression and inequality, and the ISIS regime is itself a form of dictatorship that in some important ways resembles fascism, as I have argued above. Régis Debray, when asked if ISIS volunteers from abroad resemble himself and other young people who went from advanced capitalist countries to fight guerilla wars alongside Che Guevara in Latin America in the 1960s, replies that

> we were fighting for human beings, whereas they are thinking of the afterlife. We were looking to the future, whereas they are going to the past. A passion for life as opposed to a death wish. They are regressing . . . We were not angels, and we were at times described as 'terrorists', a catch-all which served certain interests. But taking civilians hostage or killing prisoners – that was impossible. (Debray 2015: 86)

In 2015, numerous attacks linked to ISIS, including in Paris, suggested that ISIS and organisations associated with it were embarking on an intensified campaign outside of the area where it was attempting to consolidate the caliphate. In the course of the year, the violent deaths of 130 people in the Bataclan music venue and several restaurants in Paris on 13 November, and the bombing of the Russian plane flying from Sharm el-Sheikh, with the loss of 224 lives in October, were ISIS-related attacks that attracted a great deal of coverage in the Western media, along with two attacks in Tunisia, in March and June, when a total of fifty-seven people (mainly tourists) were killed. But in the course of the same year there were many other ISIS-linked attacks that received far less coverage, including in: Yemen, with 137 deaths; Saudi Arabia, with twenty-one deaths; Kuwait, with twenty-seven deaths; Turkey, where two attacks left a total of 135 dead; and in Beirut, the day before the November Paris attacks, when forty-three people died. ISIS also carried out suicide attacks on civilians in various urban centres in Syria and Iraq, including in the city of Kobani, where 220 Kurdish men, women and children were killed, and in the Shia town of Khan Bani Saad, northeast of Baghdad, killing 115 people.

The reaction on the part of Russia and France in particular, but also from the USA, was to increase the intensity and number of attacks on ISIS-held areas in Syria and Iraq and to prepare for what seemed likely to be an escalation of the violence in both the Middle East and elsewhere. But it was also clear that none of the countries intervening militarily in the Middle East had a viable plan for moving towards peace in the region after all the years of turmoil. On the contrary, it seemed likely that intervention would continue to be ill-thought-out and in pursuit of short-term interests, with the effect in the medium and longer term of generating more conflict and violence rather than increasing the likelihood of peace. In the absence of a plan for peace and stability, taking the lead from and working in conjunction with more progressive elements in the region, it seemed quite possible, in fact, that ISIS would continue to gather strength and that killing of civilians would continue in countries who were attacking it, thereby contributing to the destabilisation of European countries, in part via a further rise of the extreme right. The fact that there were connections between some of the attackers in Paris and both the St Denis Parisian suburb and the Molenbeek-Saint-Jean area in Brussels is significant. Both have high levels of unemployment, especially youth unemployment, and both have large ethnic minority populations, often by extraction from former colonies. The number of inhabitants who sympathise with jihadist attacks in these areas is small, but the ongoing failure to provide adequate jobs and general well-being is bound to increase the likelihood of ISIS recruiting from these sorts of areas in order to organise further attacks. This is not to excuse this sort of terrorism, which is indiscriminate killing in favour of a particular and acute form of oppression, but to attempt to explain it. While the attacks were taking place in Paris, the US was continuing to use pilotless drones to attack individuals and groups in various countries of the Middle East, and almost simultaneously with the attacks, four former drone operators spoke out against Obama's increased use of drones, saying in an open letter to the President that many non-combatants had been killed in the drone attacks. These deaths, they argued, 'fueled the feelings of hatred that ignited terrorism and groups like ISIS, while also serving as a fundamental recruitment tool similar to Guantánamo Bay' and they added that this was one of the most 'devastating driving forces for terrorism and destabilization around the world' (cited in *The Guardian* 18 November 15).

* * *

We conclude this chapter, in a sense, where it began, with a comparison of terrorism from above and terrorism from below. I argued at the beginning of the chapter that in order to understand the ruthless nature of some terrorism from below we need to understand the still more ruthless nature of terrorism from above. I mentioned the terror bombing of German cities in World War Two and elsewhere in this book we examined US foreign policy during the Cold War and beyond, which involved a great deal of terrorism from above. Not only have various states themselves killed and tortured many more people than non-state groups, but Western governments have in the past fifty years supported various terrorist organisations that have killed hundreds of thousands of people; these organisations include The National Union for the Total Independence of Angola (UNITA) in Angola (at war from the mid-1970s to the late 1990s), the Contras in Nicaragua and the *mujahideen* in Afghanistan.

If we confine our argument, for the moment, to the situation in the Middle East since the invasion of Iraq in 2003, there has been a great deal of terrorism from above in the form of 'collateral damage', in other words the killing of non-combatants in the pursuit of goals where the main targets of violence were combatants. We have seen how this has encouraged not only terrorism from below in Iraq, Afghanistan and elsewhere in the Middle East itself, but also increasing amounts of terrorism from below in other countries, including in Western Europe, much of it (at the time of writing at least) organised by ISIS and its proxies. This is, arguably, terrorism of a new form. Terrorism organised or sponsored by a state has been seen before, but the way in which ISIS combines extreme violence in the caliphate itself with targeting civilians in large numbers abroad, carried out by people prepared to die, means that there is a new form of fighting that is particularly difficult to combat. This also means that, in the short term, the response by the West and its allies in the Middle East is potentially particularly dangerous. In the past, the West has often been able to retaliate against terrorism from below without fear of substantial counter-attack, but this is no longer the case. The mistakes of the past are having repercussions in a particularly clear and unpleasant way.

As mentioned above, ISIS warfare combines elements of both terrorism from above and terrorism from below. It may be argued that the source of the word 'terrorism', namely the Terror after the French Revolution, also combined both types of terrorism, when in 1793–4 Robespierre and others sought to defend the revolution by use of state Terror, that is, systematic execution of opponents of the revolution. It may therefore be argued that there are similarities between the two forms of new-state violence in very different epochs. But this would be to ignore the dramatically different ideologies behind the two forms of terror. Certainly, the Terror after 1789 was almost certainly bloodier than it needed to be in order to defend the Revolution, and it had to an extent a violent dynamic of its own. But it sought to move forward towards a more just and equal society and to ward off counter-revolution. ISIS, as we have seen, is attempting to create through barbarism a state based on extreme forms of exploitation, inequality and indeed slavery and a perpetual state – in both senses of the word – of violence.

The question must now be posed: are acts of terrorism (from below) ever justified? The answer must be no, assuming we are talking about acts that involve the loss of life of non-combatant civilians. Not only is there no moral justification for such acts, but they allow governments to introduce more repressive measures than existed previously. Various liberation movements, including the Front de Libération Nationale in Algeria, killed civilians as well as combatants in large numbers and this sort of violence almost certainly had a negative effect on the post-independence situation in Algeria.

Injustice and inequality breed terrorism from below of various kinds, as does terrorism from above. Terrorism from below is usually neither morally justifiable nor tactically fruitful. But it will continue as long as there is substantial injustice and as long as societies continue to base themselves on substantially other considerations than equality combined with peace.

CONCLUSIONS

Both the starting point and conclusion of a study of violence in the pursuit of emancipation must be that any violence, whoever it is against and whoever perpetrates it, is tragic and must be avoided if at all possible. This means that in struggles for emancipation minimum necessary violence must be used in any combat against those defending the unjust and violent status quo and that even the most violent opponent must be treated humanely and with justice. That is the only correct starting point. But it is not a pacifist one. It is not pacifist because in order to achieve a state of affairs where emancipation in various domains is achieved, violence may regrettably be necessary – in other words it cannot be ruled out.

This perhaps resembles in a superficial way the starting point of many, especially liberal, approaches to the question of violence in the process of profound change, which insist in theory at least that minimum violence must be used at all times. But we need a far profounder commitment to non-violence and peace than has been practised by regimes that combine liberal democracy with capitalism, not to mention more authoritarian governments. We have seen that supposedly peace-loving and peace-seeking governments have promoted a great deal of violence in various ways. Throughout the period we call modernity, extreme violence has been perpetrated by the powerful against the weak, supposedly in the interests of 'progress', but often in fact in the interests of maintaining a thoroughly unequal and exploitative status quo. In the post-Second World War era, colonies, former colonies and any country that seemed likely to move closer to the Soviet Union were liable to become the target of armed and extraordinarily ruthless intervention. For the USA, Latin America became the theatre of brutal attack in the 1970s in particular, in the name of stemming the tide of anti-imperialist, anti-capitalist and egalitarian movements; no action was too violent and no dictator too bloodthirsty to earn the support of the US and its allies as long as they appeared to be repressing egalitarian groups and movements. Since the end of the Cold War and the triumph of neo-liberal economics in much of the West, poorer countries have remained targets for violent intervention, particularly if they threaten the economic or political – the two are often the same, in practice – interests of the West. Thus, for example, Saddam Hussein in Iraq went from being a war-crime-perpetrating dictator who was a friend of the West to still being a war-crime-perpetrating dictator, but who became a target of the West, which used sanctions against Iraq causing the death of hundreds of thousands of civilians, followed by military intervention with disastrous consequences. Since then, the scale of death and destruction in the Middle East has been incalculable, and it continues without end in sight. The West's long history of intervening in the region and making the plight of its people much worse looks set to continue.

It is thus not difficult to demonstrate that the status quo is profoundly violent, and if we also take into account the death and suffering caused by uneven distribution of resources, both within nation states and between nations on a global scale (structural violence), we are left in even less doubt; thousands of people, many of them children, die every day due to limited access to adequate food, water, basic hygiene and simple medication. Moreover, this situation is ongoing; in other words there is no proper plan to alter this situation, either from a political point of view or from an economic (often distribution of resources) point of view, and other examples abound – domestic violence, especially against women and children, violent prison systems, gang warfare encouraged by drug dealing for vast profits, sex trafficking, and so on. In some respects both agent-related violence and structural violence have become worse over the past thirty years, due to the actions of the world's only remaining superpower and its allies, and the ravages of neoliberalism. It is possible to imagine how oppression, repression and violence could become worse still if the periodic crises of capitalism cause widespread social unrest, if there is ecological catastrophe, or both.

But when thinking about the ethics of violence for change it is not enough simply to explain that the status quo is violent and that it needs changing, and we cannot simply move from that position to one of arguing that peaceful and egalitarian ends justify violent means of struggle to attain them. In the nineteenth century this was more plausible, perhaps, when in Europe and North America, as well as in the rest of the world, violence and suffering were so prevalent and clear to see that the need for armed insurrection was almost axiomatic. When Lenin argued, after Marx, that the 1871 Paris Commune had failed and been so violently suppressed by the Versailles government in part because the Communards had not taken military action seriously enough, this seemed to make perfect sense and the Bolsheviks acted very differently; they learned many lessons from conventional, bourgeois warfare and applied them in the wake of 1917 when confronted with civil war within Russia and attacked by numerous other states from without. But we cannot take the same approach now as in the nineteenth century and early twentieth and above all we cannot proceed as if the communist experience of the twentieth century had not happened. The Soviet Union brought many benefits to its people compared with the previous regime, which had offered hardship and cruelty over many centuries. The benefits under Soviet communism included vastly improved healthcare, increased life expectancy, better housing, education and general standard of living. Indeed some of these deteriorated sharply in the decade after the break-up of the Soviet Union. But communism also brought death and suffering on a huge scale, in particular during the process of forced collectivisation of agriculture, repression towards dissenters from the party line, involving minimal or non-existent judicial process followed by execution or long-term incarceration in the harshest of conditions during the purges of the 1930s, not to mention the Gulag. Much the same can be said of China, and especially Cambodia and North Korea. However we may wish to explain these terrible episodes and the ongoing political injustices that were an integral part of the communist experience of the twentieth century – either by degeneration under the rule of Stalin and Stalin's attempt to create socialism in one country, by Mao's optimism regarding the Great Leap Forward and Cultural Revolution, or by the extreme hostility of the West towards communist states and the failure of working people of enough other countries to overthrow capitalism – we cannot escape the fact that in the name of greater equality and indeed human emancipation, enormous and ongoing suffering was caused.

In other words, we need a framework for examining the ethics of violence in pursuit of emancipation that takes on board the failures of historical communism without accepting that there is no better possible future than ruthless capitalism combined with liberal democracy, whose democracy even in its heartlands is wafer-thin. This sort of arrangement is indeed, for the moment at least, a more effective way of maintaining the status quo than the situation in the nineteenth century where there was more overtly class-against-class capitalism, more effective because the experience of mass consumerism and mass production of ideological instruments of conformity (advertising, newspapers, television, the Internet and so forth) is more subtle than the cannons, the guns and the bayonets used so frequently in nineteenth-century and early twentieth-century Europe against the oppressed.

In an earlier chapter I examined in some detail both Fidel Castro's declared ethics of revolt and the actual experience of Cuba before, during and since the revolution of 1958–9. Castro is virtually alone among insurgent leaders in having an ethics of revolt that strictly limits violence against the enemy and against party members who step out of line. This was demonstrated time and again in Castro's and his comrades' actions, and is explored in many of Castro's speeches, writings and interviews. Certainly, we need to bear in mind that the Cuban revolution took place in very particular circumstances and was at first as much a revolt against the loathed and unscrupulous dictator Fulgencio Batista as a revolution in the cause of profound equality and wider emancipation. Moreover, the role of the Soviet Union in protecting Cuba from US military attack and in softening the effects of the US economic blockade was crucial to the survival of the revolution in a form that was roughly speaking true to its origins. In some ways, Cuba is an exception in the galaxy of twentieth-century communism in that its revolutionary path was relatively straightforward, especially compared with the giants of the communist experiment of the twentieth century, namely Russia and China. We also examined some of the ways in which the Cuban revolution has failed its own people and has even perpetuated violence against it, although not on the scale of almost any major capitalist state today and without remotely resembling the cruelty of the various regimes in the decades and indeed centuries preceding the 1958–9 revolution. All of this notwithstanding, it is vital that we examine further the case of Cuba and in particular the approach of Fidel Castro when thinking about the future direction of violence in revolt. Castro had direct experience of the ruthless violence of Batista, but he also pointed to what we have been calling structural violence with particular clarity when in 1962 he declared:

> [O]n this continent of semi-colonies about four persons per minute die of hunger, curable illness or premature old age, 5,500 per day, two million per year ... A holocaust of lives which in fifteen years has caused twice the number of deaths of the First World War, and it still continues. Meanwhile, from Latin America a continuous torrent of money flows to the United States: some four thousand dollars a minute, five million dollars a day, two billion dollars a year ... For each thousand dollars which leave us, there remains one corpse: that is the price of what is called imperialism! (Castro [1962] 2008: 112)

Another aspect of my argument is that when examining violence in revolt, we need to take notice of the many indications that the prospects for peace are good. This, I have argued, is the other side of modernity that is still going strong despite the aspects of modernity and capitalism that allow violence of so many types to continue. Notwithstanding the violence of capitalism and of historical communism, modernity has brought a strong egalitarian impulse and a strong peace dynamic. This continues to be expressed in a myriad of ways, from increasing revulsion towards domestic violence to ever-more demands for medical research and treatments that benefit all members of society; from recognition of the need for equality between men and women to widespread discussion about and defence of minority rights for many groups; from the huge numbers of people who donate money to charities with the intention of relieving suffering to enshrining basic tenets of anti-violence in international law. The importance of this peace dynamic to my argument is both that it puts a different perspective on the prospects for a more humane form of revolt, and that in the longer term, non-violence may be integrated into the fabric of a far more egalitarian and just society. Certainly, this peace dynamic, which is in every case associated with an egalitarian impulse, is in some cases and in some periods subject to serious reversals that can only be resisted through activism and political action of various kinds; it is activism, resistance and revolt against oppression and exploitation that has brought about many of these advances – and indeed brought modernity itself – and it is only these acts of defiance and activism that will maintain and enhance them.

I have suggested in this book that too many socialist activists and intellectuals have, for too long, shunned the idea of 'imagined futures', or what is often termed utopian socialism. There is much truth in the idea – as put forward by Marx and in particular by Engels – that the utopian socialists of the nineteenth century were unrealistic in their view that islands of emancipation and equality could be constructed within a sea of almost untouched capitalist inequality and exploitation. There was much that was both elitist and unrealistic about the nineteenth-century utopian socialists' approach, which did little for the mass of impoverished and deeply exploited ordinary people. But my argument is that the baby was thrown out with the bathwater. Imagining possible futures as a way of enriching the socialist project was almost completely shunned. We now need once again to imagine a far more equal and just society, and in fact we need to be able to do this in some detail. In the language of Ernst Bloch, we need a 'warm stream' approach as well as a more scientific, 'cold stream' perspective. In particular – for the purposes of this book but in its own right as well – we need to imagine a future that is profoundly non-violent and peaceful. If we do this, we will quickly find that equality and peace are inextricably bound together.

Inequality and the maintenance of inequality, as I have attempted to show, have themselves generated and continue to generate a great deal of violence of many kinds. Moving beyond violence will mean moving beyond inequality and exploitation. If the two phenomena – equality and peace – are not paired in order to eradicate violence, violence will not disappear or will re-emerge, either as obvious exploitation within a particular country or region, or between countries and regions, or more likely both. At present, the international division of labour between richer and poorer nations produces a great deal of structural and other types of violence, dividing the world into what Etienne Balibar calls 'life zones' and 'death zones'.

How, then, does this shed light on the question of violence in pursuit of emancipation? Most importantly, I suggest that the utopia-inspired idea of a peaceful, non-violent society should be at the heart of any progressive struggle for change. The goal of peace and profound equality must inform the means by which people struggle. It is not possible to construct an ethical guide that indicates precisely how to and how not to behave, regardless of the detail of the circumstances. There is no timeless set of measures that is applicable in all circumstances regarding how violent we can be in revolt – when we can kill and when we cannot, when we take up arms and when we do not, when we negotiate or make concessions and when we confront reactionary forces. To date, all guidelines of this nature that have existed have been ideologically motivated, that is motivated by the goal (the end) and thus these guidelines change over time and according to the circumstances. Most guidelines of this kind suggest that it is legitimate to be violent in defence of the status quo, that is, to defend it violently against attack and attack violently those who prevent a society similar to the one being defended from coming about. Once the 'just' society is achieved, people must lay down their arms and leave violence to the police and the army; in all societies to date, the powers that be want very limited participation in politics once that 'acceptable' society is established – they want depoliticisation. This is the argument put forward by liberalism and by Just War Theory, but this has also been the argument of historical communism and of groups who struggle for national liberation. My own view is not that individuals need to be permanently armed and ever ready to take part in uprisings – far from it. But we should recognise that in a more just society there would need to be sufficient democracy that uprising would be unnecessary; constant debate and participation in politics (broadly defined) would be needed instead of depoliticisation.

Again, it is impossible to give guidelines as to what is right and wrong for all situations and indeed ethics can never be wholly dissociated from questions of strategy and theory; reflection must inform on-the-ground decisions and vice versa. As Kate Soper has put it regarding means and ends more generally:

> The rule we might do better to follow is the rule that no absolute rule applies; that all situations requiring moral decisions are concrete and have to be judged on their merits; and that in making such judgements what counts morally more than any adherence to principle is our possession of a certain moral intuition or sensibility. To act morally, I would suggest, is often to act in a regretful spirit of compromise: it is to be aware of what kinds of things in general are right and wrong, and in that sense to act in the light of general rules; but it is also to be aware that some of what we shall actually feel called upon to do will be in contradiction with one or other of those principles. (Soper 1987: 113)

This is one of the ways in which Just War Theory is deeply flawed, namely in attempting to have ethical standards that apply to all situations and that all claim to be ideology-free. My belief is that one cannot have a proper discussion regarding ethics and violence in an ideological vacuum. In this book I attempt to make a contribution to ways in which an alternative discussion can take place. Liberalism is not entirely flawed by any means. It at least purports to recognise the importance of freedom, some types of equality and the flowering of the individual, and liberalism also defends certain important rights, such as freedom of expression. As I have attempted to show, however, liberalism is very un-ambitious in each of these respects and is, moreover, often fully prepared to suspend these principles when other interests are threatened.

Some readers may react to the line of argument in this book by suggesting that it is anachronistic and of only historical interest. They may point out that in the richer countries violent revolt in the cause of equality and emancipation took place in the nineteenth century and early twentieth but that since then it is extremely rare, because capitalism has managed one way or another to provide circumstances that are sufficiently pleasant for enough people that they are not tempted by serious revolt, that any stirrings of real revolt are effectively quashed at an early stage and that we all buy into an ideology or various ideologies that emphasise the benefits of capitalism as it exists and play down its disadvantages. I would understand this reaction, but I wish to make various comments in response.

First, if we look to many parts of the developing world, there are groups taking up arms in the pursuit of substantial change; this is not always in the cause of equality for all and is in some cases it is for deeply reactionary purposes, as we have seen. But this is not always the case and, perhaps just as importantly, will not always be the case in future. Another part of the equation is that the capitalist status quo may well become more violent and still more ruthless. Immanuel Wallerstein and others have come to the conclusion that capitalism is in the autumn of its years. This is neither an optimistic nor a pessimistic view, but a fairly detached judgement based on the contemporary reality of the capitalist system combined with analysis of several centuries of its history. Given that capitalism is dependent for its survival on ceaseless accumulation and that this in itself is impossible in the longer term, together with the fact that it is now possible to envisage real limits to capitalist expansion, not to mention ecological catastrophe that ceaseless drive for profit is now in grave danger of causing, a qualitatively new – and perhaps terminal – phase of the capitalist system is quite plausible. The political economists examined in Chapter 2 do suggest strongly that a far more violent form of capitalism – more violent not only in developing countries but also in what is now the liberal democratic West – is a distinct possibility, with fascist-type regimes being used as the means by which capitalism would attempt to save itself, at least in the medium term. The alternative is a far more egalitarian arrangement after the demise of capitalism, whereby the economy, the political system and society generally is organised in such a way that human needs are the driving force, that equality of all human beings is taken for granted and that democracy is deeper than the world has ever known it before.

There are various possible futures for the human race and the different parts of it, but, as I have just suggested, questions of violence, non-violence and equality are likely to be among the ones that forward-looking people consider when looking towards those futures. The jihadi violence that is so prevalent at the beginning of the twenty-first century is certainly in part a reaction against decades and indeed centuries of oppression, exploitation and short-sighted military intervention, which gets worse with every intervention the West makes. But this particular insurgent violence, which has adopted religion as its mobilising focus, is violence against certain types of oppression – 'neo-imperialism' is the best shorthand term for them – and it is also violence whose goal is often profoundly unequal, where women are at best second-class citizens and religious and other minorities are treated with brutal contempt. The most extreme form of this at present is Islamic State, or ISIS, whose boastful barbarism and ruthless sectarianism is part of its core identity. The other part of Islamic State's identity is of course its seizure of land in Iraq and Syria that has become its caliphate. ISIS may or may not succeed in its attempt to create a durable Sunni-Islamic homeland with a fascist-type approach to governing, but even if it does not, the idea of a religious fundamentalist caliphate that benefits economically from oil and protects itself with the most deadly weapons available is likely to re-emerge in the region. The countries of the Middle East that have aided the rise of jihadi groups and the countries in the West that have been attacking without sufficient thought for the consequences of their actions are playing a very dangerous game.

Taking all of these various points into account, then, my argument is that we need a dialectical approach to the question of violence in pursuit of emancipation. This involves taking into account the extreme violence of both capitalism and historical communism – and we may now add the violence of religious fundamentalism. It also involves taking on board, however, the very real peace dynamic that surrounds us in the West in particular, but also in other parts of the world. Equality and long-term peace remain the key considerations in any approach to questions of means and ends in relation to violence for a better future. It is the combining of these elements and an insistence that they should not be disaggregated that allows for a constructive debate.

BIBLIOGRAPHY

Agwani, Mohammed Shafi (1969), *Communism in the Arab East*, New York: Asia Publishing.

Alison, Miranda (2009), *Women and Political Violence: Female Combatants in Ethno-National Conflict*, London: Routledge.

Amin, Samir (2008), 'The defense of humanity requires the radicalisation of popular struggles', in Leo Panitch and Colin Leys (eds), *Violence Today: Actually Existing Barbarism. Socialist Register 2009*, Rendlesham: Merlin Press, pp. 260–72.

Amnesty International (2015), 'Cuba', *Amnesty International Report 2014/15*, February, <https://www.amnesty.org/en/countries/americas/cuba/> (last accessed 1 September 2015).

Anderson, Perry (2013), *American Foreign Policy and its Thinkers*, special issue of *New Left Review*, 83, September/October, pp. 5–167.

Andress, David (2005), *The Terror: Civil War in the French Revolution*, London: Abacus Books.

Arblaster, Anthony (1990), 'Bread first, then morals', in David McLellan and Sean Sayers (eds), *Socialism and Morality*, London: Macmillan Publishers, pp. 81–99.

Archer, John, 'Testosterone and human aggression: An evaluation of the challenge hypothesis', *Neuroscience and Biobehavioral Reviews*, 30, 319–45.

Arendt, Hannah (1969), *On Violence*, London: Penguin Books.

Aron, Raymond (1975), *History and the Dialectic of Violence: An Analysis of Sartre's* Critique de la Raison Dialectique, Oxford: Blackwell Publishing.

Aronson, Ronald (1984), *The Dialectics of Disaster*, London: Verso Books.

Atack, Iain (2012), *Nonviolence in Political Theory*, Edinburgh: Edinburgh University Press.

August, Arnold (2013), *Cuba and its Neighbours: Democracy in Motion*, London: Zed Books.

Badiou, Alain ([1988] 2013), *Being and Event*, London: Bloomsbury Publishing. (Translated by Oliver Feltham)

174

Badiou, Alain ([1997] 2003), *Saint Paul: The Foundation of Universalism*, Redwood City, CA: Stanford University Press. (Translated by Ray Brassier)

Badiou, Alain (2007), 'One divides itself into two', in Sebastian Budgen, Stathis Kouvelakis and Slavoj Žižek (eds), *Lenin Reloaded: Towards a Politics of Truth*, London: Duke University Press, pp. 7–17.

Badiou, Alain ([2009] 2010), *The Communist Hypothesis*, London: Verso Books. (Translated by David Macey and Steve Corcoran)

Balibar, Etienne (2004), *We, the People of Europe? Reflections on Transnational Citizenship*, Princeton: Princeton University Press.

Balibar, Etienne (2010), *Violence et civilité*, Paris: Editions Galilée.

Balibar, Etienne and Bertrand Ogilvie (1995), *Violence et politique*, special issue of *Lignes* 25, May.

Bauman, Zygmunt (1989), *Modernity and the Holocaust*, Cambridge: Polity.

Benjamin, Walter ([1921] 1978), 'Critique of violence', in *Reflections*, New York: Harcourt Brace Jovanovich, pp. 277–8.

Berman, Marshall (1982), *All that is Solid Melts into Air: The Experience of Modernity*, London: Verso Books.

Bernstein, Richard (2013), *Violence*, Cambridge: Polity.

Bessel, Richard (2015), *Violence. A Modern Obsession*, London: Simon & Schuster.

Blackledge, Paul (2012), *Marxism and Ethics: Freedom, Desire and Revolution*, New York: SUNY Press.

Bloch, Ernst ([1938–47] 1986), *The Principle of Hope*, 3 vols, Cambridge, MA: MIT Press. (Translated by Neville Plaice, Stephen Plaice and Paul Knight)

Bloch, Ernst ([1918] 2000), *The Spirit of Utopia*, Redwood City, CA: Stanford University Press. (Translated by Anthony A. Nassar)

Bloch, Ernst ([1968] 2009), *Atheism in Christianity*, New York: Herder and Herder. (Translated by James Swann)

Bloch, Ernst and Mark Ritter (1976), 'Dialectics and hope', *New German Critique*, 9(9), autumn, 3–10.

Blum, Deborah (1997), *Sex on the Brain: The Biological Differences between Men and Women*, New York: Viking Press.

Blum, William (2014), *Killing Hope: US Military and CIA Interventions since World War II*, London: Zed Books.

Bourke, Joanna (1999), *An Intimate History of Killing: Face-to-Face Killing in Twentieth-Century Warfare*, London: Granta Books.

Brenkert, George G. (1983), *Marx's Ethics of Freedom*, London: Routledge.

Brie, Michael (2008), 'Emancipation and the left: The issue of violence', in Leo Panitch and Colin Leys (eds), *Violence Today: Actually Existing Barbarism, Socialist Register 2009*, Rendlesham: Merlin Press, pp. 239–59.

Budgen, Sebastian, Stathis Kouvelakis and Slavoj Žižek (eds) (2007), *Lenin Reloaded: Towards a Politics of Truth*, London: Duke University Press.

Camus, Albert ([1951] 2000), *The Rebel*, London: Penguin Books. (Translated by Anthony Bower)

Carter, April (2005), *Direct Action and Democracy Today*, Cambridge: Polity.

Carver, Terrell (1989), *Friedrich Engels: His Life and Thought*, London: Macmillan Publishers.

Castro, Fidel ([1953] 1987), 'History will absolve me', in Marta Harnecker (ed.), *From Moncada to Victory: Fidel Castro's Political Strategy*, New York: Pathfinder Press, pp. 79–153. (Translated by Margarita Zimmermann)

Castro, Fidel ([1962] 2008), 'Second declaration of Havana', in *The Declarations of Havana*, London: Verso Books, pp. 86–120. (Introduction by Tariq Ali)

Castro, Fidel and Frei Betto (1985), *Castro and Religion: Conversations with Frei Betto*, Melbourne: Ocean Press. (Translated by Mary Todd)

Castro, Fidel with Ramonet, Ignacio (2007), *My Life*, London: Penguin Books. (Translated by Andrew Hurley)

Cavanaugh, Mary (2012), 'Theories of violence: Social science perspectives', *Journal of Human Behavior in the Social Environment*, 22(5), 607–18.

Caygill, Howard (2013), *On Resistance: A Philosophy of Defiance*, London: Bloomsbury Publishing.

Chasin, Barbara H. (2004), *Inequality and Violence in the USA: Casualties of Capitalism*, 2nd edn, New York: Humanity Books.

Chenoweth, Erica and Maria J. Stephan (2012), *Why Civil Resistance Works: The Strategic Logic of Non-violent Conflict*, New York: Columbia University Press.

Cherki, Alice (2002), 'Préface à l'édition de 2002', in Franz Fanon, *Les damnés de la terre*, Paris: La Découverte, pp. 2–15.

Child Poverty Action Group (CPAG) (2015), *Facts and Figures*, <http://www.cpag.org.uk/child-poverty-facts-and-figures> (last accessed 1 December 2015).

Chomsky, Aviva (2015), *A History of the Cuban Revolution*, 2nd edn, Oxford: Blackwell Publishing.

Chomsky, Noam (2005), 'Simple truths, hard problems: Some thoughts on terror, justice and self defence', Royal Institute of Philosophy Lecture, <http://www.chomsky.info/articles/200501--.pdf> (last accessed 6 April 2015).

Chomsky, Noam (2015), 'L'arme des puissants', *Le Monde diplomatique* 14, special issue on terrorism, April–May, pp. 67–9. (Based on a lecture delivered at the Massachusetts Institute of Technology, 18 October 2001.)

Chomsky, Noam and André Vltcheck (2013), *On Western State Terrorism: From Hiroshima to Drone Warfare*, London: Pluto Press.

Coatsworth, John H. (2010), 'The Cold War in Central America, 1975–1991', in Melvyn P. Leffler and Odd Arne Westad (eds), *The Cambridge History of the Cold War vol 3: Endings*, Cambridge: Cambridge University Press, pp. 201–21.

Cockburn, Cynthia (2012), *Anti-militarism: Political and Gender Dynamics of Peace Movements*, Basingstoke: Palgrave Macmillan.

Cockburn, Patrick (2007), *The Occupation: War and Resistance in Iraq*, London: Verso Books.

Cockburn, Patrick (2015), *The Rise of Islamic State: ISIS and the New Sunni Revolution*, London: Verso Books.

Coltman, Leycester (2003), *The Real Fidel Castro*, New Haven, CT: Yale University Press.

Corm, Georges (2012a), *Pour une Lecture profane des Conflits: sur le 'retour du religieux' dans les conflits contemporains du Moyen-Orient*, Paris: La Découverte.

Corm, Georges (2012b), *Le Proche-Orient éclaté (1956–2012)*, Paris: Gallimard.

Courtois, Stéphane (ed.) ([1997] 1999), *The Black Book of Communism: Crimes, Terror, Repression*, Cambridge, MA: Harvard University Press. (Translated by Jonathan Murphy and Mark Kramer)

Crouch, Colin (2004), *Post-Democracy*, Cambridge: Polity.

Cummings, Bruce (2010), *The Korean War: A History*, New York: Modern Library Chronicles.

Dawisha, Adeed (2003), *Arab Nationalism in the 20th Century*, Princeton: Princeton University Press.

Debray, Régis (1970), *Strategy for Revolution*, London: Jonathan Cape Publishers. (Translations by *New Left Review*, Richard Seaver, Lorrimer Publishing and Monthly Review Press)

Debray, Régis (2015), 'Le désert des valeurs fait sortir les couteaux', *Le Nouvel Observateur*, 2619, 14–21 January, pp. 83–7.

Deutscher, Isaac (1972), 'Marxism and non-violence', in *Marxism in Our Time*, London: Jonathan Cape Publishers, pp. 79–91.

Deutscher, Isaac (1984), 'Violence and non-violence', in *Marxism, Wars and Revolutions. Essays from Four Decades*, London: Verso Books, pp. 256–62.

Dilla Alfonso, Haroldo and William I. Robinson (1996), *La Democracia en Cuba y el diferendo con los Estados Unidos*, Havana: Ediciones CEA.

Dillon, Michael and Julian Reid (2009), *The Liberal Way of War*, London: Routledge.

Dodd, Lindsey A. and Andrew Knapp (2008), 'How many Frenchmen did you kill? British bombing policy towards France (1940–1945)', *French History*, 22(4), 469–92.

Doran, Christopher (2012), *Making the World Safe for Capitalism*, London: Pluto Press.

Douzinas, Costas and Slavoj Žižek (eds) (2010), *The Idea of Communism*, London: Verso Books.

Eagleton, Terry (1999), 'Utopia and its opposites', in Leo Panitch and Colin Leys (eds), *Necessary and Unnecessary Utopias: Socialist Register 2000*, Rendlesham: Merlin Press, pp. 31–40.

Eckstrand, Nathan and Christopher Yates (2011), *Philosophy and the Return of Violence: Studies from this Widening Gyre*, London: Continuum.

Economist, The (2013a), 'Iraq ten years on: The slow road back', 2 March.

Economist, The (2013b), 'Jailhouse nation: How to make America's penal system less punitive and more effective', 20 June.

The Economist (2015), 'Islam and slavery: The persistence of history', 22 August.

Elias, Norberto ([1939] 1994), *The Civilising Process*, Oxford: Blackwell Publishing. (Translation by Edmund Jephcott)

Elkins, Caroline (2005) *Britain's Gulag: The Brutal End of Empire in Kenya*, London: Random House.

Engels, Friedrich ([1880] 1968a), 'Socialism: Utopian and Scientific', in Karl Marx and Friedrich Engels, *Selected Works in One Volume*, London: Lawrence and Wishart, pp. 394–428.

Engels, Friedrich ([1883] 1968b), 'Speech at the graveside of Karl Marx', in Karl Marx and Friedrich Engels, *Selected Works in One Volume*, London: Lawrence and Wishart, pp. 427–8.

Engels, Friedrich ([1875] 1970), 'The Peasant War in Germany', in Karl Marx and Friedrich Engels, *Selected Works in One Volume*, London: Lawrence and Wishart, pp. 242–7.

Engels, Friedrich ([1878] 1975), *Anti-Dühring: Herr Eugen Dühring's Revolution in Science*, London: Lawrence and Wishart.

Engels, Friedrich ([1844] 1999), *The Condition of the Working Class in England*, Oxford: Oxford University Press.

Evans, Martin and John Phillips (2007), *Algeria. Anger of the Dispossessed*, New Haven, CT: Yale University Press.

Fanon, Frantz ([1961] 2001), *The Wretched of the Earth*, London: Penguin. (Translated by Constance Farrington)

Ferro, Marc (2010), *Le Livre noir du colonialisme*, Paris: Fayard.

Fiala, Andrew (2004), *Practical Pacifism*, New York: Algora Publishing.

Fiala, Andrew (2008), *The Just War Myth*, New York: Rowman and Littlefield.

Fiala, Andrew (2010), *Public War, Private Conscience: The Ethics of Political Violence*, London: Continuum.

Finlay, Christopher J. (2006), 'Violence and Revolutionary Subjectivity. Marx to Žižek', *European Journal of Political Theory*, 5(4), 373–97.

Finlay, Christopher (2015), *Terrorism and the Right to Resist: A Theory of Just Revolutionary War*, Cambridge: Cambridge University Press.

Fisk, Robert (2001), 'Terror in America', *The Nation*, 13 September.

Fisk, Robert (2007), *The Great War for Civilisation: The Conquest of the Middle East*, New York: Vintage Books.

Fisk, Robert (2015), 'Who is bombing whom in the Middle East?', *The Independent*, 4 May.

Foix, Alain (2015), *Che Guevara*, Paris: Gallimard.

Fotion, Nicholas (2007), *War and Ethics*, London: Continuum.

Fotion, Nicholas, Boris Kashnikov and Joanne K. Lekea (2007), *Terrorism. The New World Disorder*, London: Continuum.

Frazer, Elizabeth and Kimberly Hutchings (2008), 'On politics and violence: Arendt contra Fanon', *Contemporary Political Theory*, 7(1), February, 90–109.

Frazer, Elizabeth and Kimberly Hutchings (2014a), 'Feminism and the critique of violence: Negotiating feminist political agency', *Journal of Political Ideologies*, 19(2), 143–63.

Frazer, Elizabeth and Kimberly Hutchings (2014b), 'Revisiting Ruddick: Feminism, pacifism and non-violence', *Journal of International Political Theory Ideologies*, 10(1), February, 109–24.

Fromm, Erich (1961), *Marx's Concept of Man*, New York: Frederic Ungar Publishing.

Galtung, Johan (1969), 'Violence, peace and peace research', *Journal of Peace Research*, 6(3), 167–91.

Gandhi, Mahatma ([1986–7] 2008), 'Non-violence as political action', in *Essential Writings*, Oxford: Oxford University Press, pp. 309–74.

Gentleman, Amelia (2012), 'Inside Halden, the most humane prison in the world', *The Guardian*, 18 May.

George, Alexander (ed.) (1991), *Western State Terrorism*, Cambridge: Polity.

Geras, Norman (1996), 'Socialist hope in an age of catastrophe', in Leo Panitch (ed.), *Are There Alternatives? Socialist Register 1996*, Rendlesham: Merlin Press, pp. 239–63.

Geras, Norman (1999), 'Minimum utopia: Ten theses', in Leo Panitch and Colin Leys (eds), *Necessary and Unnecessary Utopias: Socialist Register 2000*, Rendlesham: Merlin Press, pp. 41–52.

Gleijeses, Piero (2010), 'Cuba and the Cold War, 1959–1980', in Melvyn P. Leffler and Odd A. Westad (eds), *The Cambridge History of the Cold War, Volume II: Crises and Détente*, Cambridge: Cambridge University Press, pp. 327–48.

Goldschmidt Jr, Arthur and Lawrence Davidson (2010), *A Concise History of the Middle East*, Boulder: Westview Press.

Gott, Richard (2004), *Cuba: A New History*, New Haven, CT: Yale University Press.

Graham, Stephen (2010), *Cities under Siege: The New Military Urbanism*, London: Verso.

Greenwald, Glenn (2009), 'The suppressed facts: Deaths by US torture', *Salon*, 30 June, <http://www.salon.com/2009/06/30/accountability_7/> (last accessed 13 July 2015).

Gross, Michael L. (2015), *The Ethics of Insurgency*, Cambridge: Cambridge University Press.

Guardian, The (2015), 'Obama's drone war a "recruitment tool" for ISIS, say US air force whistleblowers', 18 November.

Guevara, Ernesto Che ([1952] 2004), *Motorcycle Diaries: Notes on a Latin American Journey*, London: Harper Perennial. (Translation by Anne Wright)

Guevara, Ernesto Che ([1965] 2015), 'Socialism and Man in Cuba', Marxists, <https://www.marxists.org/archive/guevara/1965/03/man-socialism.htm> (last accessed 12 July 2015).

Guevara, Ernesto Che (1968), 'Socialism and man in Cuba', in John Gerassi (ed.), *Venceremos!: The Speeches and Writings of Ernesto Che Guevara 1928–1967*, London: Weidenfeld & Nicolson, pp. 390–402.

Halebsky, Sandor and John M. Kirk, (1985), *Cuba: Twenty-five Years of Revolution, 1959–1984*, New York: Praeger Publishers.

Halliday, Fred (2011), *Political Journeys*, London: Saqi Books.

Harnecker, Marta (1987), *From Moncada to Victory: Fidel Castro's Political Strategy*, New York: Pathfinder Press.

Harris, John (1974), 'The Marxist conception of violence', *Philosophy and Public Affairs*, 3, 192–220.

Harvey, David (2000), *Spaces of Hope*, Berkeley and Los Angeles: University of California Press.

Harvey, David (2003), *The New Imperialism*, Oxford: Oxford University Press.

Hegel, Georg ([1837] 2009), *The Philosophy of History*, London: Frederick Ellis Publishers.

Henry, Michel (2015), 'Rana Plaza: les "esclaves" du textile toujours sans droits', *Libération*, 23 April.

Hilary, John (2013), *The Poverty of Capitalism: Economic Meltdown and the Struggle for What Comes Next*, London: Pluto Press.

Hobsbawm, Eric (1994), *The Age of Extremes: The Short Twentieth Century. 1914–1991*, London: Michael Joseph.

Honderich, Ted (2003a), *After the Terror*, Edinburgh: Edinburgh University Press.

Honderich, Ted (2003b), *On Political Means and Social Ends*, Edinburgh: Edinburgh University Press.

Honderich, Ted (2003c), *Terrorism for Humanity: Inquiries in Political Philosophy*, London: Pluto Press.

Honderich, Ted (2006), *Humanity, Terrorism, Terrorist War: Palestine, 9/11, Iraq, 7/7 . . .* , London: Bloomsbury Publishing.

Hutchings, Kimberly (2007a), 'Feminist ethics and political violence', *International Politics*, 44, 90–106.

Hutchings, Kimberly (2007b), 'Simone de Beauvoir and the ambiguous ethics of political violence', *Hypatia*, 22(3), 111–32.

Iraq Body Count (n.d.), *Iraq Bodycount Database*, <https://www.iraqbody count.org/database/> (last accessed 3 December 2015).

Iraq Body Count (2005), 'A dossier of civilian casualties in Iraq, 2003–2005', 19 July, <https://www.iraqbodycount.org/analysis/reference/press-releases/12/> (last accessed 5 November 2015).

Jackson, Mark (2014), *The History of Medicine*, London: Oneworld.

Jameson, Frederic (2004), 'The politics of utopia', *New Left Review*, 25, January– February, 35–54.

Jameson, Frederic (2005), *Archaeologies of the Future*, London: Verso Books.

Jayatilleka, Dayan (2007), *Fidel's Ethics of Violence: The Moral Dimension of the Political Thought of Fidel Castro*, London: Pluto Press.

Jayatilleka, Dayan (2014), *The Fall of Global Socialism: A Counter-narrative from the South*, Basingstoke: Palgrave Macmillan.

Kamenka, Eugene ([1962]1972), *The Ethical Foundation of Marxism*, London: Routledge.

Kant, Immanuel ([1795] 1983), *Perpetual Peace and Other Essays on Politics, History and Morals*, Indianapolis: Hackett.

Karol, K. S. (1970), *Guerillas in Power: The Course of the Cuban Revolution*, New York: Hill and Wang. (Translated by Arnold Pomerans)

Kautsky, Karl ([1919] 1920), *Terrorism and Communism: A Contribution to the Natural History of Marxism*, London: Allen and Unwin. (Translated by W. H. Kerridge)

Kennan, George ([1946] 1967), 'Telegraphic message of February 22, 1946', in *Memoirs, 1925–1950*, London: Hutchinson, pp. 271–97.

Kennedy, John F. (1960), 'Speech of Senator John F. Kennedy, Cincinnati, Ohio, Democratic Dinner', presidency.ucsb.edu, <http://www.presidency. ucsb.edu/ws/?pid=25660> (last accessed 27 July 2015).

Kiernan, Ben (2008), *The Pol Pot Regime. Race, Power and Genocide in Cambodia under the Kmer Rouge, 1975–79*, New Haven, CT: Yale University Press.

King, Martin Luther (1995), 'Love, law and civil disobedience', in *A Testament of Hope: The Essential Writings and Speeches of Martin Luther King Jr.*, San Francisco: HarperSanFrancisco, pp. 263–72.

Laïdi, Ali (2006), *Retour de Flamme. Comment la mondialisation a accouché du terrorisme*, Paris: Calmann-Lévy.

Lane, Christopher (2006), *The Peace of Illusions: American Grand Strategy from 1940 to the Present*, New York: Cornell University Press.

Languepin, Olivier (2007), *Cuba. La faillite d'une utopie*, Paris: Gallimard.

Larsen, Neil (2004), 'Thoughts on violence and modernity in Latin America. In light of Arno Mayer's *The Furies*', *Krisis*, 31 December, <http://www. krisis.org/2004/thoughts-on-violence-and-modernity/s> (last accessed 15 October 2015).

Law, Stephen (2008), *Israel, Palestine and Terror*, London: Bloomsbury Publishing.

Le Fanu, James (2011), *The Rise and Fall of Modern Medicine*, London: Abacus Books.

Le Goff, Philippe (2015), 'The militant politics of Auguste Blanqui', doctoral thesis, University of Warwick.

Lenin, Vladimir Ilyich ([1908] 1972), 'Lessons of the commune', in *Lenin Collected Works*, vol. 13, Moscow: Progress Publishers, pp. 475–8.

Lenin, Vladimir Ilyich ([1917] 2008), 'The state and revolution', in Paul Le Blanc (ed.), *Revolution, Democracy, Socialism: Selected Writings by V. I. Lenin*, London: Pluto Press, pp. 262–77.

Lenin, Vladimir Ilyich ([1918] 2015), 'Speech at the First Congress of Economic Councils', Marxists, <https://www.marxists.org/archive/lenin/works/1918/may/26b.htm> (last accessed 3 June 2015).

Lessing, Doris (2012), *The Good Terrorist*, London: Fourth Estate.

Levitas, Ruth (2013), *Utopia as Method: The Imaginary Reconstruction of Society*, Basingstoke: Palgrave Macmillan.

Lister, Charles R. (2015), *The Islamic State: A Brief Introduction*, Washington, DC: Brookings Institution.

Losurdo, Domenico ([2006] 2011), *Liberalism: A Counter-History*, London: Verso Books. (Translated by Gregory Elliott)

Losurdo, Domenico ([1996 and 1998] 2015), *War and Revolution: Rethinking the Twentieth Century*, London: Verso Books. (Translated by Gregory Elliott)

Luizard, Pierre-Jean (2015), *Le Piège Daech. L'Etat islamique ou le retour de l'histoire*, Paris: La Découverte.

Lukács, Georg (1919), *Tactics and Ethics*, Marxists, <https://www.marxists.org/archive/lukacs/works/1919/tactics-ethics.htm> (last accessed 17 March 2015).

Lukács, Georg ([1923] 1971), *History and Class Consciousness: Studies in Marxist Dialectics*, London: Merlin Press. (Translated by Rodney Livingstone)

Lukes, Steven (1984), 'Marxism and utopianism', in Peter Alexander and Roger Gill (eds), *Utopias*, London: Duckworth Publishers, pp. 153–67.

Lukes, Steven (1985), *Marxism and Morality*, Oxford: Oxford University Press.

Luxemburg, Rosa ([1918] 1961), *The Russian Revolution and Leninism or Marxism*, Ann Arbor: University of Michigan Press.

Mandela, Nelson (1970), 'The case for a violent resistance movement', in Wilfred Cartey and Martin Kilson (eds), *The Africa Reader: Independent Africa*, New York: Random House, pp. 319–32.

Mandela, Nelson (1995), *Long Walk to Freedom*, London: Abacus Books.

Mann, Michael (2005), *Incoherent Empire*, London: Verso Books.

Marcuse, Herbert ([1965] 1968), 'Ethics and revolution', in Richard T. De

George (ed.), *Ethics and Society: Original Essays on Contemporary Moral Problems*, London: Macmillan Publishers, pp. 133–48.

Marcuse, Herbert ([1965] 1969), 'Repressive tolerance', in Robert Paul Wolff, Barrington Moore, Jr and Herbert Marcuse, *A Critique of Pure Tolerance*, London: Jonathan Cape Publishers, pp. 93–138.

Marcuse, Herbert (1970), 'The end of utopia', in *Five Lectures: Psychoanalysis, Politics and Utopia*, London: Allen Lane, pp. 62–82. (Translated by Jeremy J. Shapiro and Shierry M. Weber)

Martí, José (2002), *Selected Writings*, London: Penguin Books. (Translated by Esther Allen)

Marx, Karl ([1844] 2009), *Critique of Hegel's 'Philosophy of Right'*, Cambridge: Cambridge University Press.

Marx, Karl ([1867] 1954), *Capital: A Critique of Political Economy*, vol. I, London: Lawrence and Wishart. (Translated by Samuel Moore and Edward Aveling)

Marx, Karl ([1875] 2009), *Critique of the Gotha Programme*, Gloucester: Dodo Press.

Marx, Karl and Friedrich Engels ([1848] 1968), *The Manifesto of the Communist Party*, in Karl Marx and Friedrich Engels, *Selected Works in One Volume*, London: Lawrence and Wishart, pp. 35–95.

Marx, Karl and Friedrich Engels ([1850] 2010), 'Address of the central committee to the Communist League, March 1850', Marxists, <http://www.marxistsfr.org/archive/marx/works/1847/communist-league/1850-ad1.htm> (last accessed July 2014).

Matthews, Herbert (1969), *Castro: A Political Biography*, London: Penguin Books.

Mayer, Arno (2000), *The Furies: Violence and Terror in the French and Russian Revolutions*, Princeton: Princeton University Press.

Mazzetti, Mark (2013), *The Way of the Knife: The CIA, a Secret Army, and a War at the Ends of the Earth*, London: Penguin Books.

Merle, Robert (1965), *Moncada, premier combat de Fidel Castro*, Paris: Robert Laffont.

Merleau-Ponty, Maurice ([1947] 1969), *Humanism and Terror: An Essay on the Communist Problem*, Boston: Beacon Press. (Translated by John O'Neill)

Miliband, Ralph (1994), *Socialism for a Sceptical Age*, Cambridge: Polity Press.

Morris, Emily (2014), 'Unexpected Cuba', *New Left Review*, 88, July/August, 5–45.

Morris, William ([1890] 2009), *News from Nowhere*, Oxford: Oxford University Press.

Neocleous, Mark (2014), *War Power, Police Power*, Edinburgh: Edinburgh University Press.

Ogilvie, Bertrand (1995), 'Violence et représentation. La production de l'homme jetable', *Lignes* 26, October, 25–39.

Onwuanibe, Richard (1983), *A Critique of Revolutionary Humanism: Frantz Fanon*, St Louis, MO: Green.

Panitch, Leo and Sam Gindin (1999), 'Transcending pessimism: Rekindling the socialist imagination', in Leo Panitch and Colin Leys (eds), *Necessary and Unnecessary Utopias. Socialist Register 2000*, Rendlesham: Merlin Press, pp. 1–30.

Parekh, Bhikhu (1990), 'A critique of the liberal discourse on violence', in David McLellan and Sean Sayers (eds), *Socialism and Morality*, London: Macmillan Publishers, pp. 116–38.

Payne, Stanley G. (1995): *A History of Fascism, 1914–1945*, Madison: University of Wisconsin Press.

Perrault, Gilles (1998), *Le Livre noir du capitalism*, Paris: Le Temps des Cerises.

Philip, George and Francisco Panizza (2011), *The Triumph of Politics: The Return of the Left in Venezuela, Bolivia and Ecuador*, Cambridge: Polity.

Pinker, Steven (2011), *Better Angels of our Nature: The Decline of Violence in History and its Causes*, London: Allen Lane.

Popper, Karl (2002), 'Utopia and violence', in *Conjectures and Refutations. The Growth of Scientific Knowledge*, London and New York: Routledge, pp. 355–63.

Porter, Roy (2002), *Blood and Guts: A Short History of Medicine*, London: Penguin.

Primoratz, Igor (2013), *Terrorism. A Philosophical Investigation*, Cambridge: Polity.

Ramonet, Ignacio (2007), 'A hundred hours with Fidel', in Fidel Castro with Ignacio Ramonet, *My Life*, London: Penguin Books, pp. 1–22. (Translated by Andrew Hurley)

Ramonet, Ignacio and Carlos Alberto Montaner (2007), 'Was Fidel good For Cuba?', *Foreign Policy*, January–February, pp. 56–64.

Ray, Larry (2011), *Violence and Society*, London: Sage Publications.

Rengger, Nicholas (2013), *Just War and International Order: The Uncivil Condition in World Politics*, Cambridge: Cambridge University Press.

Rice, Donald (1992), *The Rhetorical Uses of the Authorizing Figure: Fidel Castro and José Martí*, New York: Praeger Publishers.

Roberts, Les and Gilbert Burnham (2004), 'Mortality before and after the 2003 invasion of Iraq: Cluster Sample Survey', *The Lancet*, 364 (20 November), 1,857–64.

Robinson, Geoffrey (1996), 'The post-coup massacre in Bali', in Daniel S. Lev and Ruth McVey (eds), *Making Indonesia*, New York: Cornell Southeast Asia Program Publications, pp. 118–43.

Robinson, William I. (2004), *A Theory of Global Capitalism: Production, Class and State in a Transnational World*, Baltimore: Johns Hopkins University Press.

Robinson, William I. (2008), *Latin America and Global Capitalism: A Critical Globalization Perspective*, Baltimore: Johns Hopkins University Press.

Robinson, William I. (2014), *Global Capitalism and the Crisis of Humanity*, Cambridge: Cambridge University Press.

Robinson, William I. and Mario Barrera (2012), 'Global crisis and twenty-first century Fascism: A US case study', *Race and Class*, 53(3), 4–29.

Ross, Daniel, *Violent Democracy* (2004), Cambridge: Cambridge University Press.

Roy, Olivier (2007), *The Politics of Chaos in the Middle East*, London: Hurst.

Ruddick, Sara (1995), *Maternal Thinking: Towards a Politics of Peace*, Boston: Beacon Press.

Rummel, Rudolf J. (1998), *Statistics of Democide: Genocide and Mass Murder since 1900*, Münster: Lit Verlag.

Ryan, James (2012), *Lenin's Terror: The Ideological Origins of Early Soviet State Violence*, London: Routledge.

Salem, Paul (1994), *Bitter Legacy: Ideology and Politics in the Arab World*, New York: Syracuse University Press.

Saney, Isaac (2004), *Cuba: A Revolution in Motion*, London: Zed Books.

Sartre, Jean-Paul ([1961] 2001), 'Preface', in Frantz Fanon, *The Wretched of the Earth*, London: Penguin Books, pp. 7–26. (Translated by Constance Farrington)

Sen, Amartya (1981), *Poverty and Famines: An Essay on Entitlement and Deprivation*, Oxford: Clarendon Press.

Serge, Victor ([1942–3] 1963), *Memoirs of a Revolutionary*, Oxford: Oxford University Press. (Translated and edited by Peter Sedgwick.)

Singh, Gopal (1976), 'Politics and violence', *Social Scientist*, 4(11), 58–66.

Sjoberg, Laura (2012), 'Feminist reflections on political violence', in Marie Breen-Smyth (ed.), *The Ashgate Research Companion to Political Violence*, Farnham: Ashgate, pp. 261–79.

Skierka, Volker (2004), *Fidel Castro: A Biography*, Cambridge: Polity. (Translated by Patrick Camiller)

Slahi, Mohamedou Ould (2015), *Guantánamo Diary*, London: Canongate Books. (Edited by Larry Siems)

Soper, Kate (1987), 'Marxism and morality', *New Left Review*, 163, May/June, 101–13.

Sorel, Georges ([1908] 1999), *Reflections on Violence*, Cambridge: Cambridge University Press. (Translated by T. E. Hulme)

Stannard, David E. (1992), *American Holocaust*, Oxford: Oxford University Press.

Stockholm International Peace Research Institute (SIPRI) (2015), *SIPRI Military Expenditure Database*, <http://www.sipri.org/research/armaments/milex/milex_database> (last accessed 14 October 2015).

Stora, Benjamin (1995), *Histoire de la Guerre d'Algérie (1954–1962)*, Paris: La Découverte.

Streeck, Wolfgang (2013), 'The crisis in context: Democratic capitalism and its contradictions', in Armin Schäfer and Wolfgang Streeck, *Politics in the Age of Austerity*, Cambridge: Polity, pp. 262–86.

Streeck, Wolfgang (2014a), 'How will capitalism end?', *New Left Review*, 87, May–June, 35–66.

Streeck, Wolfgang (2014b), *Buying Time: The Delayed Crisis of Democratic Capitalism*, London: Verso Books.

Therborn, Göran (2013), *The Killing Fields of Inequality*, Cambridge: Polity.

Thomas, Hugh (1971), *Cuba, or The Pursuit of Freedom*, London: Eyre and Spottiswoode.

Tilly, Charles (2003), *The Politics of Collective Violence*, Cambridge: Cambridge University Press.

Tone, John Lawrence (2006), *War and Genocide in Cuba, 1895–1898*, Chapel Hill, NC: University of North Carolina Press.

Toscano, Alberto (2010), *Fanaticism: On the Uses of an Idea*, London: Verso Books.

Trotsky, Leon ([1938] 1969), *Their Morals and Ours*, New York: Pathfinder Press.

Trotsky, Leon ([1909, 1911, 1937, 1939] 1980), *Against Individual Terrorism*, New York: Pathfinder Press.

Trotsky, Leon ([1920] 2007), *Terrorism and Communism*, London: Verso Books. (Foreword by Slavoj Žižek, Preface by H. N. Brailsford)

Turse, Nick (2013), *Kill Anything that Moves: The Real American War in Vietnam*, New York: Picador.

United Nations Children's Emergency Fund (UNICEF) (2014), *The State of the World's Children 2014*, 28 November, <http://www.unicef.org> (last accessed 13 October 2015).

Valentino, Benjamin A. (2004), *Final Solutions: Mass Killing and Genocide in the Twentieth Century*, Ithaca: Cornell University Press.

Villa, Dana R. (2000), *Politics, Philosophy, Terror: Essays on the Thought of Hannah Arendt*, Princeton: Princeton University Press.

Wahnich, Sophie (2012), *In Defense of the Terror: Liberty or Death in the French Revolution*, London: Verso Books.

Walker, Phillip L. (2001), 'A bioarchaeological perspective on the history of violence', *Annual Review of Anthropology*, 30, 573–96.

Wallerstein, Immanuel (2013), 'Structural crisis, or why capitalists may no longer find capitalism rewarding', in Randall Collins, Michael Mann, Georgi

Derluguian, Craig Calhoun and Immanuel Wallerstein, *Does Capitalism Have a Future?*, Oxford: Oxford University Press, pp. 9–36.

Walzer, Michael ([1977] 2006a), *Just and Unjust Wars: A Moral Argument with Historical Illustrations*, 4th edn, New York: Basic Books.

Walzer, Michael (2006b), 'Preface to the fourth edition', in *Just and Unjust Wars: A Moral Argument with Historical Illustrations*, 4th edn, New York: Basic Books, pp. ix–xviii.

Webb, Darren (2000), *Marx, Marxism and Utopia*, Aldershot: Ashgate.

Webel, Charles P. (2004), *Terror, Terrorism and the Human Condition*, Basingstoke: Palgrave Macmillan.

Webel, Charles P. (2011), 'The "ethics" of terror and terrorism', in Charles P. Webel and John A. Arnaldi (eds), *The Ethics and Efficacy of the Global War on Terrorism*, Basingstoke: Palgrave Macmillan, pp. 29–43.

Williams, Eric ([1942] 1990), *Capitalism and Slavery*, London: Deutsch.

Winter, Yves (2009), 'Marx and Engels's theories of violence reconsidered', Paper delivered at the Western Political Science Association's Annual Meeting, 19–21 March.

Wood, Ellen (2001), 'Contradiction: Only in capitalism?', in Leo Panitch and Colin Leys (eds), *Socialist Register 2002: A World of Contradictions*, Rendlesham: Merlin Press, pp. 275–93.

Wood, Graeme (2015), 'What ISIS really wants', *The Atlantic*, March, <http://www.theatlantic.com/magazine/archive/2015/03/what-isis-really-wants/384980/> (last accessed 7 May 2015).

World Bank (2015), 'Mortality rate under-5 (per 1000 live births)', Data worldbank, <http://data.worldbank.org/indicator/SH.DYN.MORT> (last accessed 14 October 2015).

World Health Organization (WHO) (2002), *World Report on Violence and Health*, 3 October.

World Health Organization (WHO) (2014a), *World Health Statistics, 2014*, <http://www.who.int/gho/publications/world_health_statistics/en/> (last accessed 15 September 2015).

World Health Organization (WHO) (2014b), *Global Status Report on Violence Prevention*,<http://www.who.int/violence_injury_prevention/violence/status_report/2014/en/> (last accessed 28 October 2015).

World Health Organization (WHO) (2015), *Global Health Observatory Data*, <http://www.who.int/gho/child_health/en/> (last accessed 1 October 2015).

Wright, Erik Olin (2010), *Envisioning Real Utopias*, London: Verso Books.

Žižek, Slavoj (2007a), 'A Leninist gesture today: Against the populist temptation', in Sebastian Budgen, Stathis Kouvelakis and Slavoj Žižek (eds), *Lenin Reloaded: Towards a Politics of Truth*, London: Duke University Press, pp. 74–100.

Žižek, Slavoj (2007b), 'Introduction. Robespierre, or, the "divine violence" of

terror', in Maximilien Robespierre, *Virtue and Terror*, London: Verso Books. (Texts selected and translated by Jean Ducange, translated by John Howe), pp. vii–xxxix.
Žižek, Slavoj (2008), *Violence. Six Sideways Reflections*, London: Profile Books.

INDEX